Kobe House P.O.W. #13

Kobe House P.O.W. #13

A.J. Locke

Old Guard Press

Published in the United Kingdom in 2013
for Old Guard Press by
Shearsman Books
50 Westons Hill Drive
Emersons Green
Bristol
BS16 7DF

Shearsman Books Ltd Registered Office
30–31 St. James Place, Mangotsfield, Bristol BS16 9JB
(this address not for correspondence)

ISBN 978-1-84861-228-0

Copyright © A. J. Locke, 1998.
Copyright © The Estate of A. J. Locke, 2013.

The right of A. J. Locke to be identified as the author
of this work has been asserted by his Estate in accordance with the
Copyrights, Designs and Patents Act of 1988.
All rights reserved.

Kobe House P.O.W. #13 was first published
in a limited private edition in 1998.
This is the first commercial edition.

Contents

	Foreword	9
1.	Clark Field	11
2.	The First Two Weeks	15
3.	Bataan	19
4.	Quinauan Point	26
5.	Interlude	34
6.	Guests of the Emperor	38
7.	The Bataan Death March	43
8.	The Schoolhouse	51
9.	Better Than Walking, But Not Much	53
10.	Camp O'Donnell	54
11.	Back to Bataan	59
12.	Bilibid Prison	61
13.	On the High Seas	69
14.	Kobe House	73
15.	Settling In	76
16.	Kyotsuki!	80
17.	Heigh-Ho, Heigh-Ho, and Off to Work We Go	83
18.	And More Work	87
19.	On the Inside	91
20.	Merry Christmas	95
21.	A New Year	97
22.	My Fellow Americans	102
23.	And Our Guards	106
24.	POW Coolies	110
25.	Monotonous Misery	115
26.	I've Been Working on the Railroad	119
27.	Spring, 1943	124

28. New Arrivals	128
29. The Mad Doctor	130
30. The Australians	134
31. 1943	139
32. Den of Thieves	144
33. A New Job	150
34. Tempus Fugit — Very Slowly	154
35. Another New Year	159
36. Two More Moves	163
37. Aches and Pains	168
38. Summer Drags On	173
39. Autumn and Another New Job	177
40. And Another New Year	185
41. War Comes to Kobe	190
42. Sweating It Out	195
43. We Lose Our Home	200
44. Wakinohama	204
45. All Over But the Shouting	208
46. Farewell to Kobe City	214
47. Homeward Bound	216
48. Random Thoughts	219
49. Fifty Years Later	221

Dedication

This book is dedicated to all my fellow prisoners of war, American, Australian, English, or Scottish, who lived, worked and suffered with me in Kobe House from October 1942 until its destruction by fire on the 8th of June 1945. They will remain in my memory for all time.

Acknowledgments

I wish to thank my Australian friends who were so generous in giving me a free rein to use their book of collective memories, *The Story of 'J' Force*, in any manner I wished while writing this book, including the use of most of the photographs, which otherwise would have been unobtainable. It was an immense help while trying to remember names, dates and other trivia which happened more than fifty years ago.

I must also include my dear wife, Lorraine, whose encouragement and help, while enduring months of my typing, kept me going until the book was finished.

Last, but not least, are all those friends who kept urging me to write about my experiences while a prisoner of the Japanese. May they enjoy my book!

A.J. Locke, 1998.

The author, Honolulu, 1937.

Foreword

Kobe House P.O.W. No. 13 was previously self-published by my father, Arthur "Bud" Locke, in 1998, in a limited edition. I loved the book, learning so much about my father, who never really talked about his experiences to me growing up, and encouraged him to republish it. Mom showed signs of Alzheimer's around that time and he had all he could do with caring for her, as her symptoms rapidly progressed. Mom passed away in November of 2005 and Dad died peacefully in 2007.

I am very proud to be their daughter, proud of the lives they lived and the sacrifices they both made. I am republishing Dad's memoirs to honor him and to pass on a bit of history that should not be forgotten. I learned where my own strengths came from in reading the book and I hope to do the annual Bataan Death March Memorial Walk in New Mexico in the near future. One of Dad's favorite sayings was you can do anything if you put your mind to it—that was how he lived and I miss them both!

Linda Locke Parkin

Chapter 1

Clark Field

World War II began, for me, about nine on the morning of Monday, the 8th of December 1941. It was the 8th instead of the 7th because the Philippines are a day ahead of the United States, due to the International Date Line, which is located in the middle of the Pacific Ocean.

I had been stationed at Clark Field since the middle of November, when my outfit, Headquarters and Headquarters Squadron, Far East Air Service Command had been activated. On December 1st, the Squadron had been moved to Nielson Field, just outside the city of Manila, where Far East Air Force Headquarters was located. I was the Squadron 1st Sergeant, and had remained at Clark along with my Supply Sergeant to finish up the paper work concerned with the transfer, and was ready to leave Clark and rejoin my outfit as soon as I had cleared the base.

I had been down to Manila for the weekend and slept in. By the time I woke up, Pearl Harbor had been bombed, the war had begun, and Clark was on alert status. I was the only one left in our old barracks and of course no one had bothered waking me up. As usual in the morning, I turned my radio on to get the news from Manila, and of course the air was filled with news about the attack on Pearl Harbor. At breakfast, I found out what was going on. After Clark Field had been put on alert status, all our B-17 bombers had taken off so they wouldn't get caught on the ground in an air raid, and were loafing around over the center of Luzon. Our pursuit squadron was also in the air patrolling to the north, a large group of Japanese bombers having been reported from northern Luzon. The Japanese failed to show, having bombed Baguio and other targets up north. By eleven o'clock, all our aircraft were back on the ground to be refueled and take on their bomb load for a raid on Formosa, while the air crews went to their mess halls for lunch.

I had finished packing my gear and had early chow, then walked down to Base Headquarters, which, at Clark, was located on the flight line, to turn in my paperwork and get my clearance to depart Clark. It was about twenty past twelve when I climbed up the stairs to the Personnel Section which, to my surprise, was empty. I found this rather odd, as someone should have been on duty. There was a lot of noise outside, but most of the time engines were being run up, so I didn't think too much about it. I did walk over to the window to see what was going on, as it did seem louder than usual. I saw four P-40 fighters on their take off runs, all crowded together with an old sea-plane we called the "Duck" trailing along. As I was looking at them, everything seemed to explode in my face. Twenty-seven Japanese twin-engine bombers were making their bomb run across Clark Field and bombs were dropping everywhere. Two of the P-40s taking off were hit, and the old "Duck" disintegrated right in front of my eyes. Talk about being surprised! All the engine noise had prevented me from hearing the bombers or any other warning. Seeing all those bombs exploding right in front of me was quite a thing. All this had happened so unexpectedly that I hardly realized what was going on, and I just froze in place and kept looking out the window. It was almost as if I was watching a war movie. I wasn't even scared until the bombs stopped exploding and I had a moment to think about it. The quiet only lasted about half a minute and then another twenty-seven bombers were dropping their loads. This time I hit the deck pronto, but being ten feet above the ground, I might just as well have stayed looking out. By this time, I was really scared. It was a wonder that I hadn't soiled my britches, as a lot of people would have done if they had been in my situation. After the second flight of bombers had gone away, it became really quiet. It was like being in a church after all that noise. Actually, I suppose it was because I had been deafened by the blasts. After I had gotten my wits together, I took off down the stairs and ran back to the barracks, where a nice V-shaped slit trench had been dug during the past week.

The dust hadn't even settled from all the bombing when swarms of Zero fighters were all over Clark like hornets. I can tell you I was glad to be in my slit trench and below the level of the ground. Three of our Filipino mess boys were already in the trench, huddled together at one end. I could hear them crying "Husmariosep", which is garbled English for "Jesus, Mary and Joseph", most of the Filipinos on Luzon being Catholic. In our V-trench, we could move from one leg of the trench to the other leg, if necessary, to get the most protection. After one Zero had gone by, you had to stick your head up to see when the next one was coming, then move to the leg of the trench which was not in his line of flight. For the next hour or so, it was like a game of musical chairs, with me and the boys dashing from side to side. At first I tried to tell them what to do, but found that my voice was gone. I guess I must have been scared worse than I thought. Not being able to shout at them, I shoved them around like chickens until they finally figured out what they were supposed to do. The Zeros shot up everything in sight for more than an hour with little opposition. Two or three of our fighters did get off the ground and shot down a couple of the Zeros before they ran out of fuel and had to land. The antiaircraft batteries around Clark manned by the recently arrived 200th Coast Artillery (AA) were firing for all they were worth, but much of their ammunition was defective, the effective range of the guns wasn't high enough to reach the bombers, and of course being in their first action didn't help. Those Zeros did as much or more damage that day than the two flights of bombers. All those bombs had wrecked most of the buildings and the hangars and set everything on fire, but the Zeros finished off every one of our B-17s and P-40s that the bombs had missed, filling them so full of holes they looked like sieves. This first air raid just about finished the American bombing capability in the Philippines, only a dozen or so B-17s which had been sent down to Mindanao remained, and these left for Australia in the next few days.

The Zeros finally ran short of fuel and ammunition and went away, so I and the boys emerged from our slit trench, all of us unscathed by some miracle. Perhaps all the "Husmarioseps" helped out. It was hard to believe that I was still in one piece after all that, and my voice even came back in a bit, thank the Lord. I knew I had better get going and rejoin my outfit, so picking my way through and around all sorts of debris, bomb craters, burning vehicles as well as a few unlucky ones who had become casualties of the bombing and strafing, I made it back to the barracks, which had been hit but fortunately was not on fire. I grabbed my gear and took off down the main road leading to the main gate and the railroad station at Dau. I didn't think that after all the excitement anybody would worry about my clearance, so I stopped at the headquarters building to say "Adios". It was still empty, and I was astounded to see the condition it was in. All the sliding windows had been blown off, the walls and floor were riddled and the roof half gone. There were a dozen bomb craters around the building less than fifty feet away. All this destruction had been done while I was in the building and I hadn't even been aware of it. How I came through all that without a scratch was beyond me. I figured then that I was born to be hung instead of being shot. In light of what was going to happen to me in the next three years, I might have been better off if I had been shot!

Leaving Clark Field for the last time, I started walking down the road heading for Dau Station, which was the junction where the road from Clark met Highway No. 1, the main road to Manila, as well as the railroad. Before I had gone halfway to Dau, a van belonging to the Post Exchange dry cleaner stopped and picked me up. This was a bit of good luck, as he was heading to Manila after making a delivery at Clark, and was happy to have a passenger. We had an uneventful sixty mile trip, and it was getting dark as we neared the city. The blackout was in force and I didn't want to get shot by some trigger-happy Filipino, so I decided to stop for the night at the Pilapil Isla, a small hotel in Caloocan where the men of my outfit usually stayed when on pass. About three in the morning, the thunder of bombs woke me up with a start. Nichols Field, just outside Manila, was being hit for the first of many times. I was certainly glad I wasn't there. I had had enough of bombing for one day. My last thought that night was that whatever happened from then on would be anti-climatic, but was I ever wrong!

Chapter 2

The First Two Weeks

The next morning I found a taxi and arrived at Nielson Field, on the other side of the city of Manila, where I was informed that my squadron had been quartered at Fort McKinley, a couple of miles away, and I was to join it there and set up the squadron orderly room. Fort McKinley was a beautiful place, the home station of the Philippine Scouts. They were already in the field, and we had moved into one of the empty barracks, the men being trucked to work at Nielson Field. Setting up the orderly room, or office, was easy. All a 1st Sgt. has, when in the field, is his field desk, which is about the size of a suit case and opens up to form a small desk. I just put it on a table and I was in business. At this time I had very little work to do, just get the men off to work in the morning and then make out the morning report. The morning report was submitted to the next higher headquarters daily, and showed the number of men available for duty as well as any change in the status of the personnel. An orderly room is normally a very busy place, with all the peacetime paper work, but paper work seemed to have been forgotten since the start of the war.

In the first days of the war, the Japanese were busy bombing and strafing all our air fields and Navy installations in an all-out effort to destroy our air and sea capabilities. Nichols Field, the fighter base just south of Manila, and the Navy yard at Cavite were each hit by seventy-six bombers on the 10th. The Navy yard was all but obliterated in these attacks, and what was left of the Far East fleet took off for safer climes in the Dutch East Indies. All that remained of the Navy was the submarine tender *Canopus* with its group of subs, a few PT boats and some harbor craft such as tugboats. The next day the Japs struck both Iba and Clark fields again, as well as destroying all the Navy patrol bombers at Olongapo Navy Base just after they had returned from patrol and were refueling. December 12 saw Del Carmen, Clark, Baguio and Tarlac getting their dose of Japanese medicine. Del Carmen, Clark, Nichols, Cabanatuan an Batangas were hit the following day. By the evening of the 14th, U.S. air and naval power in the Philippines was virtually nonexistent. Fort McKinley was the exception, never being attacked, I suppose because there was nothing there to be bombed. This was OK with me, as I had

had my fill of bombs already. We did have a ringside seat watching all the other places being bombed.

During all this activity by their air forces, the Japanese Army was also busy. They had landed at the towns of Aparri and Vigan, in the far northern part of Luzon, where they seized air fields from which their bombers could operate instead of their bases on Taiwan. The landing at Vigan was opposed by a few B-17s from Mindanao aided by the few fighters left to the 17th Pursuit Squadron, and some old P-35s of the 21st Pursuit. Two of the Jap transports were damaged and beached, one minesweeper sunk, and the other ships hit, but the damage was not enough to stop the landings. This was the last coordinated attack by our air forces, and from then on nothing but recon missions were flown by our Air Corps.

The big invasion which everyone had been expecting came on the 22nd of December at Lingayan Gulf, at the northern end of the central plain of Luzon. The beaches there were ideal for amphibious landings, and Lingayan was the logical starting point for a drive south toward Manila. The gulf area was defended by three divisions of the Philippine Army and the 26th Cavalry of the Philippine Scouts. The Filipinos had just been mobilized and were badly handicapped by insufficient training and shortages of equipment. In some of the regiments different dialects were spoken, which led to much confusion, as orders given in English or Tagalog had to be interpreted. Their officers had had a minimal amount of training, and American officers and NCOs were assigned to Filipino units to be used as a cadre. The American 31st Infantry and the two Philippine Scout Regiments were in the field but were being held in reserve and were not committed. As a result the Japanese landings at the Gulf were virtually unopposed, and by the second day they were beginning their advance down the central plain.

At this point, Headquarters Forces decided to initiate War Plan Orange-2. This was the plan to be used when the war situation became one in which the enemy forces had landed on Luzon in great strength and no immediate reenforcements could be expected from the United States. In this case, the mission of our forces was to defend Manila Bay by holding the entrance to the Bay and to deny its use to the enemy. If the enemy could not be held after landing, our forces were to fight a delaying action until all of our forces had withdrawn to the Bataan peninsula, which was to be held to the last. The withdrawal to Bataan was complicated by the fact that there was only one road into the peninsula, beginning at the city of San Fernando on the main north-south highway, and the North Luzon Force, which was opposing the Japanese who had landed at Lingayen had to hold them until the South Luzon force passed through the bottleneck at San Fernando and were on their way to Bataan. This operation was going to be touch-and-go because the Southern forces had a long way to go, as well as holding off other Japanese forces who had landed at Legaspi and other places in the south of Luzon.

While all this decision-making was going on upstairs, the lower ranks were blissfully unaware of the true situation and were proceeding to enjoy themselves as much as possible. I passed my spare time by visiting my old friends in and around Nichols Field, where I had been stationed in '39 and '40. At Nichols, the Japanese bombing had done considerable damage to the flight line and some newly built barracks, but my old barracks had hardly been touched. The new barracks, which had housed the 17th Pursuit Squadron, were almost demolished. The squadrons had already been moved out to smaller fields, and were they lucky. It was about as bad as Clark Field had been after the first raid on the 8th. Looking around inside one of the buildings, I spotted one bunk with an eight-inch hole right through the center of the mattress. A bomb had gone through the roof, the ceiling, the bed and the floor, winding up as a dud under the building. It was a good job no one had been sleeping in that bunk! The bombs the Japs were using made holes about twenty feet across and some six feet deep—quite a hole. Not many of their bombs were duds, either, at least none were that landed in my vicinity.

In the evenings, trips to Manila to sample the famous steaks at Tom's Dixie Kitchen and tall gin slings at the Poodle Dog Bar were in order. The night life in Manila seemed to have picked up quite a bit, in fact, it seemed gayer than ever. It was as though everyone sensed impending doom and tried to spend as much money as they could and have as good a time as possible before the end came. Those civilians had the right idea, although we in the Army thought that relief was on the way from America, and that they were crazy. My right-hand man, Pvt. Sandy Blau, had an old Ford and we cruised around Manila in the blackout. There was a lot of shooting going on, Americans and Filipinos all had itchy trigger fingers and were firing at shadows or what their imagination told them was a Jap fifth column. Rumors were rampant that a fifth column was in the vicinity, but as most rumors were at this time, these proved to be false. It all served to spice up our nightly adventures.

All in all, things were going smoothly at Fort McKinley. The Japanese hadn't annoyed us at all, and the squadron settled down into a nearly normal routine. That is, until Christmas Day. We always had a big turkey dinner at Christmas, and everything was in the oven about to be dished up, when Lt. Roland Barnick, our Commanding Officer, ran in and told me to get the men packed up and ready to move out in thirty minutes, as we were going to Bataan. This was quite a shock, as we had thought the war was progressing nicely and now this. All we could take with us was what we could carry, so I stuffed all the things I could think of that would be indispensable in my haversack and a barracks bag. About all one could take was a blanket, an extra pair of shoes, toilet articles, and a few pairs of socks and shorts. I also grabbed another set of khakis and a pair of mechanic's coveralls, the Air Corps working outfit. Everything else was left behind, never to be seen again, by me at least. All my photo albums, cameras, letters, anything else a soldier has squirreled away in his foot locker was gone forever. The turkeys were left in the oven, and it wasn't too long before I wished I had had sense enough to take one of them along, it was to be almost four years before I saw another, although I did dream about them.

The Squadron was trucked to Pier 7 in Manila and then had to wait until dark before boarding the *Don Esteban*, an inter-island passenger ship, for the trip across Manila Bay to the peninsula of Bataan. All was dark on the ship because of the blackout, but we found enough space on deck to lie down and get a little sleep during the 4-hour trip across Manila Bay. Early the next morning we disembarked at a little village named Cabcaben. This was the first glimpse of what was to be our home until the middle of April 1942, and I sincerely wish I had never seen the place. If I had been looking for Hades, I couldn't have done better than the peninsula of Bataan.

Chapter 3

Bataan

The peninsula of Bataan and its location relative to Manila Bay made it a very important piece of real estate. Manila Bay is roughly circular and about thirty miles in diameter. It can be pictured as a mouth, Bataan the upper jaw, and the province of Cavite the lower jaw. The mouth is partly open, with the island of Corregidor in its center, three miles from Bataan and five from Cavite. Three much smaller islands are located near Corregidor to the south. All these islands were heavily armed with batteries of heavy coast artillery to guard the entrance to Manila Bay. The Japanese would have to take these islands before they could use Manila Bay, which was the finest harbor in the Far East. Bataan guards Corregidor to the north, which is the reason all the prewar plans called for Bataan to be held for at least six months, by which time relief was expected to arrive from the United States. Supplies sufficient for forty thousand men for six months were stockpiled on Corregidor and Bataan for this purpose. Unfortunately for us, there were eighty thousand soldiers and another twenty thousand Filipino civilians who, fearing the Japanese, had fled to Bataan. With more than double the number of people planned for, it was easy to see that everything was going to be in very short supply in the near future.

The peninsula of Bataan is roughly twenty-five miles from north to south and twenty miles across. In 1941 there was just one poorly paved road, which ran down the east, or Manila Bay side, to the small port of Mariveles at the southern tip of Bataan. Mariveles was opposite Corregidor, and all the supplies being shipped to the troops on Bataan had to be transported by barge across three miles of water and unloaded there. This was going to create all sorts of problems as the war progressed. The paved road stopped at Mariveles and a gravel and dirt road went on about half way up the west coast to the town of Ragac. The entire peninsula consists of mountainous jungle, with the exception of a narrow strip of cleared land along the east coast as far as Cacaben. Mt. Natib dominates the northern half of Bataan and Mt. Bataan the southern half, both mountains being more than four thousand feet in elevation. A narrow dirt road crossed from Pilar on the east to Bagac on the west coast, running between the two mountains. This road would become the main line of resistance after the battles in January 1942.

Cabacen was a town consisting of a schoolhouse and a dozen *bahays*, or *nipa* huts, common to the Philippine countryside. There was a small dock where we landed after our trip across the bay, and a lot of the supplies coming from Manila were being unloaded there. The confusion when we arrived was indescribable, but I finally located an officer who told me to take the outfit on down the road toward Mariveles until I found a suitable spot and set up camp out of sight of the road. So down the road we went until I found a halfway decent spot by a small stream, where the tents were erected and latrines dug. All we could do then was to wait for further orders. No one seemed to know what to do with all us Headquarters people, and more just like us were coming in all the time. It quickly became apparent that the food situation was bad and not going to get better. About all we were issued the first couple of days was canned corn beef hash and rice, which we ate twice a day for breakfast and supper. Our cooks had never had to cook rice as a main dish, so we got rice mush in the morning and burned rice at night. A lot of the rice was thrown out, as we weren't too hungry as yet. On our second day on Bataan, orders came down placing everyone on half rations. This didn't sound too good. If we had to defend Bataan for six months on half rations, we would be really thin by that time. I talked to some of the men I knew who had come from Manila by truck, and found out that the warehouses on the docks in Manila were open and lots of food and other things were at hand. I was an old scrounger from way back, this would be from heaven, so I picked three good men, cadged a couple of 6x6 trucks from a Master Sergeant at the motor pool I had known for a long time, and headed back up the highway toward Manila and all that good stuff. No one was heading our way because everyone and everything were hightailing it to Bataan. At San Fernando we turned south on the main highway and made better time, getting into Caloocan about dark. We spent the night there at our usual little hotel and had the last good time we ever spent in the Philippines. The lights of Manila were all back on and we wondered why, as the blackout had been on since the start of the war. We found out later that Manila had been declared an open city after General MacArthur and President Quezon had left for Corregidor on the 26th of Dec. We didn't know at the time that combatants were supposed to keep out of an open city, so we took off for the docks. We found all the warehouses open, goods strewn all over the place, and everybody taking all they could carry away. My crew joined in and managed to fill one truck with the choicest canned goods we could find, mostly canned meat and fruit. Our other truck was filled to the brim with boxes of cigarettes, as most of the men were smokers. I will always remember those cigarettes, Piedmonts in packs of ten. We may have had a lack of food in days to come, but every man in the outfit got his ten cigs daily.

About noon we headed back up the highway to San Fernando, crossing the double bridges at Calumpit which crossed the wide Pampanga River just south of the town. These bridges were blown up by the Engineers just a few minutes after we had crossed. We hadn't known it, but we had joined the tail end of the Southern Command as it passed through Manila on its way to Bataan. No wonder the traffic had been heavy! If we had been ten minutes later leaving Manila, we would have been stranded on the south side of the river, which, as things turned out, might not have been too bad. We could have headed up into the mountains and become guerrillas. I was familiar with the area and knew many Filipinos there, so with our two truck loads of goodies we would have gotten along famously. However, fate decided otherwise, and turning left at San Fernando, we went on down the road to Bataan and Cabcaben, which we reached in the evening only to find the squadron gone. We finally found it in bivouac a few miles to the south at Little Baguio, so-called because it was located on top of a ridge about halfway from Cabcaben to Mariveles. It was named after the city of Baguio in the mountains of northern Luzon, known as the "summer capital" of the Philippines, where everyone who can afford to do so goes during the hot season. It is a clean, cool city and a nice place to be when the temperature in Manila is in the nineties. At the top of the ridge at Little Baguio there was a flat area around three hundred yards in length. Base Hospital #1 was located here, just off the road to the right. A rough trail ran by the hospital, then through a large ammunition dump, then on up the ridge. Following this trail about a quarter of a mile, we found our outfit and parked the trucks on the side of the trail. Too late for supper, we made do with cans of corned beef and fruit salad from our loot. After eating, I found a pyramidal tent and set it up for an orderly room, as well as a place to live. Thus ended a day which I considered to have been well spent.

The next morning I woke up to be unpleasantly surprised by the sight of a detail of men unloading our truck of foodstuffs and carrying it away to, you guessed it, the officers' mess. How they knew that the truck was loaded with food I will never know, because it was covered completely. But there it went, and all I ever got out of it was six cans of corned beef. If I had had the brains that a 1st Sergeant with seven years service should have had, all that food would have been distributed among the men as soon as we got in. We would have eaten a lot better in the next few months than we did with what the Army gave us. The only consolation we had was that they didn't take our cigarettes as well. From that day on, I began to be disillusioned about our officers. Officers were supposed to take care of their men before they took care of themselves, and just about all the officers I had known during my service in the Infantry did just that, but Air Corps officers didn't seem to subscribe to that theory. The excuse given to us for taking our truckload of food was that pilots had to have a special diet in order to fly in combat, but in the present situation where there were only a dozen or so planes left to fly, why did a hundred or so pilots have to be fed that special diet. We all thought it was terribly unfair and unnecessary.

We were fortunate in our location at Little Baguio. The whole mountain was covered with gigantic hardwood trees whose tops formed a canopy that provided perfect cover from enemy planes. At the base of each tree there were wings growing out for twenty or so feet. They were probably the tops of the tree roots, and a tent could be set up between two of these wings to make a cozy little spot. A small river furnished a good supply of water and a place to bathe, and due to our elevation above sea level, there was usually a cool breeze. Best of all, there were no mosquitoes and therefore no malaria, which is endemic in the lower parts of Bataan where the greater part of our troops were. In a couple of days, all our tents were up and we were snug as bugs in a rug. With plenty of bamboo at hand, the squadron clerk and I built frames for bunks and with strips of canvas nailed across the frames, had what were passably comfortable sleeping arrangements, much better than sleeping on the ground. The only fly in the ointment, and this fly was a big one, was the fact that we were on half rations, and it looked as though we would be getting less food, not more, in the foreseeable future. Breakfast was just a canteen cup of watery rice called *lugao*, sweetened with sugar to make it fit to eat, or salt if you didn't have sugar. This was supposed to last you until supper, when you were issued a mess kit of boiled rice with a small piece of whatever meat was on hand that day, together with a couple of spoons of gravy, and for the first couple of weeks, one slice of bread from the Army bakery, which was delicious. I had always heard about the corned beef which all the troops in the Great War had complained about, but strangely enough, all we ever got, infrequently, was corned beef hash. Some days we got a bit of canned salmon in place of the meat, and perhaps a few peas or carrots, but I don't recall being issued any amount of vegetables. It was inevitable that food and how to get more of it began to be our first consideration.

The first week at Little Baguio passed quietly, but on New Year's Day of 1942, our Squadron Adjutant, 2nd Lt. Harold Whitcomb, of Fremont, Ohio, showed up and informed us that as of now we had been assigned to the 2nd Battalion of the Provisional Infantry Regiment and would be in the reserve forces for use as reenforcements when necessary. This was not unexpected, as without any aircraft we were useless. The bad part of it was that only I and one of my sergeants had had any Infantry service or fired a rifle. None of our officers had any idea of infantry training, so of course it fell to me to take care of it. Everyone was issued a Springfield rifle, Model '03, bolt action, together with a bayonet. Rifle practice was simple, only five rounds of ammunition were available for training, so each man fired at a tree. About all that did was to scare all the monkeys in the vicinity. After that I had to start close order drill and the manual of arms. I couldn't imagine why we had to do close order drill when I knew if we had to do any fighting it would be in the jungle, but the Commanding Officer insisted on it, and so for a few days I marched the outfit up and down the trail all morning. Nobody ever showed up from Headquarters to see how we were doing, so after a week I quit all that foolishness and from then on, all I inspected were the rifles to make sure they were being taken care of.

By the middle of January the squadron was well settled in our pleasant home in the jungle. The latrine rumors had it that there had been a big battle up north, where we had handled the Japs pretty roughly, but the army had to fall back on the MLR, or main line of resistance, which was along the dirt road running across the center of Bataan, from Pilar to Bagac. This line was supposed to be held to the last man. So far we had not been called on, which was OK with us. The only thing Japanese we had seen as yet was a small observation plane which came over every day around noon. We could see it through the treetops as it slowly cruised along, but I doubt if it could see anything through that mass of jungle. I suppose they could get a glimpse of the hospital, but as it was well marked with red crosses, it was not being bothered at this stage of the game.

Our only worry during this period of quiet was that of the food supply. The good bread which we had been getting stopped, the supply of flour having run out, and the coffee ration got progressively smaller. The meat ration, when there was any, was carabao, or water buffalo, and it was really tough, the carabao being used as draft animals by the natives. We began to feel hungry most of the time, which affected all of us, especially those in their teens, I suppose because they were still growing and needed more food than the older guys. This called for action, so as there were a few of the men who had some hunting experience, I thought they might as well see what they could find in the jungle. Two men who were from the Tennessee back country went out to see what there was available. When they came back, they brought in some monkeys which they gave to the cooks to see what they could do with them. Monkey meat turned out to be very good tasting, as long as you hadn't seen it when it was dressed for cooking, because it looked just like a baby in that state. To me, monkey tasted almost like pork chops, and most everybody enjoyed this addition to the food ration. Hunting began to be special duty for the two hillbillies, and they went out every day. When the supply of monkeys got low, they brought in a kind of large lizard, as well as some really big snakes. Both snakes and lizards taste like chicken, and we couldn't get enough of them. Coconuts, pineapples, and sugar are also grown on Bataan, but we were up in the mountains in the jungle, where nothing at all in the way of edibles seemed to grow. I imagine a native of the region could have found plenty to eat, but we Americans were definitely not jungle dwellers. Some of the foragers found cashew nuts, and a few deaths resulted when the nuts were eaten raw. Evidently cashews are deadly poison unless they are roasted before eating. None of my hunters brought any in, so we never had any occasion to try them out. There was one form of animal life in plentiful supply—the rat. If we had but known, it, rat is one of the most tasty and the easiest source of protein that a POW can get. Most Americans would rather die than eat a rat, and at this stage of the game we weren't quite hungry enough to eat one. Later on we were not that fussy. All we did with the hordes of rats was to try to kill them. One way to do that was to put some rice in a mess kit and place it in the middle of a tent, then douse the candle, which is all we had for light. Soon we would hear a noise from the mess kit, everyone would put his flashlight on and throw his bayonet at whatever was eating the rice. A lot of fat rats hit the dust that way. We would have eaten better if they had been given to the cooks.

Malaria had already begun to affect the troops on Bataan, especially those at sea level. There were very few living as high on the mountain as we were, and nearly everyone got malaria in the next few months. We at Little Baguio were issued one quinine tablet per day. Quinine is the ultimate in bitterness, and a Sergeant had to personally see that each man took his. It would have been more sensible to have saved them for issue when we were in mosquito country. When we really needed them, there were none left. Later on, I would have given a month's pay for a few of those quinine pills.

Our stay at Little Baguio came to a sudden end on the 23rd of January. The Japanese had landed in force on the west coast of Bataan, in rear of our main line of resistance, and the Air Corps Regiment was being rushed to the danger point as a reinforcement. We were finally going to see some action. I was to go with Lt. Whitcomb and thirty men to one of the places where the Japs had landed and the rest of the squadron went to another. No one had any spare food to take along, about all we had was our mess gear and what few personal items we hated to leave behind. This was stowed in our gas mask carrier, which made a nice little knapsack after the gas mask was thrown away. There must have been about fifty thousand gas masks littering the landscape of Bataan. About midnight we boarded trucks and headed down the road toward Mariveles and the west coast and what would later be called the battle of the Points.

Chapter 4

Quinauan Point

Our truck convoy passed through Mariveles and continued on up the dirt west coast road. The west coast of Bataan as far as Bagac is all mountain ridges which run into the China Sea ending in small points of land. The road ran along the side of Mt. Bataan, and in many places where the mountain ran into the sea, was cut into the almost perpendicular mountain side. About four miles up this road, at one of these cliffhanger spots, the convoy suddenly stopped. I got out of the truck to find out why, and soon found out. There were Japanese airplanes overhead. They were dive bombers just starting to make their bomb run on a perfect target, our convoy, stuck on the side of a mountain with no cover. Just about everybody went over the left side of the road down the cliff to get away from the trucks, but I and my driver went up a gully on the right side which led up the mountain. We were probably fifty yards from the road when the bombs hit. Fortunately for us, the bombs all fell on the other side of the road. Everything was so dry and dusty, the bombs raised such a cloud of dust that you couldn't see your hand in front of your face for five minutes. When it cleared up a bit, we slid down the gully to the road and found the trucks as good as before. Every one of the bombs had landed on the seaward side of the road and right in the midst of all the men who had jumped over that side. The cliff was so steep that although they were a good distance from the road vertically, they were not far enough away from it horizontally, so they got the worst of the bombing. I lost four men from the outfit, presumably dead, as they never showed up again.

The convoy had to move on, so all the survivors boarded the trucks and we went on for a mile or so, then stopped at a trail leading down the left side of Quinauan Point. An officer at the trail head told us to go down the trail until we met opposition and then hold. We hadn't gone far when we met wounded men coming up the trail. One officer who had a bullet hole in the middle of his stomach said "Keep going, they are just ahead. Show them what Americans can do." At this point, I took the lead, having been a scout in the infantry. I didn't like the situation at all, but at least I would know what to do when we met the enemy. Not far from there we ran into a few men dug in behind trees firing a mortar. They were from a company of Philippine Constabulary, or what amounted to State Police. We joined them and started to dig in, but before we had gotten started, another officer came up and told us to go back up the trail to the coast road and take the trail down the northern side of the point. We were happy to do that, as there were Jap mortar shells coming pretty close to us at the time. Back up the trail and around we went, then down the trail on the north side. No one was on this side but a squad of airmen from the 2nd Observation Squadron and they needed help. We finally reached the tip of the point, about a half mile from the road. This part of the point consisted of a narrow ridge only about ten feet wide and fifty feet long. Lt. Whitcomb arrived in a couple of minutes and told us to dig in there to stop the Japs from going up the northern trail. On the south side of our little ridge was a small bay where the Japanese had landed. Nobody knew how many Japs had landed or just where they were, so after we had dug our foxholes, we were ordered to advance and find the enemy. This was not welcome news to me, having to take twenty-five raw airmen into action against seasoned infantry; however, orders are orders, and with deliberate slowness, we started our advance south.

The ground was fairly flat, but the jungle was unbelievably thick with vines and undergrowth, which made it impossible to move faster than a crawl. In fact, crawling on our bellies was about the only way to move at all. It was impossible to see any further than you could reach. I figured that if I did meet a Jap we would be close enough to shake hands while we shot each other. Not a nice outlook! We had advanced perhaps a hundred yards when we heard machine gun fire right ahead. In my infantry days I had checked out on machine guns, and from the sound of those firing, I knew they were Japanese and close enough to indicate that we had just about ran into their position. It was a good thing we were all hugging the ground, as bullets were zinging through the thick jungle and cutting vines about a foot over our heads. Any further advance would have been foolish, so I placed my men behind trees and prepared to do what we could to keep the Japanese where they were. Fortunately for us, they seemed content to do just that. I will never know why they didn't advance to the coast road and cut it, as they could easily have done in the first hours after they had landed on the point. Probably they were lost in the thick jungle and were as confused as we were. After a bit a messenger came down the north trail and said we had to hold the Japs right where they were. He did drop off a bag of hand grenades with me that he was glad to get rid of. He acted as if he was carrying a bag of rattlesnakes and was afraid they would bite him. I told him I would take the hand grenades and would he go back to where he had come from and tell them thirty airmen are holding who knows how many Japs and they had better get some infantry up here pronto. He gladly made his way in the reverse direction. There were about thirty grenades in the sack, and I made good use of them during the next hour. It wasn't the best place to be throwing grenades, what with all the vines and branches, but I managed to make pretty good use of them. One of the Jap machine guns sounded as though it was in grenade range, so most of my grenades were lobbed in that direction. I don't know what damage I did, but there were long periods when that gun was silent, and perhaps that helped to keep the Japs in their holes instead of advancing. The bad thing about those grenades was that they were made for the 1st World War, and a good share of them didn't explode. The rings that had to be pulled before throwing seemed to be rusted in place as well. I know one thing, if you pulled those rings with your teeth as shown in all the war movies, pretty quick you would be gumming your food!

Chow finally arrived that night about nine and you couldn't imagine what we had for supper. Each man got about ten large boiled raisins and not another thing. I had always hated raisins in any form except straight out of the box, and just looking at those repulsive things almost made me sick. It was only because my stomach was completely empty that I held my nose and ate them. It was funny, they didn't seem to taste that bad and I'm sure I could have done with a couple of hundred more.

After a sleepless night, kept awake by random firing on both sides, we were happy to be relieved by the 3rd Battalion of the 45th Infantry, Philippine Scouts, and were happy to move back to our fox-holes on the north side of the point. The Philippine Scouts were crack troops and if anyone could take care of the Japs, I figured they could. After the Scouts arrived, the Air Corps was placed on beach defense, to prevent further Japanese landings on Quinauan Point. This duty was a lot easier and much less hazardous to the health than rooting them out of the jungle, and more compatible to our level of infantry training. The few Air Corps men who had been on the point when the Japs had landed had left a .50 cal. machine gun behind in their hurry to leave, and we gladly took it over. The Air Corps Infantry had plenty of these guns, which had been removed from aircraft destroyed at Clark Field. Mounted on pipes driven into the ground, they furnished a considerable amount of firepower. As the northern side of Quinauan Point ended at an almost vertical cliff nearly a hundred feet high, we had a perfect field of fire if any Japanese attempted any landing in that direction.

The next few days were spent in relative ease. Lt. Whitcomb arrived to take charge of our little detachment, which by now had dwindled to twenty. We had started out with thirty, but four never showed up after the bombing on the way up, and others had been taken away on some officer's whim. The only officer I had much to do with on Bataan was Lt. Whitcomb, who had enough sense to take a little advice from someone who knew a bit about the Infantry, meaning me. He was a good Joe and we got along well. He made it through the war, went back to his home town of Fremont, Ohio, and was elected Mayor year after year.

It only took a day for us to improve our foxhole and to emplace our machine gun for maximum effect. With nothing else to do, the men were allowed to sleep all day. Any further landings were presumed to occur at night, and all of us had to be on guard during that time. Every hour or so I made the rounds of the foxhole to make sure the men were awake. This was tiring, so I finally settled on having just two men keeping watch for two hours at a time, then having another two take over the watch. This made more sense, as the rest of the men could get a good night's sleep. Nobody ever came around at night to check up on us anyway.

While we had it relatively easy, the Scouts were having a rough time with the Japanese holed up in the jungle. Advances were measured in feet per day, and casualties were heavy, mounting to nearly 50% when the battle ended. For some reason, the Japs never made an attempt to advance, but dug in and stayed put to fight a defensive battle. Their foxhole were made in such a way that they could curl up at the bottom in a recess cut in the side of the hole, and nothing but a direct hit in the hole would put them out of action. The hole also had a cover, and many times when the Scouts had advanced past a foxhole, the occupant would lift up the cover and start firing from the rear. The Japanese also made much use of snipers who climbed trees and then tied themselves to the tree, firing until they were finally spotted and killed. They also used bunches of firecrackers which they threw in the rear of the Scouts to make them think the Japs were in their rear. As the battle wore on, it was clear that infantry alone couldn't do the job, and the Scout artillery was called in and began to shell the Japs. About all this did was to start cutting the jungle down, as most of the shells exploded above the ground due to all the trees. After a few days of this, the Japanese had been pushed back gradually until they occupied a small area about the size of a football field.

Evidently the Japanese had working radios, because now they began to use air drops for supply. A small cargo plane would fly down the west coast and across Agloloma Bay about twenty feet above the water, then zoom up over our position and make the drop. Half of what they dropped missed the target, and after each drop I sent some men out to see what they could find. Happily, a good share of the drop was edible. At first glance, it looked as though the Japanese were dropping dog biscuits, but after sampling one or two, they tasted pretty good, so we decided they must be the Jap emergency ration. We recovered enough so that each of us got about ten pounds, a welcome addition to the scanty rations we were getting at the time. In fact, we were almost starving. Our rations, such as they were, arrived once a day after dark, and had to last us all the next day. We began to find out that the further one was from Mariveles, the less one got to eat. Rice was never issued on the points, and soup was unheard of. Most of the time what we did get was one can of salmon between two men, along with a few of those boiled raisins and a canteen cup of cold coffee. Actually, we were getting more and better food from the Jap air drops. Along with the dog biscuits we found what looked like large brown pills filled with an odd-smelling liquid. No one wanted to try one; we should have, because some medic told us later that it was vitamin B, which we were sadly lacking in our present diet. Besides being short of food, we were also on very short water rations. One canteen full of water per man per day didn't amount to very much as most of it went for drinking, leaving just a bit to splash on your face. That was all the washing we were able to do, and before long we were a pretty dirty bunch.

The Japs kept the air drops coming, the same plane showing up about every couple of hours. It came across the bay on a direct line and right over our position, so after we got used to it, I thought we might as well do something about it, and had our .50-cal. gun manned and ready. The next time it showed up, we opened fire at about two hundred yards. We must have fired hundreds of rounds at that miserable little plane and never knocked it down, even though we could see the tracers hit it right on the money. It is a mystery to me how it came through all that lead. It was just as well that we didn't hit it, and after we started getting the stuff they dropped, we quit trying to shoot it down.

On the evening of the 1st of February we had been on the point a week, and were taking things easy after enjoying our supper of a cupful of rice, two spoonfuls of salmon and our daily cup of coffee, when we saw a couple of flashes out to sea. In a few seconds two shells landed on the coast road. They had been fired from what we took to be a cruiser but was actually a mine layer. That woke us up a bit, as the Japs had been pretty quiet of late. Nothing more happened until about midnight, when we were alerted by machine gun fire from the shore to our right. Looking out in the bay, we saw a group of boats heading for the shore. In no time, every gun on the cliff and on the bay shore was firing as fast as it could be loaded, including all the artillery within range. Tracers lit up the bay like fireworks on the 4th of July. A few minutes later, all four of our remaining P-40s arrived on the scene dropping bombs and strafing the boats. This was all pretty exciting, especially when some of the big guns on Corregidor began bracketing the point we were sitting on. Anyone who has ever heard a 155mm shell overhead will know how we felt with those things going by on either side. They sounded like a freight train to me. I was so worked up I must have eaten a pound of my dog biscuits without even knowing it. In the meantime, I was dropping hand grenades over the edges of our narrow ridge to discourage any Jap who might be trying to climb the steep cliff. It was fun until one of the grenades hit a bamboo tree and dropped to the ground ten feet away from us. I shoved Lt. Whitcomb down in his foxhole and made like a turtle myself. Of course that grenade had to be one of the live ones, and although we were showered with stones and dirt, neither of us was hurt.

Despite all the lead thrown at those Jap barges, half of the Japs made it ashore north of our point, where they were to cause a lot of confusion and trouble for the next few days. In the meantime, they overran my old outfit, the 17th Pursuit Squadron, killing a number of my old buddies. Again, the Scouts had to be called in to finish them off, as all the airmen could do was to try to keep them pined down.

A couple of days after the Japanese had tried their night landing, some of our remaining tanks were brought in to help the Scouts. This combination worked well, the tanks keeping the Japs down in their holes while the Scouts finished them off by dropping a hand grenade down each foxhole. This did the business, with the exception of a few survivors who holed up in caves under the cliffs at the tip of the point. These last had to be rooted out by the Navy, using dynamite. The dead Japanese on Quinauan Point were found to belong to the 1st Battalion of the

20th Infantry Regiment. All the seven hundred men of the battalion had been annihilated in the battle, having fought to the death. Not one had surrendered.

With fighting at an end, we could relax a bit and try to enjoy life more, even though we were still being starved. The daily food ration was still the same, just enough to sustain life. At least we could get in a good night's sleep. One thing we all did was to tour the area where the last of the fighting took place, which was about a hundred square yards covered with black, bloated, horribly smelling Japanese bodies. It was so bad that we all tried not to breathe. Nobody lingered after picking up a few souvenirs such as Japanese rifles, flags, pictures, etc. Before I left, I saw something I could hardly believe. It was a chaplain taking wrist watches off the dead Japanese, and I will never forget it. He was the only chaplain I had seen since the war started and I'm sure he must have had better business to attend to than that. Another thing that astonished me was the fact that every single growing thing in that jungle had been cut down by gunfire. Not a tree or bush had been left standing in the area where the Japanese had holed up during the battle.

The battle of the Points taught the Americans a hard lesson. They found that when the Japanese were on the defensive they were very difficult to handle. Their Bushido training and spirit didn't include the word surrender. Any soldier who surrendered was permanently disgraced, and return to Japan and family was impossible. This made it necessary to kill every one of them. The Japanese soldier was also well trained in jungle fighting. His foxhole was invisible until you fell into it, and snipers tied into trees for days were so hard to spot that any tree that held one had to be sprayed with automatic fire to silence them. They also lived on rations that no American could normally survive on. I say normally, because I am sure that my men and I had been living on less food for the last three weeks than the Japanese we were fighting.

A couple of days after the end of the battle, we were taken back to Little Baguio by truck. No place had ever looked as good to us as our old camp did after our three-week stint in the field. The first order of business was to take a good bath in the little river running by the camp. We were the dirtiest group of men you could ever imagine, after living on our water ration of one quart per day. Not much can be spared for washing in that situation, you may be sure. We all had a good start on a beard, and our coveralls were so stiff with dirt and sweat they could stand by themselves. A couple of hours of scrubbing and we were back to a clean, but still hungry, condition. It was nice to be back to what we called home, in February 1942.

As far as our first experience of actual combat went, I suppose that we accomplished our mission, which was to keep the Japanese tied down until the Scouts arrived on the scene. I will never know whether or not I killed any of the enemy as I never really saw one in the thick jungle, but as I heaved about fifty grenades, I suppose that I may have caused a few casualties in the enemy ranks. One or two killed would have made no difference in the outcome—they all died anyway.

Chapter 5

Interlude

The last two weeks of February passed quietly, the enemy having pulled back from the front lines to rest and await reinforcements after the January battles and the abortive landings on the west coast which had resulted in the loss of an entire Japanese regiment, one battalion at Quinauan Point and the rest at Longoskawayan Point near Mariveles. Sailors turned into Infantry and a few Marines kept this landing under control until the indispensable Scouts arrived. This action ended the same way as that on our point, with every one of the Japs killed. This left the Japanese short of men, and as many of their troops had come down with malaria, they were forced to suspend any offensive action for the time being. Some thoughts were given to an American push, but as half of our troops had malaria, as well as a universal loss of body strength due to the inadequate food ration, the idea of an offensive was soon scratched.

We at Little Baguio were better off than most, due to the absence of the malaria mosquito at our higher altitude. Our food was a bit better, too, due to the many pilots and high ranking officers in the Far East Air Force who lived near us and got better food than anyone else. That is, if you could call a mess kit of *lugao*, or watery rice, for breakfast, and another issue of rice with a few small bits of whatever was available, added to it for supper. By this time everyone had lost whatever body fat they had accumulated in the good days before the war. My normal weight had been around one hundred and seventy-five pounds but after six weeks of one-third rations, I doubt that I weighed a hundred and fifty. Everyone was in the same boat. Even the coffee was running out, and that was just about the limit. A dog-face without his hot cup of coffee is miserable, and we all tried to find a substitute which would serve. I found that roasting banana leaf and then boiling it resulted in something faintly resembling coffee. At least it was better than hot water.

Another bright idea came down from the brass. This was an order to clear a field of fire to our north, but being in the middle of nothing but giant trees up to twenty feet in diameter, all we could do was to cut out the undergrowth. No one had the energy to do any more. Close order drill came up at times, but this silly idea was disregarded. Everything not connected with food was soon forgotten. I finally came up with a bright idea; cigarettes were scarcer on Bataan than food and we were fortunate in owning a truck full of Piedmonts. A few good scroungers with a haversack of Piedmonts might do better than our hillbilly hunters, who, by this time had just about denuded the jungle of edible animal life. "Operation Piedmont" was put into operation, and the results were almost too good to believe. The high-rankers who lived next to us had a lot of canned food to trade for cigarettes and which we added to our slim suppers. The squadron was now down to thirty men, due to the loss of the rest, who had been sent to Longoskawayan point and had been kept there as coast defense, so four cans of corned beef split between thirty, meant that each man got a good addition to his rice and soup. Those on the front line areas were worse off by far that we were in the matter of food, so my traders had little luck in that area. A much more fertile field was the rear area in the vicinity of Mariveles, where most of what remained of the navy was located, and who were eating better than the Army, due to the submarine tender *Canopus*, which had been beached in a small bay near Mariveles. Its electrical system was still operating to keep the ship's stores in good shape, including the ice cream machine, as my traders reported. The *Canopus* turned out to be a gold mine when offered cigarettes, and became a regular trading stop. One memorable day our booty included a can of condensed milk for each man. Our cigarettes brought in a lot of odds and ends, but not enough to make much of a difference in the end. We were a lot better off than the poor guys on the front lines, who got just enough food to keep themselves alive. Half of their ration was lost, strayed, or stolen on the long supply line from Corregidor. As always, those who needed the most wound up with less.

About the end of February, an old buddy of mine, Nick Metta, transferred into the Squadron. I had come across him our first day on Quinauan Point, and had told him that if he could arrange a transfer, I would see that he made Staff Sergeant. Nick and I had been in the same company in the 13th Infantry and had transferred to the Air Corps for duty in the Philippines, arriving in Manila in October of 1939. Although being in different Squadrons, we were still buddies and went out together. He was a good pinochle player, and we spent many hours playing the game for a cent a point by candle light in the orderly room tent. This can run up to quite a sum, as I remember owing old Sgt. Adcock, of Shreveport, Louisiana, about $300. Old Adcock was in his fifties at this time and was an old alcoholic. He made it through the war, somehow, but died in the 1950s before I could pay him.

The 1st Provisional Infantry Battalion, all Air Corps personnel, was now holding a sector of the front line on the Manila Bay side, so Nick and I took a few days off to visit them and look up a few of our old buddies. We filled our haversacks with Piedmonts and caught rides down the east road to find the Battalion well dug in at the east end of the line. We saw a lot of people we knew from Nichols Field, including George Manzi. George had been in the 13th Infantry with Nick and me, and had come over with us. We fixed him up with a half dozen packs of Piedmonts and spent the night talking about old times. The next day we volunteered to go out on the morning patrol of ten men. This patrol went out five kilometers to the front to locate the Japs and to see what they were doing. We walked in single file through the dry rice paddies until we reached a little barrio on the shores of Manila Bay, about a half mile in enemy territory, where some of our Piedmonts were traded for a kilo of brown sugar, some bananas and a scrawny chicken. This made our little trip a success. We never saw a Jap, fortunately, and back in our lines we had a better than usual meal, thanks to our cigarettes.

What I saw while at the front lines opened my eyes to the reality of our situation on Bataan. The men there were in much worse shape than we were, as being at the end of the food chain, they were lucky when they got the full one-third ration. Most had malaria as well as the beginnings of another deadly disease caused by malnutrition. This was a disease unknown to any of our doctors, but familiar to all Filipinos. They called it beri-beri, and it was as deadly as malaria or dysentery, certainly worse in its long time effects. Medicine was almost nonexistent, and about all the sick could do was to suffer. I doubt that more than a quarter of the men on the main defense line were in good enough shape to do any fighting. We were sure glad to get back to our camp at Little Baguio.

Nick and I made one more trip about the middle of March, to visit those of the Squadron who were still at Longoskawayan Point. At the foot of the hill we paid a visit to the *Canopus*. They still had plenty of food, as usual with the Navy, and we had a good meal (including ice cream!), for which we traded two packs of Piedmonts. Smokes were $20 a pack at this stage of the game and not many were available. With full stomachs, we arrived at the Point, where we and our smokes were welcome. We spent the nice moonlight night visiting and drinking hot cocoa made by Cpl. Mike Alinell, one of my cooks. Next morning we spent exploring the point, which, unlike Quinauan Point, was nearly all rock. Fortunately, it was in plain view from Corregidor and they were able to bring some of their big guns to bear on the Japanese, who had trouble digging in on almost bare rock, a big help to the Scouts in their attack. All the three hundred Japs who had landed on Longoskawayan had met their maker there.

On our way back to Little Baguio, we crossed Mariveles Field, which was being built to take all the fighters which were being sent from the U.S. to rebuild our four-plane air force, so we were told. All during the month of March we had been hearing about these reinforcements on the short wave radio. I personally heard one of the announcers say, "The largest convoy in the history of the world is now heading your way," and I, along with all the rest of Bataan, was sucker enough to believe it. This was just about the cruelest thing done to us, to make us think that help was on the way, when the powers that be in Washington had in fact written off the Philippines as early as December of 1941. I will always believe that we were done in by one man, General Dwight D. Eisenhower, who had been placed in charge of the relief of the Philippines by Gen. Marshall, the Chief of Staff. Eisenhower had been in the Philippines in the 1930s under Gen. MacArthur, and had never liked him. I fully believe that Eisenhower hung us out to dry because he hated MacArthur so much, and Marshall and President Roosevelt let him get away with it. If they had been honest about it and told us that we were on our own and nothing could be done to help us, it would have been more merciful. To keep our hopes up, when in fact there was no hope, was the cruelest part of it all. I, for one, will never forget that, as long as I live.

The news that Gen. MacArthur had been ordered to Australia and had left on 11 March didn't improve the outlook, either. It was just another nail in Bataan's coffin. Many of the men felt betrayed when they heard about it, calling the General a coward and a deserter who cared only for his own skin. This was just sour grapes, as any one of us would have given everything he had to be on the same boat with him. The same ones called the General "Dugout Doug" because he lived in the Malinta Tunnel on Corregidor, when in fact he had proved his bravery many times in World War 1 and had to be forced into the tunnel during bombing raids on Corregidor. In any case, he had to obey a direct order by President Roosevelt, who knew he was the best man available to command the American forces in Australia. I expect that Gen. MacArthur would have had some rough treatment if he had been taken by the Japanese!

Chapter 6

Guests of the Emperor

Our quiet life at Little Baguio ended on April 3, the day before Easter Sunday, 1942. Late in the afternoon we heard the roar of Japanese heavy artillery, the opening act of the final assault on our front lines, and from then on the guns never ceased. Japanese bombers swarmed over the entire front line and the east road, making any movement on it impossible during the day. We felt lucky to be up here on the mountain under the trees and not under that storm of shells and bombs. Soon, streams of wounded men began struggling up the road into Hospital #1, our neighbor at Little Baguio, while a trickle of unwounded and unarmed men began to pass on their way down the road toward Mariveles and safety, or so they thought. During the next few days, this trickle became a solid river of men and trucks.

Finally, on the morning of April 8, Lt. Whitcomb told me to get the men ready to march. I assumed that we were finally going to do some fighting, but as orders came down to destroy anything we had in the way of Japanese souvenirs, I began to get the drift of what was really happening. So into a slit trench went my field desk, squadron records, most of my money, wrist watch and high school ring, to be buried four feet deep. Burying my money was a terrible mistake, as I sure could have used it in the future. I expected to be back in the near future to recover everything, so I took care to mark the nearest tree in order to be able to find the right spot when I got back. How wrong can you get? I never got back until 1958, on leave from Okinawa. When I told my story to the Stars and Stripes in Manila, they furnished me with a car, a shovel, and a reporter who went along for the story. When we arrived at Little Baguio, I found the road leading up past the old hospital without trouble. We followed the old road winding through the big trees until we reached the last curve. Almost there, I thought, but when we rounded the curve, what did we see but a monster grove of banana trees! All the giant trees where our old camp had been were gone, as were my hopes of finding my buried treasure. Money, records, trophies, all are still under some banana tree, unless some lucky Filipino farmer found them while planting his trees.

About 11:00 P.M. the squadron fell in and I marched them down to the road, where we expected to turn north to join the battle, but instead were told to head down the mountain toward the town of Mariveles. We joined up with the mass of walking wounded, vehicles of all kinds, groups of filthy and exhausted men, very few of whom were in any kind of formation. In other words, what we were seeing was a defeated army in full retreat. Having been in semi-isolation in Little Baguio, we hadn't realized just what the true situation was, and it was quite a shock to us. Another shock came as we were passing the big ammunition dump, which was blown up by the engineers just as we were leaving Little Baguio. Talk about the 4th of July! No celebration ever held could compare with what we saw when that dump disintegrated. With the road packed by marching men, it was a wonder none were hurt by all the exploding shells and ammunition. It felt as if the whole mountain was shaking, which in fact it was, and not just from the explosions, but from, believe it or not, an earthquake which was occurring at the same time! What a night that was!

As we marched down the mountain, I think that we were the only ones in any formation, but as we went along, the general attitude of defeatism began to take over. I tried for a while to keep the squadron together, some sort of organization and discipline always being better in such a situation, but nothing helped now. What I got for my pains was the answer, "To hell with you, you're no better than we are, now." Finding it was useless to reason with them, I soon resolved to take care of myself and let the devil take care of the rest, if that was what they wanted. At least my buddy Nick Metta stayed with me, so we had some mutual support.

We finally reached the bottom of the mountain early on the 9th of April and joined a great mass of men in a area near the air field. There we were told to told to disable any weapon we were still carrying, and throw it on a pile. This was quite a wrench, as we knew then that this was the final act to the drama and that our part in the war, such as it had been, had come to an end. After Nick and I had added our .45s to the pile, we settled down to await further developments. No food was forthcoming, so we ate very sparingly from the meager food supply that we had managed to carry along. Together we had a half dozen assorted cans of food that we had managed to hoard. Along with these in our haversacks we both had an extra set of khakis, underwear and a spare pair of shoes and socks. Most of the thousands around us had discarded everything except the clothes they were wearing, being too weak or sick to carry any extra weight, so we were in better shape than most.

During the morning, we learned that Gen. King had surrendered Bataan to the Japanese commander, Gen. Homma, his command having disintegrated and being incapable of any more fighting. All we had to do now was to await our fate. More men were arriving, and a great mass of men were huddling together. In all, some sixty-four thousand Filipinos and twelve thousand Americans had been surrendered, the greatest defeat in the history of American arms. It was no fun to be part of such a debacle. Many felt that it was a disgrace to have surrendered, but fighting for four months on almost no food, with no air support or reenforcement of any kind, the majority sick with malaria, I don't think that we on Bataan were disgraced in any way. We did the best we could do with what we had.

Finally, about three o'clock, the suspense came to an end. A couple of Japanese tanks hove into sight, along with a few trucks loaded with soldiers, who herded us into a tight mass of men along the slope of a small hill. Many years later, reading the official history of the campaign in the Philippines, I came across a picture which looked familiar, and lo and behold, there in the center of the crowd, I found myself and Nick. Even at the beginning, it showed that I had been smart enough to stay out of the front ranks. If you were in the front rank when some Jap soldier went amok, you were in trouble, for sure. Pretty soon an officer arrived and gave us a speech, which nobody understood, it being in Japanese. We sat there in the hot sun waiting for further orders. During the afternoon, some of the Japs found a discarded American motorcycle which they finally started and promptly ran into a big tree. Needless to say, nobody laughed. Finally, in early evening, we were prodded into a column and marched west across the air field to the road which ran up the west coast. This was the way to Quinauan Point and Agloloma Bay, where we had killed the six hundred Japanese. I had an idea that we were being taken to the Point where we would be shot in turn, and was mightily relieved when after about a mile, we were shunted off to the right into a dry rice paddy, where we spent the next two days. The next morning a rumor went around that all food we were carrying was going to be taken away from us and that we should eat what we had before we lost it. I should have known better than to believe anything like that, but not wanting to take the chance of losing what we had, Nick and I did as all the rest did, and crammed it all down. I remember having a can of abalone, which I had never eaten before. It was just like chewing rubber, and tasted like it, too. Of course it turned out that the rumor was false, as rumors usually are, but left us without anything to eat at all. I suppose we were lucky to have had anything at all to eat, as the great majority had nothing. For the next two days we sat there just waiting, no food or water being given us, and without latrines of any kind. The area we were in became pretty filthy, as one can imagine.

The Japanese had been separating the Americans from the Filipinos all this time, for reasons of their own. The Filipino Scouts, who were actually in the American Army, tried to stay with us Americans, but were weeded out and forced to go with the Philippine Army. One of the Scouts who I had known at Nichols Field gave me a sock full of unhusked rice, which I was glad to get. I had ideas of cooking it later, when I got to where I was going. Around noon, on our 3rd day in the rice paddy, we were formed up into groups of two hundred and marched back across the airfield with a Jap soldier in the lead and another in the rear, both with loaded rifles and fixed bayonets. As we crossed the airport, we had to run a gauntlet of Japs who searched men at random, taking their rings, watches, money or anything that looked good to them. If anyone was reluctant about giving up his possessions, he was soon made to see the light by being hammered with a rifle butt or poked with a bayonet. Any POW found with Japanese money was beaten into a bloody pulp and taken away, for what purpose you could only imagine. Neither Nick or I had a watch or ring, so all we got was a couple good whacks with a bamboo sword to hurry us up. For once, I was lucky, as I still had my wallet with fifty pesos in it. Those fifty pesos came in handy later on! I still have that wallet, tattered and torn, the only thing that remains of all my prewar possessions.

When we finally made it across the airfield, the Japs herded us into our group of two hundred again, and we started off up the mountain towards Little Baguio. We didn't realize it at the time, but we had just started on the long trek which was to become famous as the Bataan Death March.

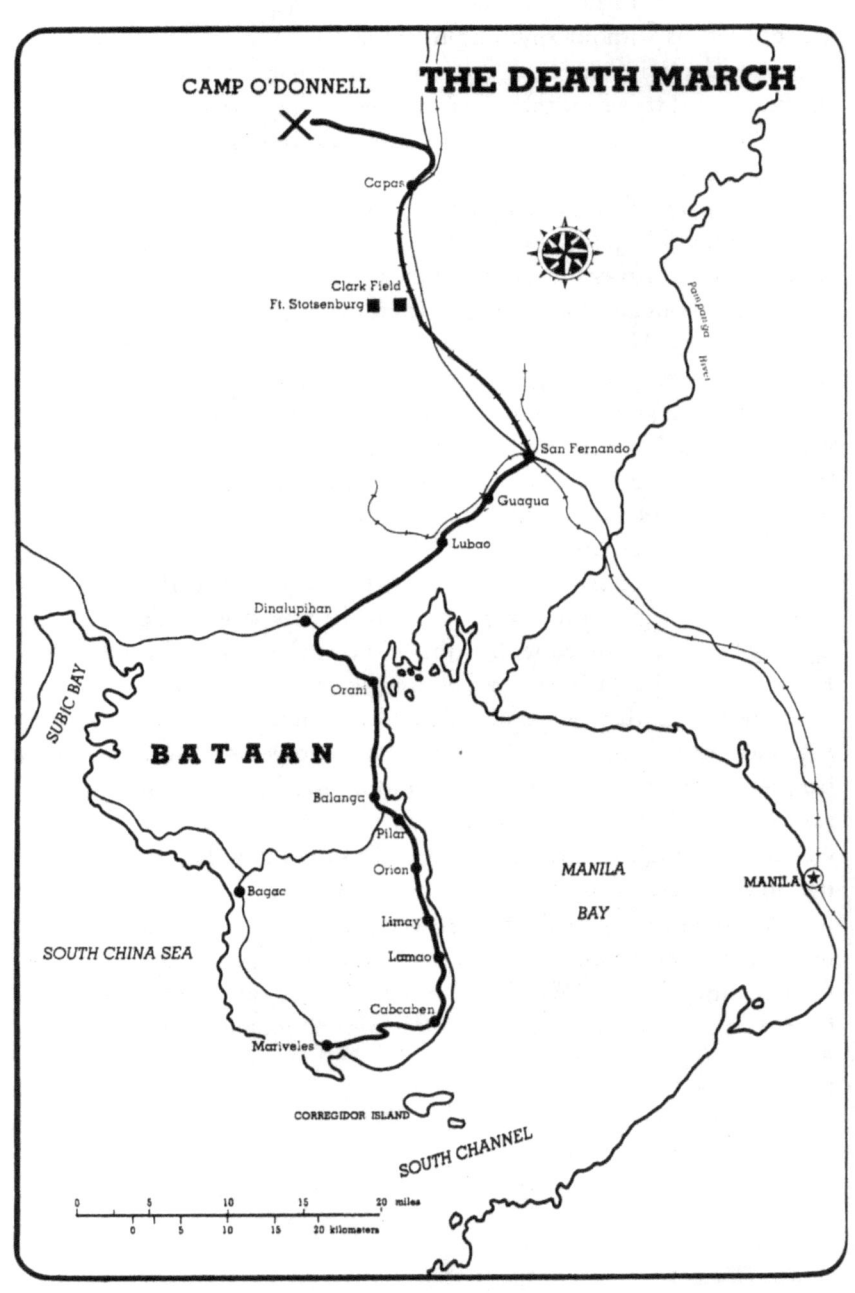

Chapter 7

THE BATAAN DEATH MARCH

Our first day on what was to become famous as the Bataan Death March found our group of two hundred struggling up the steep, winding road which led to Little Baguio, then down the other side of the mountain to Cabcaben, and thence on up the east coast of Bataan. It had been paved, after a fashion, before the war, but after all the traffic and bombing, it was just a gravel road with dust inches deep. Needless to say, everyone became coated with it. Even though this was the first day on the road, there were a great many having a hard time. A lot of the men had been in the final battle, had walked twenty or so miles from the front to Mariveles, and were now having to cover the same ground again in the opposite direction. It would have been a lot easier on Nick and I if the outfit had stayed up at Little Baguio and surrendered there, which would have saved us a lot of hard walking. By the time we were half way to Little Baguio, men began to fall out from weakness and from malaria. Some of these were helped along by their buddies, if they happened to have any, while the weakest just passed out in the ditches by the side of the road. We didn't know what happened to them, but we began to hear random shots, as well as to see dead bodies here and there by the road, so we could guess what had happened to those who couldn't keep up. I finally began to realize what a tough situation we were in. My conception of POW life had been quite different from what we were now seeing. We had expected to be fed and the sick given medical care. Instead, we got no food or medicine at all, and had been robbed and beaten, to say nothing of being shot out of hand by the trigger-happy guards. Things were becoming very serious.

Our progress along the road was slow, as we were continually being shoved off the road by the Japanese trucks and troops heading to Mariveles. It was night when we finally reached the top of the hill and Little Baguio, where we hoped to get a little rest. What we did get was a change of guards, who started us down the other side of the mountain with shouts of "Speedo," which became familiar as the first Japanese command we could understand, no translation needed. Going down the mountain was a bit easier than climbing it, but it was still near ten in the morning when we finally reached Cabcaben, the tiny barrio we all knew well. What greeted us there was a barrage of shells coming from the guns of Corregidor, firing counter battery at some Jap artillery emplaced near the school house. Our guards hurried us past at our best speed, which wasn't too fast, considering that most of us were half dead from our ten-mile trip up and down the mountain. Shells were exploding as we passed, and we had some satisfaction in seeing one Jap gun take a direct hit. We felt like cheering, but that wouldn't have been a very good idea at the time. We got past without anyone being hit, and after another mile up the road, our guards herded us off the road into another dry rice paddy and packed us together in a sitting position, where we stayed for half the day under the blazing sun. In the Philippines, the hot, dry season begins about this time of the year, and that sun was hot! Many of us had no head cover and began passing out. Others had lost their canteens and were going crazy for lack of water. The majority of those that still had canteens had drunk all their water and were almost as bad off. Nick and I still had a little left, perhaps a half pint. Our infantry training had been a great help so far, as we knew how to conserve our water. You can live for a long time without food, but not without water, and this became our greatest worry on the march.

We remained sitting there for about four hours, when the guards, who had been sitting in the shade of a coconut tree, finally woke up and started us off again. The sun treatment in the morning, and marching in the afternoon, became standard procedure for the future. We were glad to be on the move again, even though about a dozen of the group had to be left behind because they couldn't even stand. I suppose the Jap cleanup detail took good care of them. The highway from Cabcaben north ran along the coastal plain with no hills to climb, which was nice. There were deep ditches on both sides of the road filled with muddy water, burned out vehicles, dead animals and lots of dead bodies, American as well as Filipino. The majority of our bunch were so crazy to get water that they would drink out of the ditch and fill their canteens there too, if they had a canteen. This was a good way to get dysentery, which, if there is no medicine available, is fatal to about 98% of those coming down with it. The guards didn't seem to mind, but then, I'm sure our welfare wasn't on their minds. I had a sip of water left, but even if I had had none at all, I knew it was death to drink that water, and I never did. Pretty soon, we began passing artesian wells gushing nice clear water. They were all located across the ditch, perhaps fifty to a hundred yards from the road.

We could see men from the groups ahead of us running across the ditch to the wells, but only a couple would get there before their guards fired a shot or two into the air and they had to run back or be shot. Nick and I were out of water by now, though, and we made up our minds to get some of that good stuff coming out of the ground, so when we saw one well which was closer to the road than most, away we went and filled our canteens, as well as our stomachs, with pure aqua. We did this all the way up the east coast of Bataan. We must have lucked out in drawing two good guards, because nothing ever happened to us, while others were shot doing the same thing. The story told after the war that there was no water available on the Death March just was not true. You just had to have the guts to go and get it.

Another few miles and we arrived at the barrio of Limay and were shunted off into another dry rice paddy for a repeat of the previous night. This time, we were allowed a bit more space and freedom of movement, so I scouted around to see what I could scrounge. Scrounging is an art, and I was good at it. The first thing I spotted was a half dozen rotting onions in the bottom of a ditch. I cleaned them up and soon had what was left cooking in my mess kit over a grass fire. This was our first food in four days, and we really enjoyed those rotten onions. We had learned our first lesson as POWs. To survive, you had to eat whatever was available, whatever it was and however distasteful it looked. Everything edible has vitamins of some sort. A lot of people I knew died because they wouldn't learn this lesson.

The next day was a repeat of the previous two. It became a matter of just putting one foot ahead of the other, and as weak as we all were from lack of food, even that became difficult. More and more were falling by the wayside, never to be seen again. The hundreds of men who were suffering from malaria were having a terrible time trying to keep up with the rest of us. With the temperature around a hundred degrees, no food for a week, not enough energy to find drinking water, a blazing tropical sun, and guards only too willing to bash you with their rifles, it was a wonder that any of them were able to go on. The majority of those whose bodies littered the roadside had certainly been suffering from malaria. Some were lucky enough to get a little help by being half carried along by someone they knew until those helping them ran out of steam. As an example, Nick and I saw one of our old friends from Nichols Field, a Sgt. Carter, and gave him an arm each for a mile or so. He was pretty bad off with malaria, but he made it through the war. I met him at a POW reunion, and he told me that we had saved his life. I doubt that we had, but who knows. I'm sure others must have helped him, too. It seemed that most of those who gave up were the younger men, who would have benefitted by the discipline they had so quickly discarded. The majority of the Air Corps when the war began were just teenagers who had arrived in the Philippines late in 1941 and they were dropping like flies. Those of us who had been in the tropics for some time suffered less from the heat than the newcomers did. I would suppose that the younger ones also needed more food than those fully matured, such as Nick and I. We were both twenty-six years old when the war began, and although pretty hungry by this time, were still perking on all six cylinders. Neither of us had gotten malaria as yet, and of course this was a help.

Late in the afternoon we staggered into the barrio of Orion and were jammed into a small school yard where, wonder of wonders, we each got a rice ball about the size of a baseball, and a pinch of salt. Not very tasty or filling, but welcome all the same, it being the first food we had gotten since the surrender. We were crammed in like sardines in the little school yard, which was one of the filthiest places I had ever seen. Nowhere on the march had there been any sanitary facilities, nor were we allowed to dig a latrine trench. In any case, we had no tools or even the strength to dig one. If someone felt the call of nature, all he could do was drop his pants and let go, with grass, if you could get any, making do for the toilet paper. Locating a clean spot to bed down was an impossibility. Every place we stopped was the same, and before long everyone was a filthy, dust covered, crap-smeared, stinking specimen of humanity.

The seemingly endless night finally ended and we went on our weary way. Around noon we came to the town of Pilar, where the single road from the west coast joined ours. Streams of men who had surrendered on the west coast joined those from Mariveles. Some were carrying stalks of sugar cane found on the way, and I was fortunate enough to get a piece a foot long, on which I happily sucked for the next hour. I doubt that I got much energy from the sugar, but it sure tasted good. A half mile beyond Pilar we came to the town of Balanga, which was the capital of Bataan Province, a busy place in peace time but nearly deserted at present. Our group was stuck into a vacant lot beside the Talisay River, which was a bit cleaner and more roomy than any of our previous camping spots. In fact, we were able to roam around a little. In the middle of the afternoon and everybody was trying to get some sleep, but for some reason, I didn't feel sleepy, and I kept looking at that nice cool looking river, thinking how nice it would feel if I was in it. Our two guards were having their siesta, so I thought, what the hell, I'll take a stab at it. So I went down to the river bank, took my filthy coveralls off, got out my soap and razor, and waded out till I was knee deep in the water. I managed a quick wash, then soaped my face and was just about to shave, when I heard a mad scream from the shore. One of our guards was standing there about ten feet from my clothes and gear, with his rifle pointing at me. I gathered from the way he was acting that he desired my presence on shore as fast as possible. He was between me and my possessions and his bayonet looked pretty sharp, so I warily circled around him, naked as a jay-bird, grabbed up my clothes and pack and took off up the bank. I figured I might as well be dead as to survive naked, as I surely would have been without any clothes in that sun. I did get a bit cleaner than I had been, even if I hadn't had time to shave. We stayed in Balanga that night, and I guess the mosquitos liked the taste of a cleaner skin, as I was unmercifully bitten all night long.

The next day's march was a pretty long one, through the barrios of Abucay and Orani to Hermosa, about ten miles. Nothing eventful happened that day, just the continuous staggering along that horrible road, ankle-deep in dust and as hungry as anyone could be. It seemed as though we had been on that march forever. If there was any hell on earth, we certainly were in it. Another rice paddy was on hand, and we gratefully tottered into it. No food again, so Nick and I sucked on a handful of the raw rice that I was still carrying. We had more room than was usual, the guards seemed to be in better humor. I suppose they thought that we were in such a sad state that we couldn't cause them any trouble. Nick and I found a nice spot on clean grass for a change. We were on the edge of the crowd and were looking forward to a more comfortable night's sleep, but the guards saw where we were and chased us back into the mass of filthy humanity. There went our peaceful night's rest.

The following day was one of the worst ones of my entire life. I thought it had been bad before, but I hadn't known just how bad it was when you had malaria. When I woke up that morning, I found out how malaria felt, because I had just come down with it. No one took my temperature, but it must have been a hundred and three or four. I found that malaria affects you in cycles. For three or four days you are in a fever cycle, then for the next few days you shiver and shake with cold chills. After that you might have a week or so where you are almost normal, then back into the fever and chills. Of course you lose your appetite and have to force down what food you have. This wasn't a problem on the Death March, as we had no food to force down. I started the day's hike feeling red hot and stayed that way all day. I can't imagine how those who had malaria before the march started ever made it. A lot of them did, but it must have been hell.

A couple of miles up the road we came to the bridge across the Culo River, and as we crossed, said goodbye to Bataan. From here it was twenty long miles to San Fernando, the longest, most miserable hike I had ever taken. The road here was better, but just about every hundred yards there was a bridge, the country around here being lowland near the delta of the Pampanga River. All kinds of traffic was heading south, columns of Japanese trucks, infantry and field artillery, some guns drawn by horses and some by soldiers hauling the guns with ropes. Of course there wasn't room for all that and us POWs at the same time, so we had to wait until a bridge was clear, then run across and keep running until we caught up with those ahead of us. As sick and as weak as we all were, this was a horrible experience, not helped in any way by our guards, who helped us along with blows delivered smartly with rifle butts, bamboo clubs and sword scabbards. This part of the march separated the men from the boys!

Our mob of poor POWs staggered through the barrios of Lubao and Guagua, the Filipino population lining the roadside passing out fruit, cold drinks and rice balls to whatever POW they were able to reach while dodging around our guards, who used their rifle butts and bayonets on anyone within reach. Just outside Guagua, I was lucky enough to have a banana leaf parcel shoved at me from a clump of bamboo. I never saw anything of the giver but a hand, but I blessed whoever owned it. My parcel turned out to be rice mixed with pieces of chicken—literally manna from Heaven. I still remember how delicious it tasted.

I don't know how I ever made it to San Fernando, and I was in better shape than most. The day's march must have been twenty torturous, never ending miles, and it was a killer. Bodies lined the ditches at every step of the way. Many had been killed trying to escape, this section of the road being close to a swampy jungle on the right side. If a man was healthy enough to be able to run, and wasn't shot crossing the ditch, he had a good chance of making a getaway. I knew people in the area, too, but in my condition all I could think of was to try to keep going. At this stage of the march, nearly all of the POWs had thrown away everything they had, being too weak to carry anything but the clothing they wore. I still had my haversack, but was rapidly getting to the point where I would have to get rid of it. I was just about at the end of my rope.

At last, just in time, we came to the large town of San Fernando and my bunch was shunted off to the left of the road into a fenced-in school yard and we all dropped to the ground where we were. Nothing mattered but getting some rest and something to eat. We got the rest that night, but nothing to eat. We had what was left of my sock of raw rice for supper.

We didn't know it at the time, but we had just finished the infamous seventy-mile Bataan Death March. The exact number of POWs who made the march is not known, but approximately ten thousand Americans and sixty-two thousand Filipinos who were surrendered on the 9th of April started on the march, and around 90 percent finished it. There were many reasons why the march became such a disaster; the Japanese never expected to capture so many—their own Bushido code of honor required all Japanese to die before surrendering, and they did not understand why we preferred captivity to death. They were too busy attacking Corregidor to worry about us; all their transportation was busy bringing supplies to their staging areas near the town of Mariveles, and although there had been a plan for dealing with the POW situation, poor supervision and confusion reigned. Added to all this was the attitude of the guards toward us. The Japanese private soldiers, who were routinely beaten and slapped by their superiors, were pleased to find some human that they could take out their resentment on. We were a good target, especially as we happened to be POWs, who couldn't fight back. This brutality was common, and rarely checked by their officers or NCOs.

Some made the march in three days, some, like me, took ten long days. A fortunate few were lucky enough to ride the whole distance. The rate of march seemed to depend on the whims of the guards in charge of your group of two hundred. I know that our group spent a lot of time sitting in the sun while others passed us. We did seem to be pretty fortunate in those guards in charge of us. None of us were shot or badly beaten by our guards, but we always had to be ready to dodge when truck convoys were passing on the road if they were carrying troops. They always seemed to have bamboo sticks with which they tried to decapitate any POW within range, usually a man so sick and dazed he didn't have the strength to duck. Many POWs have written about all the atrocities they saw committed on the march, such as prisoners being beheaded, bayoneted, shot or buried alive. By the number of bodies I saw along the road, it was entirely possible that such atrocities did in fact occur, although I never personally saw any. Every POW has his own story to tell, and in many cases the story is embroidered, more or less, in the telling. We all agree on one thing, the Death March was certainly aptly named, an experience none of us can ever forget and wouldn't care to do over again. No one knows the exact number of deaths occurring on that sixty mile trek, the best estimation was that six hundred to seven hundred Americans and from five to ten thousand Filipinos. I know one thing, those that made it all the way were both lucky and tough. I know I was lucky and I must have been tough.

No one ever knew just why the Japanese did what they did to us. I can understand why we had to march; there was no transportation available at the time. I can also understand that to feed that number of POWs was impossible at the time. What we could never understand was why we were forced to sit in the sun, packed in a mass, when there was plenty of shady places and more room available, or why we were forbidden to get water at the plentiful artesian wells when it would have been easy to stop a few minutes while we all filled up our canteens. A man can last a long time if he has plenty of water, even if he doesn't have food. The night stops could also have been arranged so that we could have cleaned up in one of the many rivers we passed. We all wound up doing hard manual labor for the Japs, so why didn't they try to keep us healthier. I really think that they wanted to humiliate us before the Filipinos to show them that we were no longer kings of the hill as we had been for so many years. Some Filipinos never had accepted American rule, but the majority liked the American soldier. Every town we passed through on the march was packed with Filipinos of all ages, who risked their lives by trying to give us food, or hiding those who had escaped. There were those who had welcomed the Japanese, but the Filipinos soon found that the Japanese were no liberators, but occupiers, as the Americans had been. The brutality of the Japanese brought the Filipino back to reality in a short time. In addition, the Filipino POWs were treated worse than the American POWs, for no good reason. Any way you looked at it, the Japanese weren't very likeable.

Chapter 8

The Schoolhouse

After an uncomfortable night trying to sleep on the hard, bare ground, we looked around to see what new hell-hole we had landed in this time. What we saw was a typical Filipino building, tin roof, sliding windows, set on posts. It was an elementary school empty of students. The school grounds were about two acres in extent and fenced in, providing a good holding area for hundreds of American POWs. Nick and I were in a corner of the front yard. On the side and rear of the school building there was a much larger area, also filled with POWs. More were coming in at the gate, and others leaving. As sick as I was, I didn't care much who came or went or what was happening. I just lay there in a stupor of misery. Malaria had me in its clutches. At noon, rice balls were given out, and I choked mine down even though I didn't want it. I still had enough sense to realize that I had to eat to live, so down it went.

After the so-called meal, some of the fittest men were sent out on a work detail, including my buddy Nick, who was doing better than I was. He was only five feet four inches tall, and I suppose could get along better on what food we were getting than I could, at six feet two. While he was gone, I guarded our few possessions, and between bouts of fever and chills, managed to get some water at the single tap, waiting in line for an hour, and was able to clean up my blistered, bloody feet. The school house was being used as a first aid station, and a corpsman painted my blisters with purple gentian, which was all he had. A clean pair of socks from my haversack improved things a bit. I also washed some of the dirt and sweat from my face.

Sanitation at the schoolhouse consisted of a latrine trench a couple of feet wide. It was here that I made my acquaintance with maggots. Maggots filled the latrine trench to the brim with a wriggling, white mass. I had never seen anything in my life like that and made sure that I didn't get close to the edge. If anyone had fallen into that trench, I doubt they would ever had gotten out. Fortunately, I had no desire to empty my bowels. That would have been pretty dangerous.

Nick came in about dark, and shared with me a couple of cans of fruit and a half dozen bananas which he had been able to scrounge during his day's work. It wasn't a bad night, with something in our stomachs and not as tired as we had been. We spent a couple of hours just talking about home and the good times we had had together since we had met at Ft. Devens, and wondering what was in store for us in future.

My second day in the schoolyard passed slowly and just as miserably as the first day. Nick went out early on another work detail and before he left I gave him all the money I had, which was about forty pesos, to buy what food he could. Waiting for his return, I spent the day on the hard ground in the sun with my temperature still in the hundreds, while bunches of POWs came in and went out of the main yard. I thought, Oh, for a couple of the quinine pills which we had grudgingly taken at Little Baguio, where there had been no mosquitos and therefore no malaria! Alas, now when they were needed, there were none to be had.

Night finally arrived, but no Nick. In fact, I never saw him again until the war was over and we were both in the hospital at Ft. Devens. The detail he had been on had been shipped to Cabanatuan, where a large new POW camp was being built. I would really miss him, it was a lot easier to have a good buddy to talk to and to share the hardships of POW life. Besides that, I had lost all the money I possessed, and without a red centavo my chances were pretty slim.

Another day dawned and I was still there on the stony ground, but things were about to change. Those in the small front yard were rounded up and herded out the main gate and on toward the center of town. It looked as though we were starting another march, but after a fifteen minute walk, we arrived at the railway station, where we were lined up beside the track. Crowds of Filipinos lined the streets all the way to the station, all trying to slip us food and drink. Most all of us got something, and I and all the rest will be forever grateful to those people who defied Japanese bayonets to help us. In a few minutes a train of box cars stopped in front of us. What now, we thought?

Chapter 9

Better Than Walking, But Not Much

The train we were about to board consisted of box cars, much smaller than American cars. They were about thirty feet long and eight feet wide. One hundred prisoners had to fit into this small space, but the Japanese, being experts in this business, proceeded to cram each car full to the brim. There were no windows or air vents in the metal cars, and of course the temperature went sky high. My good luck held, as I was among the last to get aboard and the last half dozen were allowed to sit in the doorway with their legs hanging outside. At least we could breathe fresh air, while the unfortunate ones who were first on board suffocated. Our car was one of the few with the doors open, those on the majority of the cars had been closed and locked. This resulted in many deaths from the heat and lack of water, some of whom had been literally roasted alive. Those who suffered from malaria must have gone through hell.

The train crept along, stopping at all the stations on the way. Every station had its crowds of Filipinos evading the guards in order to give water and fruit to those POWs they could reach. All of us on the train were Americans, but this made no difference to those wonderful people, who treated us as if we were their own. Sitting in the open door of our car, I was lucky enough to catch an orange and a couple of bananas, which I promptly ate. At this stage of the game, sharing with others had been forgotten; unless you had a buddy, you gave nothing edible away.

The seemingly endless train trip finally came to an end at the town of Capas. It had taken us four hours to make twenty-five miles. We were lined up in front of the station and started hiking again, on a dirt road leading west. I was almost finished by now, and knew I would never make the next mile, but would you believe it, there was a rickety old Pambusco bus standing there crammed full of people who were in the same shape I was. It was just starting to move when I managed to get to it and fell through the door onto the floor boards, where I lay in a daze while the old bus made the rough trip to what was to be our new home; the infamous hell-hole of Camp O'Donnell.

Chapter 10

Camp O'Donnell

The trip on the bus lasted about fifteen minutes, when we trundled through a gate into a large area enclosed by barbed wire. The passengers were dumped out without ceremony and herded together and forced to sit down in front of a small platform in the blazing sun. We sat for an hour or so, until all those who had been on the train had made it into the camp to join us. Another hour's wait until a short, runty Japanese Captain appeared, who mounted a little stage to give us his speech of welcome. The gist of his speech, relayed to us by an interpreter, was that since Japan hadn't signed the Geneva Agreement, we were not POWs, but guests of the Emperor of Japan, and the lucky ones were those who had died on Bataan. All Americans were dogs and would be treated like dogs. He was certainly right on that prediction!

After the Jap Captain waddled off, a detail of soldiers went through all our gear, searching for any anything Japanese we might have been dumb enough to keep. As always, a few men were caught, and marched away for punishment, what and where unknown. The search over, we were allowed to sit there in the sun. While we waited, who should amble up to me but George Manzi, who I had last seen on my trip to the front lines in March. We talked a bit, but as we were both down with malaria, he soon wandered away. I never saw Manzi again, as he didn't make it through the war. An hour later, we were marched to another area where there were rows of *nipa* huts, each holding a hundred POWs crammed in pretty tight. None of the huts were in very good condition, and ours had a lot of holes in the roof. At least there were bamboo platforms to sleep on, although quite a few had to sleep under the floor due to lack of space. It looked as though our trek had finally come to an end. It was about time! No food was in sight, and everyone was so beat that we all just found a place to lie down and tried to get some sleep.

Next morning an American officer showed up to give us the lowdown on the camp rules and regulations. Evidently some sort of organization had been instituted, with an American as camp commander under the Japanese commander. As I was a 1st Sergeant, I was put in charge of our hut. My duties were to keep a roster of the men in our hut and make out the work details. I also rated a corner of the building with a table and chair. The first detail I dealt with was the water detail. Two men strung half of our canteens on a pole and got in the water line, which was a hundred yards in length. When the camp was opened, there was only one faucet for the thousands of POWs. The situation had improved by the time I arrived, but water was still very critical and it took hours for the detail to make a water trip. As soon as the first detail returned, another two men were sent on the same errand, and these two trips furnished everyone with a quart of water per day, just about enough to keep us alive in the hot weather. No one could wash or shave, and as for doing any laundry, just forget it. Nobody had the energy anyway.

One piece of good news, kitchens had been set up and we were to get two meals a day. Those of us able to walk weaved their way to the mess line, where I spotted Cpl. Mike Alinell, one of my cooks, who I had last seen on Longoskawayan Point in March. He was as glad to see me as I was to see him, and in addition to the half canteen cup of *lugao*, he handed me a couple of small *camotes*, a form of sweet potato, from his private store. This tiny amount of food tasted better than any Thanksgiving dinner I had ever had, and was twice as welcome. During the rest of my time at O'Donnell, *lugao* in the morning and a little rice at night, with perhaps some whistle weed or a tiny bit of carabao meat added to the rice, was the daily ration. This diet amounted to less than a thousand calories, with almost no protein or vitamins. No wonder the sick got sicker and those in fair shape soon got sick. Beri-beri, the vitamin-deficiency disease, soon became prevalent, probably 90% of us had malaria, and dysentery was everywhere. Dysentery was the real killer at O'Donnell, and I was glad that I never drank any water from those ditches and streams on the Death March. Mike Alinell had installed a can of boiling water at the mess line, in which I never forgot to dip my mess gear, before and after eating. This probably saved my life, because the death rate from dysentery was almost 100%.

The next couple of weeks passed slowly. In between bouts of chills and fever, I made up the work details required by the Japs, usually ten men a day, if there were ten of my hundred well enough to work. These details were able to scrounge fruit and other sorts of food, so I picked men for the work details who would give me a portion of whatever they brought back in. I guess you could call this one of the prerequisites of being a 1st Sergeant, and if I hadn't taken advantage when I had the chance, I might never have gotten another chance. As a result, I was able to lay in a few cans of fruit for future use. Another detail I had to fill was the burial detail. This was difficult, as men able to carry bodies and dig graves were pretty scarce. Men were dying at a rate of fifty a day, and bodies were stacked up under the so-called hospital like cord wood. They were buried in mass graves after an orderly had removed one of their dog tags. The rains were beginning at this time of year and if the ditches were full of water, the bodies had to be held down while dirt was thrown on them. It became so bad that it was the almost dead burying the already dead.

At this stage of the game, everyone was in a terribly depressed state. Many had lost their desire to live and just gave up, while others could not adjust to the rice diet and died because they wouldn't or couldn't eat it. Their ration was quickly snapped up by others, like me, who could eat anything. The days were spent talking about home and food. It was a type of daydreaming, but it was something to take your mind off the situation we were in. I seemed to be in a state of suspended animation, not even wanting to go to the latrine. I hadn't had to relieve myself since the day we were captured and still didn't feel the urge. I presume that what little I had to eat was completely absorbed by the needs of my body, with nothing left over to dispose of. In any case, it was better to stay away from the latrines, which were populated by those who had dysentery and just sat there until some more able POW helped them along to the hospital, where they lasted a few more days before being thrown onto the stack. More than one just fell over into the latrine trench and died in it. The hospital was always full, and although there were doctors and medics, they had no quinine for the malaria or sulpha drugs for dysentery, so about all they could do was to try and keep the flies away. Speaking of flies, they were the curse of the camp.

Swarms of big black ones laid their eggs at the latrine, and then, in search of food, came after ours. It was a constant battle to keep them from getting your rice before you did. We had no mosquito nets or anything to make a net out of, so the best we could do was to keep the lid on your mess kit and try to sneak a spoonful of rice into your mouth before a big, black, filthy fly landed on it. Some times they were so thick that was impossible, and I can testify that having a big, black, dirty fly in your mouth is no fun!

After about three weeks in Camp O'Donnell, I could feel myself going downhill at a good clip. Malaria was still with me, and I was losing weight fast. I couldn't see the use of just going on as I was, so I thought that maybe, just maybe, if I went to the hospital something might be available that I didn't know about which would give me a little relief, so one morning I managed the quarter of a mile trek to the hospital, where I was told to find a place to sleep under the building, as the wards were overflowing. I tried to find a smooth spot to park my carcass, but with stones covering most of the ground, I just gave up and flopped. In the next two days, I didn't even see a doctor, to say nothing of any quinine. All we got was a bowl of soupy rice once a day. I was under one leg of the L-shaped building and they kept moving me down the leg in the direction of the corner. If you turned the corner, you were in St. Peter's ward, and you know what that means. On my third morning under the hospital, the men on either side of me had died during the night, and I began thinking that if I stayed there one more day, I would be turning the corner into St. Peter's ward, and at the end of that ward was the cordwood pile of bodies waiting for the watery ditch. Right then I made the best decision I could have made. I said to myself, "Locke, if you don't get out of here, your bones will stay in the Philippines and you sure don't want that to happen, so let's get up and go!", which was what I did. Nobody cared whether I left or not, so I just got up and made my way back to the hut. I could barely move, but taking my time and resting every ten feet or so, I finally made it. My trip to the hospital had been a great big bust.

The Japanese had begun to ship out large working parties of those POWs they considered healthy enough to perform hard manual labor, and just about everyone who could still move tried to qualify. Any place would be better than Camp O'Donnell, was the universal sentiment. It didn't matter where the work detail was headed, just as long it was out of O'Donnell. Rumors came into the camp that the work details were going all over the Philippines, to repair blown-up bridges and railroads, or back to Bataan to collect and repair the hundreds of disabled American vehicles. Being determined to get out of O'Donnell before I kicked the bucket, I decided to volunteer for the next detail. It was easy to add my name to the next list, as I made them out myself, at least the one from my group. It so happened that a detail was to leave the next morning, so I put my name down at the head of my list, and with the help of a couple of my buddies, reported at the assembly point, only to be told that the detail wouldn't be leaving until the next day. I was too sick and miserable to go back to the hut, so I just sat down in the shade of another hut to wait. During the evening, it started to pour rain. I tried to get under cover in the hut, but for some reason the occupants wouldn't let me in. I didn't really care much, as the cool rain felt good on my hot body. There was a ditch nearby full of rainwater, and it looked so cool that I just naturally laid myself down it and let the water cool me off. I hadn't felt that good since I had first came down with malaria. When morning came, I was just about able to get back to where a half dozen trucks were lined up ready to take the work detail to wherever it was going. No one seemed to be in charge, so with the help of a couple of men, I made it into one of the trucks, where I wound up sitting with my back against the cab. The convoy moved out at last, and I can remember going out of the gate and thinking I had finally made it out of O'Donnell without leaving my bones there!

It was a good thing I did get out, as when the camp closed down about the end of May, fifteen hundred of the nine thousand Americans interned there had died. No one knows how many Filipinos died there, but it must have been close to ten thousand. I had seen a continuous line of Filipinos coming down the road, two men carrying a body slung between them on a pole. We Americans had been separated from the Filipinos at O'Donnell, and I doubt if their area was as good as ours. If anything, the Japs treated them worse than they did us, so they must have had it pretty bad.

Anyway, I was still alive and kicking, however feebly, and on my way to some better place. It had to be better, as no place could be as bad as Camp O'Donnell.

Chapter 11

BACK TO BATAAN

The trucks carrying our work detail turned south at Capas and followed Route 3 to San Fernando, turned to the right again and headed toward Bataan, the Death March in reverse. Traveling down the same road I had made my weary way up a short time ago, I was pretty thankful that this time I was riding instead of walking. We crossed the bridge into Bataan, which I had hoped never to see again, and about a mile further on, the convoy stopped beside the road. Evidently it was for a lunch break, as our guards sat down under a tree and began eating. We poor POWs got no food, but had to make do with what we had, if we were lucky enough to have anything. I had a small can of peaches left, which was about all I could eat anyway. While we were eating, the truck we had been in took off down the road. The guard said, "Come back soon," but when we started up again, my truck hadn't got back, and I had lost everything I had but my mess spoon and the khakis I was wearing. This was a major catastrophe, as I had had spare clothing, extra shoes, socks, etc. in my haversack, as well as the few personal articles I had managed to hide from the Japs. From relative wealth to extreme poverty in fifteen minutes!

Jammed into another truck, I went through more suffering. There were bolts sticking out of the truck body where I was sitting, and being packed in like sardines, I couldn't get away from one that was jabbing me in the back. I can still feel the end of that bolt. We followed the coast road toward Mariveles until we arrived, in late afternoon, at the now familiar barrio of Cabcaben and pulled up in front of the schoolhouse, where we got out of the trucks and were formed up in two ranks by our guard, to be inspected by a Jap officer who came out of the schoolhouse. After looking over our sorry bunch, he surprised us by saying in English, "All sick fall out," whereupon I did just that, and with two or three others, was herded around to the back of the building into a large tent furnished with cots and mosquito nets. I had never liked sleeping on a cot, but after such a long time without any sort of bed, that cot felt like heaven.

The first thing next morning, a Japanese doctor looked us over and took our temperatures. I guess mine must have been up there, because I and two more POWs were put into a Ford sedan and taken up the hill to Little Baguio and the General Hospital there. It was still in operation, and I couldn't believe I had been lucky enough to wind up there. I was put to bed on a bamboo platform and given a dose of liquid quinine and a bowl of soup which even had a piece of meat in it! The C.O. of the hospital, Col. Duckworth, was a fantastic officer who had the Japs doing just about everything he wanted done, including providing carabao meat for the hospital when it was available. A few badly wounded Japs had been taken prisoner during the early fighting, and they had been treated and kept here at the hospital, and this probably accounted for all the favors the Japs did for the Colonel.

In a few days, my fever had gone down and I was feeling a lot better. The quinine was doing its job, in fact, it did it so well that I never had another bout of malaria, thank God. I even managed to borrow a razor and had my first shave since the surrender. I had arrived at Little Baguio on the 29th of May, so you can imagine how I looked. I was also able to take a sitting-down shower, being too weak to stand very long. A Filipino was kind enough to wash my khakis for me, and my entire wardrobe consisting of a pair of socks, shorts and khakis was clean at last. The doctors put me on a scale and my weight was ninety-six pounds, believe it or not. You can imagine how I looked, six feet two inches tall and that skinny. The doctors were amazed, as I was the first man they had seen from Camp O'Donnell. If they had been there, they would have seen plenty in worse shape than me. I know one thing, I had no meat to sit on. After a few days on that good soup, I had a feeling I would like to go to the latrine, and after sitting there for an hour, I managed to have the first bowel movement I had had in seven weeks. I know that is hard to believe, but it is the Gospel truth. Life was looking quite a bit better. I could have stayed there forever.

All good things come to an end, however, and on the 19th of June, the entire hospital was moved. The doctors and medical personnel, with all the equipment, were sent to Camp O'Donnell, to give the so-called hospital there some badly needed help. The patients, including yours truly, went by truck to Bilibid Prison in Manila. This was about a hundred-mile trip, and was much more pleasant than my previous one. I felt so much better that I was able to stand up and wave to all the Filipinos on the way, as well as to collect fruit from those kind people. In the early evening, the trucks reached the city of Manila and passed through the gates of Bilibid Prison.

Chapter 12

Bilibid Prison

Old Bilibid Prison, located in the center of Manila, had been built by the Spanish in 1865. It was shaped like a wheel, with the cell-blocks, each one hundred eighty by forty feet, radiating from the center like spokes in the wheel. It was surrounded by a high, electrified wall with guard stations spaced along the top of the wall. Americans, under a Jap commanding officer, were handling all the administration, and I was assigned to one of the cell blocks designated as a convalescent ward. There were no cells, just open space, filled with POWs recovering from malaria like me. Everyone had a mattress on the bare cement floor. Not too bad, considering my previous sleeping arrangements. At least I had a roof over my head and something to sleep on, and plenty of good water from the city water system. And, wonder of wonders, a flushing system for the latrines, using fifty-five gallon drums cut in two on a diagonal and mounted on a steel rod. A stream of water from a tap ran into the drum, which automatically dumped its contents into the latrine trough, washing everything into the city sewer. It was fascinating to watch, and most efficient. It really kept the fly population down, and although there were flies, they were nothing compared to the other POW camps. There were no bathing facilities in our ward, but one could stand under the eaves when it rained and have a nice shower.

When the Japanese had first occupied Manila, they had shipped all the native prisoners in Bilibid to other prisons in the provinces. It was then used to confine American civilians and the few prisoners taken before the Bataan surrender, after which the civilians were transferred to Santo Tomas University. Bilibid was used as a *repple-depple*, or way station, for POWs coming or going on work details. All the POWs in Camp O'Donnell had been shipped out to one of the large camps situated near Cabanatuan, which was located sixty miles north of Manila. POW work details from these camps came through Bilibid, where they usually stopped for a day or two before going on to wherever their detail was headed. Details whose work had been finished, such as a bridge having been repaired down south, also came into Bilibid for a day or two before going back to Cabanatuan. When we arrived in Bilibid from

Little Baguio, we found out that Corregidor had surrendered on the 6th of May, and all the Corregidor POWs had been marched through Manila to Bilibid and then sent by train to Cabanatuan. Their sick and wounded were in Bilibid when I got there.

The men from Corregidor were in much better physical condition than the ones who had been on Bataan and made the Death March. While they had been bombed about every day, they all had been well dug in. Being where all the food was, they ate more and better than we on Bataan. The actual fighting on Corregidor had lasted less than one day, and after the surrender, the new POWs had been kept in a garage area for a day or two, then were carried by boat to the beach a few miles south of Manila. They were then marched through Manila, which was a Japanese copy of a Roman triumph, to show the Filipinos what they had done to the high and mighty Americans. After a day at Bilibid, they were off to Cabanatuan. All the Corregidor people that I saw seemed to be in fairly good health and well dressed. Most had what gear they were able to carry, so were pretty well equipped to begin their life as a POW. All the Bataan POWs were close to death from their three-month ordeal of fighting, starvation, and bouts of malaria. To top it all off, the horrible seventy-mile Death March. Add to that a month or so in Camp O'Donnell, and it was a wonder that any of us had more than a pair of pants and a shirt, and perhaps a mess kit or canteen. All I had was a spoon, and there were many like me. I guess you could say that the Bataan boys envied the well-dressed people who had been on Corregidor. They kept what they had, too. I can't blame them for that, as I would most likely have done the same if I had been in their shoes.

Bilibid was a pretty good place to be if you were sick. All the Navy doctors from Canacao had been brought into Bilibid. They had quite a stock of medicine as well as a complete operating room. I was given a few more doses of quinine which controlled my malaria. In fact, I never had an attack again, thanks be. There are more than one kind of malaria, and I must have had the good kind, because a lot of men I know had attacks for years. The food in Bilibid was the same watery *lugao* in the morning, and a bowl of soup made with vegetable tops and perhaps a few small bits of carabao meat or fish in it, as well as a small bowl of rice. It was a bit better than I had had previously, and you didn't have to fight the flies for it, either. I doubt if there were many calories in our food, but there must have been some, as my weight gradually rose a bit. It could hardly have gone down, or I would have disappeared. Of course all of us were continuously hungry, and all we ever talked about was food and sometimes about home. Speaking of home, we were finally allowed to fill out a card stating that we were alive and being well treated by the Japs. The card said this, and all we had to do was sign it and print the address on the front. I don't know when the card was sent, but I signed it the last week of June 1942, and my mother got it on my birthday, the 3rd of August 1943. At least she had finally found out that I was alive, a year and eight months after the war began.

My rank as 1st Sergeant came to my rescue again. I was put in charge of my ward and ran the work detail roster. Even though we were all on convalescent status, everyone able to walk had to do some work. Just after I had arrived, a small commissary, or store, had been started in one of the cell blocks. If you had any money, you could buy sugar, beans, tooth powder, pencils and small notebooks. Of course it was of little use to me, not being particularly flush with money. However, as all purchases had to be made through one man from each ward, who took the orders, bought the goods, and delivered them. I happily designated myself to be the buyer for my ward, and for the next couple of months went to the store each morning. This duty was a lifesaver for me, as it enabled me to make a little money. When sugar was bought at the store, a canteen cup holding about a pint was used as a measure. The cup was dipped into the sugar bag and emptied into a large can which would hold all the sugar bought for the ward. I made sure that my canteen cup was heaped up high when I bought any. When I delivered the sugar to the buyers in my ward, I gave them a level cup. Any sugar over this became mine, so for every four cups I sold, I accumulated one cup for myself, which I sold for fifty centavos. In this way, I accumulated a few pesos, and was able to buy things I needed. Of course some of my sugar went to make the morning *lugao* fit to eat. I suppose you could say that my shorting the sugar was dishonest, but when you are a penniless POW the rules are bent in every direction. Another of my duties was to go after the supper rice and soup with one of my buddies, and after everyone had been served, there was usually a few spoonfuls left in the bottom of the bucket, which we shared. Every POW had his own method of improving his lot. Some did laundry, mended clothes, cleaned up and waited on a wealthier one, cut hair, or scoured the prison grounds for cigarette butts from which the bits of tobacco were taken and sold.

I had quite a surprise one day when a work detail arrived from someplace down in the southern part of Luzon. One of the detail was

Sandy Blau, who had run the payday poker games for me at Clark Field. He had been on one of the points when Bataan surrendered and had made it to Corregidor. While on the island he had played a lot of high stakes poker with a bunch of officers, and being a professional gambler, had a pocket full of IOUs as well as quite a bit of cash money. We had a good visit, and before he left for Cabanatuan the next day, gave me forty pesos. This was enough to get me started in business. At this time in Bilibid, the Japanese were fairly lenient in their control, letting the American doctors run the place. There were a few guards inside, and of course we had to salute them, but beatings and slapping were rare. The guard privates were greedy for money, and it was possible to bribe the ones on the wall into buying food, cigarettes or whatever after his tour of duty. A POW wanting to use this service would hand up five pesos to the guard along with his name. The guard would tell the POW when to be at the wall to get his merchandise. This was always a surprise. The guard lowered a paper sack to you, in which you might find a bunch of bananas or some other kind of fruit, soap, tooth paste, candy or bakery goods. What you got was probably worth two pesos, but whatever it was, it was a godsend, and both POW and guard were satisfied. I always asked for penny candy, everyone being starved for sweets. The POWs had set up a market in which you could buy just about anything—if you had money. The market was set up between two of the cell blocks and looked like an American flea market. The choice spots, which were in the shade, had all been preempted by those POWs who had lost arms or legs in the Bataan fighting and were permanent residents of Bilibid. One of these had the monopoly on sandals, or "go-aheads," as we called them. These were made from used auto tires, with a strap added to hold them on. He did a rushing business, due to the fact that our shoes were rapidly wearing out and there were no new ones available. These go-aheads became standard footwear in the Philippine camps. Also sold in the market were all kinds of fruit, coconuts, cigarettes, candy, toilet articles, rice cakes, sugar, odds and ends of clothing, and sometimes the tastiest food of all, fried rat. You had to eat rat to find out just how tasty it was. They were in great demand and some of the men became expert at catching them. Next in demand was dog meat, standard fare in the Philippines. Cat was a poor third, but available at times. Hungry cats could be lured into the prison through small holes in the wall or brought in by men who worked on details in town. Needless to say, about anything that could walk or fly, especially grasshoppers, was disposed of without delay by hungry Americans. That is to say, any hungry American with pesos, and most had nothing at all in the way of money.

On days that I had been lucky enough to find a guard who would take my money and buy for me, I would find an open space along the cell block and set up shop. I usually ordered centavo candy and normally got a hundred pieces, and selling them at ten centavos each, would clear five pesos on the deal. With the money I made, I began to buy clothing and other things to replace what I had lost on *ataan*. I was really fortunate in obtaining a set of mechanic's coveralls big enough for me. These proved to be my wisest buy, although I didn't know it at the time. I was even able to buy duck eggs once in a while. Wonderful!

During the summer of 1942, time passed slowly in Bilibid Prison. As convalescent POWs were judged well enough to work, they were shipped out to Cabanatuan. I was gaining a little weight, but thin as a match stick. Our food was still the same rice and soup, but the brown sugar which went on our morning *lugao* made it easier to eat. My bunk mate was a little sailor from Texas named Arthur Connell, who made an acey-deucy board, and taught me how to play this Navy game. Thus passed many a tedious hour. Another buddy was redheaded Johnny Peterson, from Big Timber, Montana, who had been a cowboy and had lots of stories to tell. With little else to do, shooting the breeze made the time go a bit faster. Most of the talk was about food, of course, as well as guessing when the U.S. would win the war and we would be free. We knew nothing of the real situation, and our consensus was that we would be home in six months. The few pessimists were laughed at. My guess was July 1943—wrong by more than two years.

Along about the middle of August I noticed that my feet and ankles were swelling up until I could barely put my shoes on, and my legs seemed to be losing strength as well. The swelling progressed upward slowly, and by the end of the month had reached my knees. My legs had a very strange feeling, as if they were two sticks of wood with twenty pound weights attached to the ankles. They were there, but didn't feel as though they belonged to me, and just wouldn't do what they were supposed to do. If I tried to run or move quickly my legs stayed still and I fell on my face. Finally, my legs became numb and lost all feeling. I knew something was radically wrong but didn't know just what. A lot of the other patients in our ward were suffering the same symptoms and many were worse. Finally a Filipino told me that I had beri-beri. Beri-beri was a tropical disease, and none of our doctors had ever seen it before and had no idea what caused it or what to do about it, but one of our Navy corpsmen, Lester Tappy, happened to have saved a book all about diseases which I borrowed and looked beri-beri up. What I found wasn't very encouraging. I found that it was a vitamin-deficiency disease affecting the nervous system. The symptoms were swelling of the lower extremities, gradually progressing upward toward the heart. Now came the shocker—when the swelling reached the heart, there were twenty-four hours of agony, and you were dead. I could see that my prognosis wasn't too good! Along with this came pictures of people with legs like elephants and testicles swollen to the size of footballs. I had already seen this around the ward, and those people really had died. I could see that I was in for it, as there was no hope in wishing for vitamins, none being available. However, the swelling never got much above my knees, so I escaped that final agony. I didn't get any better, but stayed in the same condition. There was a native remedy used by all the Filipinos, available in all the native stores, which would have cured all of us, but our doctors didn't know about it, and the Japanese wouldn't procure any. *Tiki-tiki*, as it was called, was just a syrup made from the husks of rice, plentiful and cheap. All oriental peoples ate nothing but white rice, which had no vitamins at all, and took *Tiki-tiki* to prevent beri-beri. If we had been fed brown rice instead of white, none of us would ever have suffered the agonies and the deaths, as well as the lasting effects of this disease. Fifty-five years after the war, former Japanese POWs are still feeling these effects, and most are receiving disability compensation from the government.

Time went slowly and miserably in Bilibid Prison. A few convalescents became healthy enough to be shipped out to Cabanatuan and their places were filled by others who had contracted malaria, beri-beri, or dysentery on some detail. I began to think that I was doomed to stay there forever, as all I seemed to be doing was to hold my own, with difficulty, due to my beri-beri legs. Things change, however, in unexpected ways. On the 12th of October, a medic appeared with an announcement. Fifteen volunteers were wanted from the convalescent ward to go to Japan. A party of thirty officers and five enlisted men who had been captured on Leyte, Iloilo and Panay, islands south of Luzon, had just arrived in Bilibid en route to Japan. We had only a couple of hours to think it over. There were a lot of reasons why we shouldn't volunteer, but the more I thought about it, there were good reasons why we should go. One big reason, to me at least, was that Japan was not a tropical country. I could be sure that I wouldn't get malaria again, and most likely would get rid of my beri-beri. I was a little wrong on that, as it doesn't matter where you live; without the proper vitamins, you will still get it. Another good reason to go, and I was right on this one, was that I had an idea that if we went by ship, sooner or later those ships would be getting sunk, and at this stage of the war, it would be safer to go right now, before the U. S. Navy submarines began to do their work. I always had wanted to see Japan, anyway, and so I put my name down to go. As a POW, you never have the chance to decide anything, and when you do, you had better make the right choice. It turned out, eventually, that I made a good choice this time.

I think I was the sole volunteer, but fourteen others were picked, and we were all examined to see if we had any infectious diseases. We were then told to be at the main gate the next morning with all our possessions. Nothing was said about beri-beri or I wouldn't have made it. That evening I packed up all I had into a woven straw Filipino shopping bag, as I hadn't been able to buy a haversack or bag. Then I made a tour of the ward to say goodbye to the guys I had been with so long, and in the morning fell in with the rest of the detail. I left Bilibid on the 12th of October 1942. When we fifteen poor orphans from Bilibid joined the thirty-five who had come from the southern islands, we felt like tramps. They had never been in action, had lived off the fat of the land, and when they had surrendered after the fall of Corregidor, still had all their possessions. Most had full haversacks, barracks bags and suitcases. One Navy chief warrant officer even had his footlocker, carried by two enlisted men. They where all dressed in clean uniforms, and I am sure they must have resented our raggedly clothed presence. Out the main gate of Bilibid we marched, down the street to the Bridge of Spain where we crossed the Pasig River. This bridge had quite a steep grade toward the center, and I found my legs refusing to do their duty. Fortunately, two of the Bilibid people helped me over the hump and practically carried me the rest of the way to Pier 7, on the Manila docks. We marched up the pier to where a small ship was tied up. As we passed the bow of the ship, I noticed the name on the bow, *Ryukyu Maru*. It was a small cargo ship, I would guess of five hundred tons, but of this I am not sure. We climbed up the gangplank and were directed to the fore hatch. The hatch was battened down for the trip and we were packed on top of it, not a bad place at all when one considers how later POWs were treated on their trips to Japan. It was pretty hot sitting in the sun, but us Bataan people were used to that and it didn't bother us too much. In the evening we were issued rice and what was, to the ones from Bilibid, a most delicious soup, which had pieces of fat pork and pumpkin floating around in it. At least we found it delicious, and we ate until we were full for a change. The others turned their noses up at it and just pecked at it, which bothered us not at all, since we were ready to eat anything and everything that came our way. In the evening, a group of Filipino ladies from the Philippine Red Cross came on board to present us with sugar, coconuts and all kinds of fruit, which was greatly appreciated. This was one of the very few times that the Japanese allowed the Red Cross anywhere near the POWs, although they had tried many times. We all had a good sleep that night with a full stomach for a change, not worrying about what the morrow would bring. We had learned by now that we had to take what came anyway.

Chapter 13

On the High Seas

The 13th of October dawned bright and clear. Our breakfast of rice and soup was received with enthusiasm. Fruit left over from the evening before topped this repast, delicious to us hungry POWs. We found that our guards were very lenient, and as long as we remained in the vicinity of the fore hatch they didn't pay much attention to us. Our toilet facilities consisted of a wooden contraption hung overside on the port bow, handy when needed, which was often. A diet which was mostly liquid made it necessary to eliminate water about every hour.

Late in the afternoon, the *Ryukyu Maru* cleared the dock and headed west across Manila Bay. It was a sad farewell to Manila, which we had known and enjoyed so much in the years before the war, but that was all water under the bridge now, and we just had to forget it and look ahead. It was getting dark when we passed between Corregidor and the tip of Bataan. Corregidor resembled a desert compared to the lush tropical island it had been. The Jap bombing had destroyed all the buildings and I don't think there was a single tree left standing. The small port of Mariveles and the air field where we had surrendered to the Japanese could be seen off the starboard, bringing back painful memories. It had only been a little longer than six months since the surrender, but it seemed to me to have been eight years, considering what I had been through in that time. I watched the dim outlines of the Philippines fade away into the night with mixed emotions. I had spent two and a half good years there, which had come to a halt when Clark Field had been bombed. Now, I was leaving a place where I had almost met my maker. I could do nothing about it now. I had made the decision to leave the past behind and let the future take care of itself. In the meantime I would enjoy all that good soup!

The next day we continued heading west into the South China Sea. The weather worsened all day long and by evening the ship was bouncing around quite a bit. When supper arrived, only a few, including yours truly, were able to eat. The rest were seasick and the sight of pork fat didn't help them any. It didn't bother me at all, and I happily downed a few extra portions. Before dark, it got so rough that we were moved from our perch on the fore hatch into what was cargo space, about thirty feet square, off the starboard side of the foredeck under the bridge. With the exception of having to bunk down on bare steel, it wasn't that bad. I was becoming used to sleeping on hard surfaces by this time, and our space was warm and dry. The only trouble was that there was barely enough light to tell one hand from another, and navigating through fifty sleeping people on your frequent trips to the latrine was quite an experience. Most were forgiving when stepped on, but the warrant officer, named Shaputnick, was really offended when anyone brushed against him. He was still dressed in a spotless uniform and I guess he expected it to stay that way forever. More of Mr. Shaputnick later. Our trips to the hanging latrine were quite an adventure. The bow of the ship was plunging up and down about thirty feet on each wave, and the waves threatened to come up through the hole and wash you into the ocean. All you could do was to hold on and hope. By the next morning we were in the grip of a full-fledged typhoon. The ship headed for the Pescadores, a small group of islands off the China coast which was inhabited by a few fishermen. The anchor was dropped in the lee of one of the islands, where we stayed for a couple of days until the typhoon blew itself out.

Leaving the Pescadores, the ship headed east. Zigzagging as we went, it took two days to make port at Taihoku, on the island of Taiwan, where we anchored offshore. We were there two days, and during our stay, all POWs able to work were given tasks to take up the time. I was given some tools and spent my time chipping paint. Others had to bail out landing barges stacked three high on the ship's main deck. My work wasn't hard and it was nice to be out in the good weather where you could see the harbor and watch what was going on. Taihoku was a big port with a lot of ships coming and going. The morning we left, three other ships joined us and we made up a convoy. This made us realize that we would be in danger on the last leg of our trip to Japan. Of course this had been one of my reasons for wanting to leave the Philippines early. It didn't make me feel any better to know that I had been right.

Our ship turned north and headed for the Ryukyus and Japan, our convoy zigzagging as we went. We were probably making eight knots, as the China Sea was still very rough. I was feeling wonderfully well, eating my fill of rice and pumpkin and pork fat soup. I suppose my system was starved for grease of any kind. That is what hunger does for you, I wouldn't have eaten that stuff for anything before I became a POW. I had always hated fat. I was gaining weight and my legs felt stronger day by day, so evidently that soup had some good in it. All in all, I wouldn't have minded if I could have joined the crew and stayed on the *Ryukyu Maru* for the duration. That would have done me in, though, as the *Ryukyu Maru* was sunk in 1944, but my trip on it was one of the more pleasant times during my ordeal as a POW.

Nearing the Ryukyu Islands, just south of mainland Japan, we were making our usual eight knots when all of a sudden there was a loud explosion off the starboard side which shook the whole ship. There was a field gun on the stem, manned by some of the crew, which began firing at what we never knew. Our guards came rushing and ordered us out of our hold and up to the boat deck, where we were assigned a life boat and given life preservers. Everyone had an idea that we had been hit and not having time to pack our gear, grabbed whatever was handy. In the confusion all I took with me was a roll of toilet paper! I imagine I took it because toilet paper had become so scarce it was almost nonexistent, and worth its weight in gold. Anyway, that was all I had, and if we had been torpedoed, I would have been better off than those without. High up on the boat deck, we could see all around, and the first thing I saw was a torpedo coming our way, which fortunately missed our stern by about ten feet. It is said that a miss is as good as a mile, and we were sure happy about that miss. There must have been more than one sub, as an oil tanker next in line was hit and went down in a very short time. We stayed up on the boat deck for another hour and then were allowed to go back down to our so-called stateroom, where I happily stored my roll of toilet paper back in my shopping bag. We were safe until the next sub came along. It turned out to be the only scare we had, as we were now in among the Ryukyu Islands and nearing the entrance to the Inland Sea along the south coast of Honshu, the largest island. This was a very beautiful area, dotted with small islands and odd-shaped rocks. We cruised along the Inland Sea for a whole day and night, then on the morning of the 27th of October 1942, we arrived at the port of Kobe, just three years to the day when I had arrived in Manila in 1939. We were supposed to have landed at Moji, but fortunately for us, plans were changed and here we were in Kobe.

Kobe is the second-largest port in Japan, and we could see numerous docks along the waterfront. The *Ryukyu Maru* came alongside one of the largest docks and made fast. We fifty POWs gathered up our gear, went down the gangplank, and were marched up a street away from the docks. The street ran along a large open area which seemed to be a park or sports ground. After about a quarter of a mile, we came to a small square where there was a flower garden, next to a large railway station. We were parked here until 5:00 P.M., just sitting and looking at the Japanese civilians passing by, who naturally were looking at us, as if we were beings from another planet. After our guards had consulted with a strange Jap officer, off we went back down the street four blocks, turned right for one block, right again, and through a pair of large gates into what looked like a warehouse yard. This was to be my happy home for the duration, almost three long years. There should have been a sign saying "Welcome to Kobe House!"

Chapter 14

Kobe House

The unprepossessing place we had just entered was officially called Kobe Sub-Camp, Osaka POW Area, but given the name "Kobe House" by the inmate POWs incarcerated therein. Entering the gate, all we saw was an alley some twenty feet wide between what looked like brick warehouses. Next to the gate on the right was an open-fronted platform on which sat a Japanese Army sentry, who greeted us with a screech which would raise all the dead within hearing. Evidently it was a call to the Sergeant of the Guard to let him know that we had arrived in his domain. The Sergeant arrived and directed us up a set of stairs next to the guard post, past a small room holding three oddly dressed men, then down a half dozen steps into a bare room thirty feet square, where we all chose a spot and sat down. In a few minutes, a portly Jap Lieutenant appeared and gave a welcoming speech in Japanese, which was duly interpreted by a runty civilian. The gist of the speech was that he was Lt. Morimoto, the camp commander, and that the Emperor had given us our lives, for which we

Naka Michi Dore, Kobe, in 1967. The building on the left of the photo is on the site of "A" Block, Kobe House. *Photo courtesy of Ray Brown, 2/30 Btn AIF.*

must be thankful and work hard for him. We certainly were thankful for our lives, and we certainly worked hard. Our work was to be anywhere in the city of Kobe we were needed, and if our work was good, we would be paid and well fed. He then left and was replaced by a Sgt. Major Morita, who ran the camp under Lt. Morimoto. Sgt. Morita then laid down the rules we would have to follow while we were in Kobe House. The most important ones were that, no matter what rank we held, we must salute all Japanese soldiers, even the lowest recruit. If we were bareheaded, we must bow instead of saluting. When any Japanese spoke to us, we must come to attention with eyes to the front, and not move a muscle. While in camp we must be fully dressed with coats buttoned and shoes tied. We must also be clean shaven and have our hair cut. The little interpreter, who was nicknamed Henry, had such a poor command of the English language that hardly any of us understood what he had said. Fortunately for us, there was a marine named Hoblitt, who spoke Japanese well enough to translate Henry's translation into English that we could understand.

After this warm welcome, we continued to sit and wait. In about an hour, the door opened and a couple of the men in strange uniforms appeared with two large buckets of soup and another of rice. I must say something here about a Master Sgt. Lucas, the senior NCO in our group. Luke was a big, strong man from Georgia, who had been in the Service for many years. During the voyage up from Manila, he had claimed to have a broken neck, sustained while working on a ship on the docks there, caused by a sack of sugar falling on him. Others said that was right, but not an accident, as other POWs in his work crew had dropped it deliberately. However it may have happened, Luke kept his head rigid, not turning it one way or another. Of course, this kept him from doing anything in the way of work. This time, as the food came in the door, someone yelled "chow down," and Luke's head snapped around to see it. We knew then that old Luke was a phoney. Luke took care of himself and nobody else. Back to the food. Of course we were all hungry, as usual, and tucked in without delay. One bucket held a thick fish soup and the other an equally thick vegetable soup. With a good bowl of rice, it was just about the best tasting meal we had had since the surrender. We all agreed that if this was the normal ration at Kobe House, we would enjoy our stay.

When we had eaten, more people arrived, to issue us four blankets per man. They were made of a grey material which we didn't recognize, but turned out to be made from peanuts, how, we never found out. These blankets were very welcome, as we were no longer in the tropics and we were feeling the change in temperature. Those who had been in the tropics for a long time felt the cold worse, and I was one of them. On top of that, there was no heat in the room, or for that matter, any part of Kobe House, as we soon found out.

Our next visitor turned out to be Captain Houghton of the British Army. He informed us that he was the Camp Commander by authority of the Japanese Army. His aide, Warrant Officer Bertie Bell, took us on a little tour of the compound. It consisted of two brick warehouses which had been owned by the firm of Butterfield and Swires, a British trading company, confiscated by the Japanese when war began. The open space between the two buildings was probably twenty feet wide and some hundred twenty feet long, barred at both ends by a heavy gate topped with barbed wire. The room we had been in was the upper story of a small tea warehouse. The warehouse on the right hand side as you came in the gate, was designated "A" Block, on the ground floor of which was a latrine, cookhouse, and bathing area. The latrine consisted of a large concrete tank with a double row of wooden cubicles built on a platform over the tank. Each cubicle was about four feet square with one board missing in the center. This slot was our toilet facility, not too comfortable, as you had to squat over the hole to do what you had to do. My legs were so weak from the beri-beri that I had a terrible time. I think there should have been a rail or some other support to hold on to, but that would have been too good for a POW. You can imagine the odor that permeated this place! Oddly enough, after you had been there a few minutes, the smell disappeared. One saving grace was that each cubicle had a door. We must have had the only toilet in Japan with a door—all the ones I visited later on were wide open. The urinal was a cement trough along one side and which drained into the main tank. In short, it was a dank and dreary place, and no one lingered there any longer than he could help.

There were a lot of other men around whom we surmised were POWs too, but our area was roped off and we were ordered not to try to talk to them. Most were dressed in a dark corduroy outfit, but some had khaki shorts and shirts, and were speaking a sort of English. Along the front of the bath area there was a line of sinks, with cold water only, where we had a quick, cold, face wash, then back up to our room, where we bedded down in our brand new blankets. "Lights Out" came at 9 o'clock. Thus ended our first of many days in our new home.

Chapter 15

Settling In

The following morning we were issued our mess gear, such as it was, consisting of two small bowls for our rice and soup, the standard fare for Jap POWs. Our single eating utensil was a spoon. A spoon was sufficient, as we never got any food that needed cutting or spearing. After our bowl of rice and another of thin soup, we gathered up our belongings and moved to new quarters. The thirty officers in our group were moved across to "B" block to join a few British officers, while the twenty enlisted men were assigned to the 3rd floor of "A" block. Climbing two flights of wide wooden stairs, we arrived at a big room divided into three sections, each section having double rows of platforms eight feet wide, with a narrow aisle between the platforms.

Running up the center of this aisle was what turned out to be a table. It had folding leaves which were raised at meal times. This arrangement allowed us to eat sitting on the edge of the platform, which was about chair height. The platforms were covered with about an inch of straw and some thin straw matting on top. This soon flattened out so that essentially we were just about sleeping on hard boards. The space allotted to each man worked out to be twenty-seven inches by seven feet, which made for pretty cramped quarters, especially if two big men were next to each other. A narrow shelf at the head of each man's space held what toilet articles or clothing he had. Blankets had to be folded army fashion and went below the shelf. Shoes went under the foot of the platform. No shoes could be worn on the sleeping platform, and serious punishment would result if this rule was disobeyed.

There were three floors in "A" block, each occupied by a hundred and fifty POWs, as well as two floors in "B" block. In all, Kobe House held some five hundred other POWs, British troops who had been captured in Hong Kong on Christmas Day of 1941. The majority were in pitiable condition, all very weak, with many down sick with pneumonia. They had been through an experience about as bad as our Death March. Sailing from Hong Kong for Japan on a freighter named the *Lisbon Maru*, they were torpedoed by an American submarine in the middle of the China Sea. Packed in three holds which were battened down, those in the aft and midship holds had no chance and were all drowned when the stern of the ship went down. Fortunately for those in the forward hold, the stem hit bottom while the bow was still out of the water, allowing some to break out of the hatch and get off the ship before it went under. Surviving POWs had to swim five miles to some small islands, as the Japs would not pick them up and even shot at them in the water. The one thing that kept them alive was the life belts issued each man, especially as few were able to swim. Reaching the islands, they huddled together for warmth, the majority having only shorts for clothing. No food was available. After a couple of days, they were taken to Shanghai by some Chinese fishermen and turned over to the Japanese. There they were kept on the open docks in cold October weather, still nearly naked. Finally, they boarded another ship and arrived safely in Kobe, two weeks before we Americans got there. Eight hundred and forty-six British soldiers lost their lives when the *Lisbon Maru* was torpedoed. The seven hundred survivors had finally found a haven in Kobe House, where those not having clothes had been issued coats and trousers of the odd-colored corduroy we had seen when we arrived. They were in such bad shape that most of them were still in the sack, too weak to get up. The lack of heat in the old warehouses, together with the poor diet, would make their recovery slow and in many cases, impossible. Over one hundred of these men died during their first winter in Japan.

When we Yanks had settled down in our spaces on the platform, a Japanese supply NCO appeared, and each of us was issued a Japanese army cap with its red star removed. This was to be our headgear from now on. Those of us who had been on Bataan and had nothing to wear but a set of khakis were fitted out with discarded Japanese army breeches and coats, an overcoat, two face towels, two *fundoshis*, which were long strips of cloth with strings on one end, to tie it around the waist, for underwear. After we got used to the *fundoshi*, it wasn't too bad, and easy to wash. The uniforms were serviceable, and welcome, as everyone was feeling the cold. Unfortunately those of us who were six feet or more in height found nothing big enough to squeeze into and were doomed to shiver. The only heat in the building was provided by two brick contrivances on each floor similar to a backyard barbecue pit. Each of these were issued five pounds of coal per day, which of course didn't last too long. Most of the time the coal was saved for use in the evening, to heat hot water for the one hot drink of the day before bedding down.

We also received a small, round piece of tin on which was painted our name in *Katakana*, a form of printing used in Japan when writing foreign words, and our POW number. My number was five hundred thirty-eight, or, in Japanese, *"go byaku san ju hachi."* My name was also in *Katakana*, in four characters which read *Asa Doku*, which was the best the Japs could do with the "th" and "l" sounds, neither of which are in the Japanese language. A red circle was painted around the edge of the badge, denoting the fact that I was an NCO. This was an advantage at times, but a disadvantage at other times. The badge was attached to the left breast of whatever outfit you were wearing.

All POWs in Kobe House were assigned to a section of thirty men, two of whom were detailed as mess attendants a week at a time, to get the buckets of soup and rice at the cook house on the ground floor and carry them up the stairs to the section area, where it was measured out by the bowlful. This procedure was carefully watched to make sure everyone got the same amount. We were all so hungry that a few grains of rice or spoonful of soup made a difference. The food ration was weighed at the cook house, according to the number of men in each section, but after all of the section had been served, there was usually a small amount left in each bucket, perhaps a couple of spoonfuls of rice and a half bowl of soup. This went to the ones on mess detail, which was the reason nobody tried to avoid it. The one bad thing about it was that the buckets had to be washed in cold water, no hot water being available anywhere except in the cook house. After supper, we were free to do what we wanted until lights out at nine o'clock. No one could hit the sack until that time, so about all we could do was to shoot the breeze and to get to know your fellow POWs. We Yanks were a mongrel group, all from different outfits; I had never seen any one of them before Bilibid. Only one of the others came from New England, most were from the south or west. I became fast friends with Billy Johnson, from Lowell, Massachusetts. At least we had some things in common. He had been in the Army about as long as I had, so we got along well. I also began to talk to some of the British, those I could understand, that is. Half of them were Scots from the 2nd Battalion, Royal Scots Regiment, and the other half were from the 1st Battalion, Middlesex Regiment. About a third of them spoke an understandable English, but the Cockney dialect, as well as the broad Scots, was just impossible. It took me two more years before I was able to hold a decent conversation with most of them. I was reminded of the Lancashire Fusiliers that I had associated with in Tientsin, China, when I was in the 15th Infantry there. The north-country accent they spoke was almost intelligible. These POWs were all career soldiers, serving twelve year enlistments as compared to our four years. Most had served in India, as well as in Hong Kong, and we spent hours comparing our different ranks, pay, food, and off-duty recreation, which was remarkably like ours. Soldiers are about the same, regardless of what country they serve.

Chapter 16

KYOTSUKI!

Our first week in Kobe House was spent in rest and relaxation, if such was possible in a temperature of about forty degrees. The Japanese had an unpleasant habit of opening all windows during the daytime and letting the wind whistle through the building. As a result, most of the day was spent under the blankets trying to keep warm. This easy life soon came to an end after a week, when we Americans, or rather the twenty of us who were enlisted men, were assembled in the open space in front of the guard's platform to be initiated into the intricacies of the Japanese language and Japanese Army close order drill. Our first lesson was to learn to count, which turned out to be quite easy. It was impressed upon us that when we counted off it had better be at the top of our voices; for an hour the place resounded with *"Ichi, ni, san, shi, go, roku, shichi, hacki, ku, ju,"* which of course is "one to ten" in Japanese. After our guards were satisfied with the volume and the pronunciation, we formed up into two lines and practiced counting off for another hour, changing places in the ranks until we could count off properly no matter where we happened to be. During all this time the guards roamed up and down between the ranks, and any error in accent or lack of volume was promptly corrected by a smart slap in the chops. Of course we remained at *kyotsuki,* or "attention," at all times, and here it is necessary to say a bit about *kyotsuki* in the Japanese Army. It is similar to our position of attention, except that you cannot move a hair, eye-balls straight ahead at all times, with all muscles rigid. There was no relaxation such as we Yanks sneak when at attention for a long time, and after about fifteen minutes the muscles start to quiver, and pretty soon some guard will notice this and smarten you up fast. Not being able to move your eyeballs, you were unable to tell when you were going to be hit, and couldn't ride with the punch. Punishment by slapping was universal in the Japanese Army, everyone could, and did, slap anyone junior in rank to the slapper. Of course the lowly privates, who had been slapped by everyone since they had been in the Army, were exceedingly happy to find someone to vent their spleen on—the lowly POW. Don't think they didn't take advantage of the opportunity! Being forced to stand at attention while being slapped, kicked, or clubbed was one of the hardest lessons a Japanese POW had to learn, but learn it we did. At this stage of the game, we had learned one thing, any attempt at retaliation would be fatal. If you wanted to live, you had better stand and take it!

The counting off finally came to an end, a good thing, because by this time we could hardly croak. Lined up in a single line, we then practiced *keirei,* the Japanese Army salute. We didn't have too much trouble with this, as the Japanese salute is almost identical to ours, except that the fingertips are placed on the temple instead of over the eye. The trouble was staying at the salute for fifteen minutes, which was what it took for the instructor to check each of us in turn. The arm gets tired quickly in such a rigid position, and any quiver resulted in another good slap in the face. A couple of weeks later we watched the British, in groups of a hundred, go through the saluting drill. They had a much harder time of it than the Americans, as their hand salute was nothing like ours or the Japanese, being made with palm to the front, and changing a habit of twenty years or so was difficult. On top of that, I think they enjoyed working the guards up by not trying very hard. The guards really went insane with anger at their attempts to salute, and all afternoon the place rang with screams and imprecations, along with slapping sounds as punishment was meted out. I really think the guards were worn out and finally passed them all to get rid of them. Some of the British never learned to salute properly, and were always getting in trouble for their saluting. All the officers had to learn numbering and saluting, too, and we got a big kick out of seeing them knocked back on their heels just like we had been. Our officers had never tried to stand up for us when we got banged around for no reason, and we all had a good laugh at such poetic justice being meted out to them.

The day wasn't over yet—now we had to learn how to bow. This was very important, as when you didn't have a cap on, you had to bow instead of saluting. This bowing was done in a special way, the angle of the back to the body being critical, as well as the length of time the bow was held. Of course this was repugnant to us POWs, who had never bowed to anyone before, and some went to great lengths to avoid being caught without a cap on. We soon got used to it, however, and found that it was another form of saluting. In fact, the command to bow was the same as that for the hand salute. If we bowed to a guard, we got a salute back, so I just bowed all over the place and kept out of trouble most of the time.

It had been a long, hard, cold day, but it wasn't over yet. We formed a line and one by one we were loaded down with a sack weighing about a hundred pounds, then walked around in a circle. Now a hundred pounds isn't much to a man in good health, but to some of us who had been through Bataan and the Death March, it felt like a ton. My legs were so weak from beri-beri they would hardly move. In fact, at this time, I didn't weigh much more than that bag did. We were finally released to go back inside. It had been a long, rough afternoon, with a cold wind blowing through the alley between the two buildings. We had just enough clothing to cover our bodies, and most of the time were standing at attention. Carrying those bags was a relief, at least it warmed us up a bit. Kobe was a lot like Boston as far as cold weather goes, with the wind coming off the ocean and whistling through the streets, as well as through your clothing. Inside Kobe House wasn't much better until five o'clock, when the windows were closed.

Our supper of soup and rice was on time and very welcome after our long, cold day. The soup was hot enough to warm you a little, even if it was usually nothing but hot water with a few vegetable tops in it, and the rice, at this time, was very good. I had gotten used to rice very quickly and couldn't get enough of it. It was funny, but there were still those who couldn't, or wouldn't, eat the stuff. Most didn't last too long. The first thing I had learned as a POW was to adapt to whatever situation you found yourself in. This included eating rice, fish eye soup, ground up fish, seaweed, etc., as well as to *kyotsuki* or *keirei* when necessary. Plenty of POWs died because they never learned to adapt.

Cpl. Hoblitt appeared after supper to inform us that we were to go out to work in the morning. Sgt. Lucas, as section leader, would stay in. I was to be leader of the work detail and not have to work for the present. We had no idea of what work we were going to have to do, or where we were going to do it. I was glad I was to be leader and not work, but I soon found out that being a work leader of a POW gang was not the bed of roses it sounded like. In fact, it turned out to be downright dangerous.

Chapter 17

Heigh-Ho, Heigh-Ho, and Off to Work We Go

On a cold, windy morning in early November 1942, all the American enlisted men, less old Luke, fell in on the street outside the gate for our first day of labor for good old *Dai Nippon,* in other words, the Empire of Japan. *Bango,* or counting off, went well due to our practice of the day before. Jack Oakie and the Sgt. Major were present, to give us a pep talk on how fortunate we were to be permitted to work for the Emperor, and exhorted us to show our gratitude by working hard. We were then turned over to two Japanese civilians wearing arm bands, and one of the some twenty permanent guards stationed at Kobe House, who marched us through the city some half a mile, to an area on the city docks owned by a company called Kami Gumi. The two civilians who had collected us at Kobe House had the responsibility of overseeing us while we were working for their company. They were called *Honcho,* or foreman. Most of the honchos we worked under in Kobe were decent types, who treated us fairly as long as we did our share of the work. They were not allowed to hit us or to abuse us physically. The Kobe House guard took care of any punishment to be dealt out. If any of us got into trouble, such as getting caught stealing something to eat, we were reported to our guard, who could either dole out punishment himself, or, if the crime was serious enough, report the matter to the Sgt of the Guard when we got back to Kobe House. If that happened, there was real trouble, and we always tried to have the guard take care of it, one or two slaps was a lot better than an hour or two of *kyotsuki* in front of the guard house with every Jap in the vicinity taking a crack at you.

Work on all the Kobe docks was about the same. Cargo came in by ship or barge and was off-loaded onto the docks. It was then moved into a warehouse and stacked up in great piles. This moving part turned out to be our job. At Kami Gumi, barges were delivering round cakes of what looked like compressed beans, oats and straw, about six inches thick, a yard or so in diameter, and weighing about thirty pounds each. These had to be moved into the warehouse and stacked up some six feet high. Half of the crew were given two-wheeled dollies such as are used to move big boxes. These dollies were called *Nekko* in Japanese, and together with a *kagi,* which is a tool with a handle like a hatchet and a sharp hook an inch long on the end, you can move just about anything with comparative ease. There is a smaller *kagi* which just fits into your other hand with a four-inch hook which curling up over the hand. This short *kagi* is used with the long one when lifting bags of beans, sugar, or whatever. We soon learned to use these tools, indispensable to a longshoreman, which we were to become. It would have been impossible to do such work bare-handed.

The work didn't go too badly; each *nekko* was loaded with two of the round cakes by a POW who was shown how by an old coolie, who had done this work all his life. One side of the cake was moved with the *kagi* so that it could be lifted with the other hand and placed on the *nekko.* The POW then trundled his load into the warehouse, where another took the cakes and piled them up. This was the hardest work, and only a few of us were strong enough to throw those cakes up over their head. Fortunately, there were some who were in decent enough shape to do this stacking job. The work went OK, and at 10 o'clock everyone on the docks, including us POWs, knocked off work for a tea break. I had always hated tea, but it was nice and hot and sweet I didn't turn it down. Anything that would warm your bones up a little was welcome. We had a whole hour off at noon, when we were each given a small box about the size of a cigar box, filled with boiled rice and a couple of pieces of a pickled vegetable. This was called a *bento* box, which was the standard lunch for the dock coolies. It was a pleasant surprise indeed, since we hadn't expected such largesse. We found out later that this was part of the contract the civilian companies made in order to get labor on contract from the Japanese Army, which owned us. Another tea break was given in the middle of the afternoon, after which we worked until 5:00 P.M., then we marched back to Kobe House by the two honchos and our guard, then for another hour we went through a training session in Jap army close order drill learning such things as *Migi Muke,* "right face"; *Hidari Muke,* "left face"; *Hidari Narai,* "eyes right", etc., as we had made such a poor showing marching to work. We also had to learn to goose-step when we passed an officer and for the last hundred feet when we arrived back at camp.

We worked the whole week at Kami Gumi doing the same job. It was a relief to get out of Kobe House with its roving guards. The interior guards were from an infantry outfit stationed near Kobe and were rotated weekly. We never got to know them as well as we did those who took us to work, and they were always finding an excuse to beat up on the POWs for any little thing, either real or imagined. This, as well as the extra bit of food we got for lunch, was a good incentive not to stay all day in Kobe House if you could get out. The guards who took us to work were all men who had been wounded in the war, and who were on invalid reserve status. They were permanently attached to Kobe House, and besides guarding the work details, handled all the mess, supply, medical and administrative duties. They all had their different temperaments and habits, some of them treated us well, some made life a hell for us. We soon learned how to deal with each one. One thing they all had in common was an explosive temper which had better not be aroused.

    Being a work leader had its benefits. I was able to wander around the area at will, as I was supposed to ride herd on the POW gang. One day I noticed some small wooden crates in a stack, and using my kagi, pried up one of the boards so I could get into the box. Inside were small cans of something I knew not what, not being able to read the label. However, when shaken there was a liquid sound, so I punctured the can with my *kagi* enough to see that it was full of peas. Still having my old G.I. spoon, I got the hole big enough to get the spoon in and ate some of the peas, which were so delicious I ate the whole canful. These peas were the first decent vegetable I had had since December of 1941. The guys with the *nekkos* were coming up one aisle and going out another, so I got another can open and as each one went by my dark corner he got a spoonful of peas shoved in his mouth. This went on until a half dozen cans had been emptied and the empties dumped in the *benjo*. I even got a couple of cans to the ones who were stacking. Needless to say, we enjoyed those nice sweet peas, although I shudder to think of what would have happened to me if I had gotten caught, but I always was good (or lucky) at stealing and never was. Billy Johnson was my best buddy in Kobe House and together we worked some good heists. Each morning, a man with a hand cart filled with little bottles of hot soya bean milk visited the docks to sell his milk to the coolies. Bill was a good talker and he got the milkman's attention at one end of the cart while I sneaked a couple bottles from the other end. This soya bean milk was sweet and tasty and hot, as well as being filled with vitamins. My career as a *dorobo*, or thief, was off to a good start. In fact, if I hadn't stolen, I probably wouldn't have made it through my forty-one months as a POW. There were some who would not steal because of their scruples about sinning and who died as a result. I never had such scruples; nor did 99% of the inmates of Kobe House.

We all wondered just what the round cakes were that we worked on. They seemed to be made of a dried, compressed material which looked something like Cracker Jack. Always being hungry, I figured they might be edible, and if so, an addition to our scanty diet. So I broke off a piece which looked as if it might be edible and stuck it in my mouth. After a few minutes, it softened up some, in fact it didn't taste that bad, and at least gave a fuller feeling in the stomach. Bill liked it, too, and so I began breaking off likely bits and passed them to him. Our bellies felt nice and full when we got back home that day. After our supper soup and rice we were both really satisfied for the first time in days. About the time lights went out, we both began having pains in the stomach which bent us over. For four hours we had gas in great quantity coming out of both ends. We figured out that the stuff we had eaten must have been dehydrated, and the soup just made it expand to its pre-dried stage in our stomachs. What a night we had! Next day one of the old coolies made a sign to us with fingers like horns and mooed like a cow, so from then on we called it cow cake. I wonder what it would have done to the cows if they had to eat it dry! After this experience, we learned to soak the cow cake overnight before eating it. I found that an inch of crumbled cow cake in the bottom of my bowl would, when doused with water, swell up to a full bowl full. Then you could eat it with no gas problem. The stuff didn't have much taste, but at least filled you up.

Working at Kami Gumi wasn't that hard compared to some of those we had later. It gave us the experience we needed to work with and under Japanese civilians, who, as a rule, treated us as they would any coolie gang. There didn't seem to be any animosity towards us as enemies, which we had expected to occur. In fact Japanese civilians were all so heartily sick of the war and short rations, I think they were sorry for us. All our troubles came from the military.

Chapter 18

And More Work

The opportunities for work were unlimited. Kobe was, and still is, the 2nd largest seaport in Japan. The city is long and narrow, I would say five miles long by a half mile or so wide, being squeezed between the Inland Sea and a mountain range. It has a wonderful harbor, with at least a mile of docks and warehouses. At the west end of the harbor, the Kawasaki shipyard built giant submarines and aircraft carriers for the war. All the large Japanese companies such as Mitsubishi, Sumitomo and Mitsui, as well as many smaller companies, had large warehouses, called godowns, some on four piers, in the harbor area. We became acquainted with all of them in the near future.

After our two weeks at Kami Gumi, we were joined by a couple of hundred of the British who had been judged fit to work. We all fell out in the street where we lined up in ranks, then were detailed to different jobs, taken over by honchos of the different companies, and with a guard marched off to work. The large companies were all similar, where we unloaded ships coming up from the areas that had been conquered by the Japanese. Hemp and copra from the Philippines, rubber and tin from Malaya, and oil from Borneo were the major cargos. The hemp came in large bales and was moved from dock to warehouse by *nekko*. This wasn't too bad a job except that some of the dock area was paved with cobblestone and as the hemp bales were heavy, sometimes we got stuck in rough spots. When this happened, it took two more men to get the *nekko* going again. Most of the warehouses, or godowns, were three or four stories high and the freight elevators were busy. Crude rubber came in blocks some three feet square and weighed 100 kilos, the standard weight for most commodities in Asian countries. The square shape made it easy to move using a *nekko*. Copra, or dried coconut meat, was a horse of another color. Copra came in bags and had to be carried from the dock to the godown, where it was stacked almost to the ceiling. Not too bad at first, but when the pile got higher, it was necessary to use planks to reach the top of the pile, and getting up there was a struggle.

Beans, rice, peanuts, beside copra, were all shipped in burlap bags, and each bag weighed the standard hundred kilos, or two hundred twenty pounds. Anything that came in bags had to be carried on the shoulder from dock to stack, and the first time you were loaded with one, you wondered how in the world you were going to make it to the stack, to say nothing of climbing a series of planks to the top. A hundred kilos felt like a ton to us POWs, as most of us were hospital candidates. I was still only about a hundred twenty-five pounds in weight, and my first bag almost collapsed me, but I finally made it to the stack. The British, many of whom had worked on the docks before the war, called the carrying process "lumping." Every coolie in the world knows how to lump, but we POWs learned it the hard way. The old coolies who worked with us had heavy apron worn around the waist which they flipped up over their carrying shoulder and the side of the head. This protected their neck and ear from the rough bag. Of course we had no aprons, and when that rough bag landed on your neck it was really rough on the tender skin. Two POWs with *kagis* lifted the bags and swung them up on your shoulder, and if you were still upright after that, you staggered into the godown where you dropped your bag on the stack, or climbed up the plank to where the top of the pile was. It was quite a trick to negotiate this plank, which, due to your own weight plus your bag, tended to bend down and spring back up. In the course of time, we learned the trick of using this upward spring to our advantage, and then we seemed to fly upward in leaps and bounds. Carrying this much weight was harder for the tall men, such as I was, as our center of gravity was too high. It was especially difficult when we had to move bags from godown to freight car, as the Japanese box cars were a lot smaller than American ones, the doors being less than six feet high. Trying to get through that little door with such a heavy load on my shoulder, with my weak, wobbly legs, was just about impossible, and I usually found myself doing the lifting, which was really harder work than carrying. After finishing a carload of five hundred bags, you and your lifting partner had lifted fifty-five tons. All in all, I found lumping just about the hardest work I had to endure. Most of the British were shorter than the Yanks, and lumping was easier for them. They had a habit of making a game out of any work. When they did the lifting and you arrived for your bag, they would swing it out so it literally flew through the air, and you had to take off at the right time and speed to catch it on the run, about like catching a 220 lb. football over your shoulder. If you didn't catch it just right, the results could be disastrous. I landed on the floor a good few times with that bag on top of me before I finally got it down right. I often wonder how I ever made it through the day when on a lumping job. Needless to say, I soon learned to avoid these jobs when at all possible. Some people did like lumping, although I could never figure out why. They were welcome to it. The only good part of lumping was that it kept you warm. All the dock jobs we worked on had a crew of women who worked with the coolie gangs. They were mostly middle-aged or older, and had worked on the docks all their lives. Each gang, including us POWs, had two or three of these women who did the light work, such as sweeping up anything that had been spilled, or sewing up bags that had holes or rips in them. They were a good-natured lot, and we had lots of fun joking with them. They treated us as if we were their children, I guess as a substitute for their own sons, who were practically all in the service. We called them "Piggy" women, the nearest we could come to the Japanese *pikke,* meaning damaged or torn. They were all short and blocky, most of them stronger than I was, and could lump with the best of us. The piggy women all wore a sort of mitten made of about twenty layers of cotton cloth sewn together, then cut to shape. They were not very warm, but better than nothing, and as we had none, the piggy women made some for us out of scraps.

We POWs got along well with the other coolies and the piggy women. In fact, the longer we worked with them, we found that they liked us better than they did the Japanese military. I never met one that didn't hate the war and couldn't wait until it was over. Every civilian had to work long hours at low pay, and their food ration was little better than ours. They were really afraid of the Japanese soldiers, who didn't hesitate to knock them around, just as they did us POWs.

One cold morning my detail was taken to a flour mill, where I went through one of my worst days as a coolie. There was a round concrete platform three feet high and about six feet across the top, which was covered by a steel grate. My job was to stand on top of the grate, and as a line of lumpers dumped their hundred kilo bags of corn on top of the grate, one of the coolies cut the strings on the top of the bag. I then had to lift up the bottom of the bag so that the corn would fall through the grate. This was a hard job, as the bags came in a rush and it took some time to empty them. Of course I couldn't keep up and the honcho began screaming and raving. He must have thought that I was the strongest one of the crew, as I had been gaining a little weight and looked better than I felt. Finally, he had to put one of his own coolies on the grate, where he had always worked, and I joined the lumpers, which was hard enough work for me. The corn that fell through the grate was being ground into corn meal. The only good thing about this job was being inside, out of the cold wind. There was a stove in our break room, and we all grabbed a handful of that good corn meal, mixed it with some water, and stuck it on the side of the stove, where it baked into a kind of corn cake, not very appetizing, but tasty enough, and helped to fill up the void on our stomachs. This was our only visit to the flour mill. They must have thought we weren't worth our pay.

December passed slowly and painfully. Each day, we fell out in the morning and marched to various locations on the waterfront slaving away for our captors. In our physical condition it was some struggle to keep going. We had no news, so we knew nothing about what was happening in the world other than our miserable existence. Christmas was at hand, but nobody really looked forward to it. We just hoped to last long enough to see it.

Chapter 19

ON THE INSIDE

During our first month of work, we were given Sundays off for a *yasume* day, or a day of so-called rest in our icebox home. Hardly anybody liked this *yasume* day, the main reason being that we got no noon meal when inside, just a hot cup of tea for lunch. We were inspected by the Japanese duty sergeant at 9:00 A.M., and if he was in the normal bad mood, we spent from five minutes to an hour standing at *kyotsuki*. Old Luke, our leader, nearly always got a smack in the puss or two, he being responsible for everything the duty sergeant found wrong. The inspection over, all we could do was to sit around in the cold until after our noon tea, when we were allowed to bed down if we wanted to. I usually spent an hour or two trying to wash or mend my few articles of clothing. Hardly anyone had any soap unless he had been lucky enough to scrounge a bit on one of the jobs, and what soap we did get looked like the old brown laundry soap we used in the service, but had so much lye in it, it burned the skin. It hardly made a lather in hot water, and of course we had no hot water at all, so washing, either face or clothes, was just a dab and rinse. I had no overcoat, so I had to wear my khakis and my coveralls, working or otherwise, to keep from freezing. By this time, they were showing lots of wear and tear. Fortunately, I had picked up a sewing kit in Bilibid, so with much patching and sewing with bits of cloth I had filched on the docks, I managed to keep up with the holes.

About the middle of December, we received an issue of two packs of Japanese cigarettes, that is, two packs for NCOs. Other ranks received one pack. I had never smoked, but thought I would try it just to have something different to do. The cigarettes tasted all right to me, but all the old smokers said they were terrible. They smoked them just the same. The first ones we got were named *Kinchis*. There was a better brand named *Haycock*, which we called bombers, because there was a picture of a Japanese bomber on the package. We were never issued these, but some of the guys traded with the civilians for them. We also got an issue of so-called toilet paper, more like sandpaper then anything else. It sure did the job! Toilet paper was always in short supply, and we picked up all the paper scraps we could find while working on the docks. Nothing was worse than being without toilet paper. Some of the British who had been in Palestine or Aden used wet cloths in the Arab fashion, but I never got that bad off. The toilet paper issue was in the same ratio as the cigarettes, NCO got twice as much as privates. I don't know what the officers got, probably twice as much as the NCO.

After the washing and patching, most of us spent the rest of the day under our blankets trying to rest up a little after the week's hard labor, there being little else to do. We were allowed to play cards for one hour on Sunday, but as playing cards were almost nonexistent, nobody played. Gambling was not allowed. We had no books, so couldn't pass the time that way. I really missed being able to read, as I had always been an avid reader. So it boiled down to either sleeping or shooting the breeze with any friend we had made amongst the British. The Middlesex Regiment was based in London and most of them were real Cockneys. My ancestors had emigrated from Stepney Parish, farmland in 1636, but now part of the city of London. I found two or three who had come from there, and they told me about the modern day Stepney Parish, which had become one of the slum districts of the city of London. It took some time to become used to their brand of English, and I found it easier to talk to the Royal Scots, many of whom spoke better English than the English did. Of course, the majority had such a Scots brogue it was impossible to understand them at all. The Royal Scots had been in India before being unlucky enough to be shipped to Hong Kong, and had lots of stories to tell about their service in India.

Our so-called hospital, which was located in the large room over the guardhouse, and where we had spent our first days in Kobe House, was staffed by a couple of British corpsmen, who had the thankless job of trying to keep their undernourished patients alive under the worst of conditions. The motto of the Japanese was "No work, no eat," and anyone unfortunate enough to be hospitalized immediately went on half rations. Of course this made it almost impossible for anyone with pneumonia or the like to ever get well. As a result, during the winter of 1942-43, a hundred and twenty British died. Two of the American officers died of pneumonia, as well. As cold as we were all the time, it was a wonder more of us didn't wind up dead. Everyone, even those who actually should have been in a hospital, tried to get out to work in order not to be sent to the hospital and its half rations.

The first POWs who died in Kobe House were carried out in small coffins and had a military ceremony, but there was such a rapid increase in the death rate that the dead were put in small barrels, which were rolled out the gate to be cremated in the Japanese fashion. After we saw a few rolled down the street, the song "Roll out the Barrel" was banned in Kobe House. All ex-POWs from Japan still hate that song.

All of us suffered as the real winter arrived. It had been cold enough in late fall, but it was really bad toward the end of the year. We tried all sorts of combinations of our cheap blankets to try to get warm enough to get to sleep, but nothing seemed to help, even though we wore all our clothes to bed. The only way to keep warm was to find someone to bunk in with, which doubled the warmth provided by our blankets. We would all have preferred to have a fat girl to sleep with, but unfortunately there were only skinny men available. I finally bunked in with two Scots I had made friends with, one Tootie Greig from Aberdeen and his mucker, Duncan Cameron, from Edinburgh. This arrangement gave us four blankets on the bottom and eight on top, making it warm enough on both sides to get to sleep. Of course when one wanted to turn over, all had to turn. There were a few hardy souls who preferred sleeping alone, but nobody could convince me that they weren't cold.

Other troubles with sleeping soon cropped up. Our diet, so deficient in vitamins, or anything else, for that matter, seemed to turn to water, and everyone found it necessary to go to the *benjo* every couple of hours. This was particularly true of those suffering from wet beri-beri, which tends to edema, or retention of water. Ordinarily, these visits to the *benjo* would have been just an inconvenience, but the Japanese insisted that when we went to the *benjo*, we had to go in full uniform, all buttons buttoned and all shoe laces tied. The roving guard on duty made sure that we were following all the rules, and woe betide the poor POW who got caught sneaking down the three flights of stairs in just his underwear, hoping to save some sleeping time. With the three of us, a good night's sleep was impossible. It seemed as though someone was always going to the *benjo* and waking the others up. Of course, everyone tried to get down the stairs and back up without dressing, which saved precious sleeping time. There being only one roving guard to cover both buildings, there was a good chance he might never catch you. I got caught once, and as a result, got the worst beating of my entire career as a POW. I had just finished at the urinal trough, turned around, and who did I see standing in the doorway but the biggest guard of the whole lot. The first thing he did was yell *Kurah,* "Hey, you" in the loudest scream he was capable of. *Kurah* is the word the Japanese use when they want to get some miscreant's attention, and as I was the only one around, I knew who he meant, so I came to the approved *kyotsuki* position immediately. The guard came over and placed himself right in front of me. He then proceeded to point at my unlaced shoes and presumably my lack of coat and trousers, after which he wound up and smacked me in the chops. Of course he was trying to knock me down so he could boast about it to his buddies. That was the worst thing about being tall, some Jap was always trying to do that. Some of the guys let themselves be knocked over at the first punch, hoping that whoever did it would be so proud of himself he would quit at that point, but with the Japs, you never knew whether or not he would just start kicking you, so from the beginning, I had determined that I would stand as long as I could. Well, this Nip really put my theory to the test, because I lost count after getting hit seventy-five times. I was still standing, but just about. If he hadn't let me go at that point, I guess I would have finally gone down onto that filthy *benjo* floor. I was so dizzy that I missed the first flight of stairs and wavered my way to the other flight before I got back upstairs. My mouth was full of blood, and one front tooth had been knocked so loose than it fell out shortly. This was my first and really my worst beating in Kobe House. Normally, when someone was caught in that kind of situation, he was only slapped a couple of times, but I had run into the wrong guard, or else he wanted to show that he could beat up a big American. I know one thing, my beating cured me of the habit of sneaking down to the *benjo* without tying my shoes and buttoning up my clothes.

Chapter 20

Merry Christmas

I doubt that there were many in Kobe House who had given any thought to what was normally the happiest day of the year. We were all so tired, hungry and cold that all we could think about was keeping warm and getting enough to eat. At this time, a few of the most ill were allowed to take a day off now and then, by remaining in Kobe House to rest up a bit. A couple of days before Christmas, Al Rigdon and I managed to convince the British medic that we were sick enough to qualify for a day off. So after the work parties had left, we bundled up in our blankets for a snooze, which lasted about ten minutes, until we were rousted out and sent off to "A" block, where another so-called hospital ward had been set up on the second floor. This was right under the officers' quarters, just about the coldest place in Kobe House, and no place to be at any time. The Japs had no use for anyone who couldn't work and made things most miserable for these unfortunates. Of course Al and I weren't actually sick, but just wanted a day off, so I guess we got what we deserved. We not only got our day off, but had to stay in that ice box for the next three days! However, the third day happened to be Christmas Day, and of all things, Red Cross food parcels were issued for the first time. This was the only good part of our hospital stay, especially as those in hospital got one whole parcel each, while the rest of Kobe House had to be satisfied with one parcel between two POWs. The Red Cross parcels were a godsend, containing a veritable array of goodies, including one large can of Klim milk (powdered), a can of Nescafé instant coffee, a can of corned beef (or Spam), a box of sugar cubes, two bars of chocolate, two packs of American cigarettes, a quarter pound of cheese, and two cans of Army field rations. I guess that was the best Christmas present I ever had received in my whole life. With our noon issue of hot water, we made the best cup of coffee ever.

In the afternoon, we were sent back to our quarters, just in time to attend a Christmas concert given by the British, who were great at such things. They had been given permission for the concert by Lt. Morimoto, who was seated in the front row of the spectators with all his staff and a half dozen more from the guard section. We all sang Christmas songs in which they happily joined in. This was one of the better sides of the Japs, who knew most of the songs. They also presented us with an extra issue of cigarettes, a couple of pickled cherries to go with our rice, and a small round scrub brush. We had no idea what this brush was for, but soon found out.

All in all, I guess one could say that I and all the other POWs of Kobe House had a right merry Christmas, considering the circumstances. One thing about POW life, you learn to count every small blessing. It would have been nicer to have been at home with your family, but this being impossible, what we did have was pretty good. At least we went to bed with a full stomach for the first time since Christmas one year past, the date we first landed on Bataan.

Chapter 21

A New Year

1943 started out with a new routine. It had been decreed that all of us inmates must take fifteen minutes of P.T. each working day, before breakfast, starting with a brisk rubdown with the little brush we had been given. A long string was tied to each end of the brush, and with a string in each hand, we were able to do our poor backs with a sawing motion. I thought I would take all the skin off my back for sure, as we were stripped to the waist, with the freezing wind blowing down the street. That rub down was pure torture, although it certainly helped the circulation. The guards made sure we did a good job, too. P.T. was under the instruction of a British NCO who must have been a health nut. He had a platform to stand on, and gave us side-straddle hops, pushups, deep knee bends and all the stuff we used to get in the peacetime army. About all that most of us could do was to go through the motions, and I think the guards realized this and took pity on us for once, as nobody was slapped or screamed at. This morning P.T. continued for some weeks, but was finally discontinued when the Japs found that it was doing more damage than good.

Another new routine was the issue to each worker of a roll and a half of bread, made from potato flour. Each roll was about the size of a fat hotdog roll and tasted pretty good. These rolls were to be our noon meal, and with whatever food the company gave us, made for a fair lunch. Some companies fed well, while the lunch at others was just a plain rice ball. If you got a good company lunch, you smuggled your roll back into Kobe House, that is, if you wanted to take the chance. The rule was that you must eat your roll at work, and those found with rolls when the detail returned to Kobe House were made to regret taking the chance of a late night snack.

There were a few jobs where the opportunity of stealing food such as canned salmon, corned beef, or fruit was better than others. The procedure for working parties to go to the different jobs had been to line everyone up and the various honchos would count off as many workers from the line as they wanted that day, but, as time went on, you picked the honcho of your favorite job and lined up in front of him. In this way, a lot of the POWs went on the same job daily. Of course those who were the most able to do hard work gradually monopolized the "plum" jobs, shoving the weaker ones out of the way. This, of course, was an example of the maxim, survival of the fittest, or a case of the rich get richer and the poor get poorer, or hungrier. I usually tried for a job that wasn't beyond my physical capability, although such jobs were scarce in Kobe.

As the Japanese were finding that POWs were a cheap source of labor, new companies were constantly applying for work parties. One day three new honchos appeared and counted off thirty men each. I was included in one of the parties. Our guards marched us up the street to the large Sannomiya railway station, where we descended to the subway and were loaded onto a passenger car, part of a long train, which headed out of the station. In a few minutes the train emerged from the subway and traveled on the surface. We passed through a thickly settled region which seemed to be city suburbs, with small stations about every mile. After about ten miles or so, we got off the train at Nishinomiya Station. All the stations had signs in English, which I presumed had been for the edification of pre-war American tourists. From the station, our three groups went their separate ways, each with one guard. My group marched through the town to a large factory about a half mile from the station. Entering the factory gate, we were taken to a large, dingy shed, where we had to remove our clothes and put on company work uniforms, which looked as if they had been discarded by the dirtiest bum that had ever lived. They were made of a very loosely woven cloth which you could see through, and were filthy black. In fact, the whole factory was black. We soon found out why. The factory, called Showa Denki, made carbon electrodes of all sizes, from a half inch up to a foot and a half thick, and up to ten feet long. These electrodes were used for many things, from movie projectors to steel smelters, and were made from a mixture part graphite and part ground coke. Everything was moved from place to place by means of mine cars which ran on narrow-gauge tracks. Rigdon and I drew the job of filling a car with hot coke from the kiln, and then pushing it the quarter of a mile to the crusher on the other side of the factory where we dumped our load, refilled our car with ground coke mixed with graphite and pushed it back to the kilns, where it was baked into the final electrode shape. Filling the mine car with the hot coke was the worst part of the job, as it was red hot from the kiln, and it was all shovel work loading the car. One thing sure, we weren't cold on that job! The ground-up coke at the other end wasn't hot, but it was so fine it blew all over, coloring everything and everybody black. At the end of the day we could have put on a minstrel show and wouldn't have needed a bit of makeup.

There were a couple of good things about this job. We were given a bucket of soup, ingredients unknown but thick enough, with our bun and a half, to fill our shrunken stomachs. We were also allowed a good half hour to clean up in the communal bath. This was a large room with a dozen baths in it, as of course all the employees got as dirty as we did and had to take baths before going home. Each of us got a small bit of lye soap just about sufficient to get the black off, using a small bucket of water to lather up, then rinsing with more water before getting into the large tub which held all our work crew, for a good hot soak. For most of us, this was the first hot bath since our capture almost a year ago, and was it heavenly! It was almost worth getting filthy to get such a bath. The rest of the big tubs were filled with Jap workers of both sexes, all staring at us scrawny POWs. Any of us who were bashful got over it fast enough if they wanted to get clean. It didn't worry me any, as I always followed the old maxim which says "When in Rome, do as the Romans do." After our bath we put on our old uniforms and were marched back to the train station where we met the other two work gangs. They had worked at a steel mill, named Toyo Steel, and at Yoshihara Oil, places I was to learn more about in future. The train ride back to Kobe was almost like a commuter trip home. Even at this early date in our imprisonment we had begun to think of Kobe House as "home." At least it was the place where we hung our hats and laid our heads, some place we could rely on as being reasonably permanent.

For the next week I worked at Showa Denki along with Rigdon, pushing our mine car from one end of Showa Denki to the other. Our honcho was a small Nip we called "Speedo," which was just about the extent of his English. His bark was worse than his bite, and he was easier on us than most of them. Our daily stint was to complete seven round trips with our car, after which we could knock off and clean up. This was a great incentive to work faster, and we immediately began to "Speedo" to see who could finish work first. The network of tracks were all over the place, and we went in various directions in order to beat the other three car pusher teams. This led to a lot of overturned cars due to running off the tracks at switches or sharp turns. A derailment called for a lot of hard work putting the car back on the tracks and reloading it with the spilled load. The locals must have thought we were crazy to rush around like we did. The first couple of days we finished our quota around two in the afternoon, and spent the rest of the afternoon getting the black off and then soaking in that wonderful hot tub. Of course we found that we hadn't been too bright doing all that speedo, because the next day another round trip was added to our quota. This put a damper on our enthusiasm for getting through early. Finally we settled for eight round trips, which we completed at a reasonable pace, finishing early enough to have a hour's cleaning time. Everything considered, Showa Denki was not too bad a place to work, if you could ignore the horribly uncomfortable, filthy work clothes we had to wear, and the black dust with which we were coated with. The advantage of having the hot water to bask in, and the chance to do some clothes washing in hot water during our noon break, made Showa Denki bearable.

The next week I thought I would try one of the other factory jobs, so got a swap with one of the Toyo Steel people. This turned out to be a big mistake. I had been gaining some weight back and was up to around a hundred and fifty, and being taller than the British, I guess the Japs thought I must be pretty strong. Anyway, I was taken to a place where there was a big pile of castings, which needed to have the slag removed before the final work was done on them. The slag was removed by using a jack-hammer equipped with a chisel head. My job was to clean up a large locomotive wheel about six feet in diameter, so covered with slag it was almost unrecognizable. I had never had anything to do with a jack-hammer and had no idea how heavy one was. In my poor physical shape, it was all I could do to hold the thing upright, shifting it around was physically impossible. I finally got the chisel against the wheel and pulled the trigger, which made a terrific noise and sounded as if I was really doing the job. It would have taken me a year to have cleaned up that wheel. I was worn out by noon and welcomed the lunch break, I can tell you. We got a little rice for lunch, but Toyo Steel was always known as a poor feeding outfit. The only thing people went there was to get warm and that was easy, with all the smelters going full blast. Back I went to my jack-hammer for the afternoon, and in some fashion managed to last until quitting time. It was lucky that nobody checked up on my work that day, because if they had, I probably would have caught Old Harry back at Kobe House. My lasting impression of Toyo Steel was that it was as close to Hell as I could imagine, and if I ever go there the Devil will surely hand me a jack-hammer and show me to a locomotive wheel covered with slag. That was the last time I volunteered for Toyo Steel!

After this experience, I rarely volunteered for any strange job, no matter how well anyone spoke of it. I did get picked a couple of times for the Yoshihara Oil job, the third company at Nishinomiya. This outfit crushed peanuts, copra, cottonseeds, and other things for their oil, which was used by the Japanese Air Force. This was mostly a lumping job, moving hundred kilo bags of peanuts or seeds from barges up planks to the crushers. I never did do much lumping there, as one of our honchos was a very short Jap who took particular delight in giving tall POWs the hardest job he could find. I usually wound up scraping hardened oil off the cobblestones, using a large chisel about six feet long, shaped like a crowbar and as heavy as one. All day with this chisel and I was just about as bad off as I had been with the jack-hammer at Toyo. The only good thing about Yoshihara was that you could stuff yourself with peanuts, even though they were raw. It was also possible to dunk your bread roll in peanut oil to make it taste better, and if you were brave enough, steal some peanut oil and smuggle it into Kobe House for trading purposes. However, if you were caught with any oil, which was Army property, the punishment was pretty drastic, and not worth it, as far as I was concerned. Needless to say, Yoshihara was another job I tried to avoid.

In the course of time, these factory jobs were manned by permanent gangs of POWs who had found jobs there that they liked, for some reason or other. The only one I cared to revisit was Showa Denki, to wash my clothes and get a hot bath. Otherwise, they weren't worth the train ride.

Chapter 22

My Fellow Americans

I think that at this point in the story I should pay a little attention to the rest of the Americans who had made the trip to Kobe on the *Ryukyu Maru* and were now safely ensconced in Kobe House. The thirty officers were quartered on the third floor of "B" block, the one on the left when entering the compound, and we saw very little of them, as they were not required to work. There were some British officers as well, for a total of about fifty. Many of the American officers had been civilians working in the Philippines as engineers when the war began. Others had been school teachers, business people, etc. They had been given commissions in the U. S. Army, from 2nd Lieutenant to Major, depending on age, it seemed, as the older they were, the higher they were in rank. There were probably a dozen who had been in the Service before the war. One was a West Pointer, Captain Henry Pierce, a good officer whom I remembered as being with the 57th Infantry, Philippine Scouts, whose outfit had relieved mine at the battle of the Points. None of them, however, seemed to concern themselves about the way we enlisted men were being treated, the one thing that good officers were expected to do. They seemed content to keep out of sight and thereby out of trouble. This didn't always work, as the Japanese had no scruples about beating officers in the same way they beat the enlisted men.

As the great majority of the POWs in Kobe House were British, the Japs named one of their officers, a Capt. Houghton, to be camp commander. He lived in his office next to the so-called hospital, along with his British clerk and an American officer, Lt. Col. Franklin Fliniau, who represented the Americans. Capt. Houghton had a tough job, having to enforce the Japanese orders on the one hand while trying to keep all the POWs happy on the other, which was patently impossible. He made a fair try at it, but the Lord himself couldn't have done both.

The twenty of us enlisted men were a ragtag bunch, all from different outfits and different branches of the Service, most of whom had never seen any of the others before Bilibid. The senior NCO was M/Sgt Leroy Lucas, a big Georgian who had been in the Air Corps fifteen years or so. Being the senior NCO, he was appointed leader of our group. He was also in the unenviable position of trying to balance the desires of the Japs against the desires of the rest of us, and, as our representative, was supposed to stand up for us when we were being beaten unjustly. Unfortunately, Luke failed in this respect, most of the time meekly following the Japanese line. I have seen British NCOs brutally beaten for trying to protect their men, but never Luke. As to be expected, he was not a favorite with us, and was generally ignored inside Kobe House.

Billy Johnson had been a radio operator on a B-17 bomber, arriving in the Islands just before the war. He was a New Englander from Lowell, Mass., which was about forty miles from where I live in New Hampshire, and was a happy-go-lucky guy who liked his beer and his cigarettes, for which he traded his ration of rice. A lot of heavy smokers did this, and many died because they would rather smoke than eat. Bill's plane had run out of fuel on a bombing mission and had ditched in the Sulu Sea. The crew had been rescued by Moros and Bill always told how he stayed in a Moro house decorated with skulls and wondered if he was going to wind up as a decoration. The Moros took good care of them, though, and he eventually wound up on the island of Panay, radioman for the few Americans there. After Corregidor was overrun and surrendered in May 1942, all the Americans in the southern islands also surrendered and were shipped up to Bilibid. Bill was always good humored and liked by all. The officers needed a dog-robber to take care of their quarters, get their rice and soup, etc., and as they all knew Bill, he got the job. He was paid in cigarettes, which suited him to a "T," and he didn't have to go to work with the rest of us. He had found his niche and was happy in it.

Fred Hoblitt was a Marine Corporal, who, while in China, had learned to speak Japanese fairly well, so was used by Capt. Houghton as an assistant interpreter. He did a good job of interpreting Henry's attempt at English, which was mostly just gibberish, thereby saving us from some rule or order which was relayed through Henry and which we couldn't possibly understand. Fred slept and ate with Capt. Houghton in his office, with Col. Fliniau and the camp clerk, so we saw little of him in our quarters and never at work.

Alvin Rigdon was one of the 27th Bomb Group boys who had arrived just before the war. He came from Haynesville, Louisiana and this was his first time away from home. He and I hit it off pretty well, even though I was a Yankee and he was from the deep south, and we became good friends and "muckers," as the English would say, sharing our loot, if we had any, as well as our Red Cross parcels, when we got one, and worked together most of the time. We did have our little arguments, but on the whole got along well.

Jack Schlosser, from California, was another with whom I became good friends. Jack had been a purser on the liner *President Coolidge*, which had been in Manila when war started, and had sailed without delay. Unfortunately for Jack, who had been enjoying himself in Manila, he had been left behind. If he had known what his future was going to be, he would have remained a civilian, but not knowing this, he joined the Army. In the confusion of the time, Jack was never given a serial number, which must have caused no end of confusion when he was discharged. Jack had been all over the world and had lots of stories to tell. We had planned to take a motorcycle trip around South America when we were free again, but we were in different camps when the war ended and lost touch. I suppose he went back to sea, and I will always wonder if he was ever given a serial number!

Jimmy Barrett had been born in the Philippines. His mother was Filipino and his father an American soldier. He had enlisted in the Army when the war began, as he was an American citizen and proud of it. Jimmy could have passed as a Filipino and been released with the rest of the Filipinos, but, as he said, he was an American, so chose to become a POW with the rest of us. I learned a little Tagalog from him, as well as learning how to sing the Philippine national anthem in that language. I can still sing it.

Earl Loughner, of the Army Engineers, was a little fellow who came from Pitcairn, Pennsylvania, and had the distinction of being the only married man among us, with a son he had never seen, being shipped out before his son was born. He was a quiet guy and we were bunkies most of the time, his name being next to mine in the alphabet. Dick Morris was from the 200th Coast Artillery, New Mexico National Guard. He was the youngest of the Americans, having enlisted at the age of fifteen. He liked to work on the docks because of the opportunities to steal food, or anything else, for that matter. He was to become famous as the best *dorobo*, or thief, in Kobe House.

We had two sailors mixed in with all the Army. James Griffin, from Missouri, known as "Spider" for some strange reason, was a friendly, quiet kid liked by everyone. Mike Burnett was a tall, well-built, good-looking guy from Tennessee. Spider was another radioman who had been captured on Panay with Bill Johnson and they were good friends. Both the sailors were in good physical condition and had permanent dock jobs, Spider at Mitsui Soko and Mike at Sen Paku, the company that unloaded ships moored out in the harbor. Mike was well fed and many times passed up his supper rice, giving it to one of us less fortunate than he.

Arnold Marshall was a tall, lanky, ill-natured fellow from the Louisiana Cajun country, who had no use for any Yankee, especially me. In the course of time, he and I came to blows a couple of times, inconclusive affairs brought to a halt by the guards with rifle butts.

Jimmy Lucero was another 200th Coast Artilleryman. He was a small, dark kid from Albuquerque, New Mexico, who spoke Spanish fluently. In the course of time, he taught me quite a bit of Spanish, which was one way to pass the endless hours in Kobe House.

Others were Del Busta, North Dakota; Bill Janiec and Owen Barnett, Ohio; Walter Bohannon, Oklahoma; Sully Sutherland from Virginia, and a fellow we called "Happy," probably because he landed a job in the cook-house, and thus had it made. I don't remember his last name.

This was the small group of Americans condemned to live packed together, like it or not, for the duration. With such diverse backgrounds, we were never as close knit as the British, who were all Regular Army and had been in the same outfit for many years. They were like a large family, much more cohesive than we were, coming from the same localities and the same type of environment, while for the most part we Yanks came from widely scattered parts of the U.S., had different outlooks on life, and in many cases, an almost different language. This mixture of different types resulted in the formation of small cliques who took care of themselves in a dog-eat-dog fashion, without much help given to any of the others.

Chapter 23

AND OUR GUARDS

In contrast to the interior and gate guards, who were regular army and who were rotated weekly, there was a permanent party who was responsible for the mess, supply, and administrative and medical functions of Kobe House. It numbered some twenty-four people and was commanded by Lt. Morimoto, or "Jack Oakie" as he was nicknamed by the POWs. His right hand man was a Sergeant Major, or *So-Cho*, a pretty good guy as far as Japanese go, and although he punished POWs at times, was never cruel. Then there was the supply sergeant, "Fish-face," who had charge of the food and other supplies. He constantly stole from our meager rations, as well as looting from the Red Cross parcels stored in his supply room. I think he was the most hated Jap of them all, and after the end of the war, I believe he was the only one from Kobe House killed by revengeful POWs. "Henry," the interpreter, whose real name was Igachiguchi, relayed regulations and orders from Jack Oakie to the POWs, although we rarely understood just what he was talking about.

Some of the Japanese camp staff at Kobe House.
Photo courtesy of Artie Power, 2/30 Btn, AIF.

The majority of the permanent party were former soldiers who had been relieved from active duty due to wounds or sickness, and had been given the easy job of guarding POWs. One guard was assigned to each job and marched the gang to work and back. He did nothing while we were at work except take life easy and drink lots of tea, unless some POW was caught stealing or having an argument with the honcho, which was a common occurrence due to the language problem. Civilians were not allowed to slap or hit POWs, and our guards were zealous in this respect. I think most of them liked to lord it over civilians, whom they actually treated worse than they did us. I have seen women and children knocked for a loop if they tried to get through our ranks, especially at Sannomiya Station when we were waiting for our train.

The station was always jammed, and the long lines of POWs were quite an obstacle to people trying to catch a train. Many tried to break through, but they did it at their peril, as the guards had eagle eyes for such things. The guards overlooked our squabbles with the honchos most of the time, and as time passed and we learned more Japanese, the jobs went easier with less trouble. Most of the trouble we had was when some POW was caught stealing and was reported to the guard. It was up to him to judge the case and deal out what punishment was due. Punishment varied as to degree or length, depending on the guard and how he was feeling at the time. Usually a half dozen of his best delivered across the face was sufficient, except in those cases deemed severe enough to be reported to the Sgt of the Guard at Kobe House. This usually called for hours of *kyotsuki* in front of the gate along with suitably severe beatings with a wooden sword, depending on who happened to be on duty that day.

Each of the guards had different personalities and habits, which we tried to figure out but never really did. They were all unpredictable, some all the time, some part of the time. We gave all of them nicknames, usually because of some physical characteristic, such as "Fish-Face," the supply man, whose face came to a point. Then there was the "Chinless Wonder," which is self-explanatory. "Gentleman Jim" was a good-looking fellow who took great care in his appearance, which trait was not common to many Japanese soldiers. Unfortunately, he was one of the most unpredictable of the guards, and you never knew when he was going to fly off the handle. I was a victim of his one day at Kami Gumi when I was the group leader. For some reason, Jim decided that I must work along with the rest, and when I objected, as leaders were not supposed to have to work, he went mad and straightened me out with some solid rights. Needless to say, I went to work! On other days he was most congenial, giving me his rifle to demonstrate the American manual of arms, and showing me pictures of his wife and family. I found that this was a good way to get on good terms with most Japanese. Just asking them about their families was a good icebreaker. Of course you had to tell them all about your family and how many *kodomos,* or children, you had. The more *kodomos* you had, the better the conversation.

One of the bad ones was "Horse face," who had lost an eye and had a wooden hand which really hurt when you got whacked with it. I think perhaps that some American had shot his hand off, the way he treated us. I remember one morning when we were lined up waiting to go to work. It was the rule that we all had to have our roll and a half with us for lunch, but some of those who were headed for a job where they ate well or could steal food, such as Sen Paku, where Mike Burnett worked, left theirs at Kobe House in order to have a late night snack. They were out of luck this morning, as Horseface was on duty, and the first thing he did was to go up the line checking each man to see if each man had his roll and a half. Of course he began to find that some didn't have theirs, and the wooden hand began its work. Working his way up the line, Horseface found more and more who had left their ration inside, and he rapidly lost his cool. Mike Burnett was at the end of the line, and for once he had his roll and a half, which he was waving around while laughing to see the others get whacked. Unfortunately for him, Horseface was now so livid with rage he began knocking around everyone he could reach, and Mike got his share, which the rest of us appreciated. I had been one of the first in line and could safely watch the mayhem as Horseface went up the line.

Then there was Wingy, also with a hook, Mickey Rooney, Betty Boop, the Boy Wonder, the Angel and Darkie. The Angel was a big, ugly man who openly declared to us that he would never strike a POW, and, to my knowledge, never did. Darkie was the best one of all the guards. He wasn't very good-looking and was about the darkest Japanese I ever saw. I never saw him hit a POW and he took good care of us, making sure that the companies gave us our full ration at noon, that our *yasumes* were on time and that we had enough coal in our huts to keep us warm. It was too bad that there weren't more guards like the Angel and Darky, but I guess we were fortunate even to have two good ones out of that lot. Many of the Japanese prison camps never had one good guard, to say nothing of two.

Most of the time our guard disappeared as soon as we reached the job, only coming around a couple times during the work day. I'm sure they had no worries in respect to any POW trying to escape—that was the last thing any of us thought about. Swimming seven thousand miles would be just too much trouble.

Chapter 24

POW Coolies

Early spring of 1943 saw all of Kobe House working on the Kobe docks, and of course the three factory jobs. It was still very cold and windy, but I had finally been given an old Japanese army overcoat that was big enough, so at least I was a bit warmer going back and forth to work. It also kept me a bit warmer at night. The food ration, together with our company lunch, was better and more nutritious than what we had been issued in the Philippines, helped my beri-beri to improve gradually, although the weakness would never leave my legs, and I had gained enough weight to take me out of the skeleton category. Another good thing was that I never had another malaria attack. Everything seemed to be coming along better, and I figured that volunteering to go to Japan had worked out OK. So far, anyway.

Another nice thing that happened was that the bath in Kobe House had been activated, and on our *yasume* day we could enjoy a hot bath. We went into the bath by sections, thirty men at a time, for twenty minutes. The bath was about fifteen feet square and almost three feet deep. Of course our dear officers got first crack at the water when it was nice and clean. We were all supposed to wash up before getting into the bath, but not everyone did this, wanting to get into the hot water and warm up. If you were in one of the last sections to get in, the water wasn't what anyone could call clean, in fact it was filthy dirty, but wonderfully hot, so the filthiness didn't make that much difference to us. Being up to your neck in red-hot water was pure heaven to a perpetually frozen POW, and at least the dirt got loosened up some. There was a row of showers in the bath room, but no hot water, just cold water from the mountains in back of Kobe, and I mean it was pure liquid ice. I doubt if there were more than ten men who took a shower after their hot bath, but I was one of them, as I couldn't stand being slimy dirty. Fifteen seconds was just about all you could stand it, just long enough to rinse the gunk off. It was funny, though, after coming out of that shower, I stayed warm for a couple of hours. Everything seemed warmer after that!

Working on the docks became easier as we got used to it. We got to be pretty good, as good as any of the coolie gangs and better than some, as none of the regular coolies seemed to be very enthusiastic. It was easy to tell that none of them were happy about the war, and wished it was all over. We were right with them on that! During our lunch hour, we were let alone to do what we wanted, as long as we didn't stray too far. Our main thing was to scout around in whatever godown we were working in to see what was loose enough to pick up. Most of the godowns were three or four stories high, and held lots of interesting things, from sugar to soya beans, as well as canned goods. Most POWs became thieves by necessity, as anything edible you could find to put in the soup pot for lunch, or smuggle into Kobe House for trading purposes, increased your chances of survival. I would guess that at least 99% of Kobe House tried their hand at stealing.

The Japanese War Ministry had determined that the food allowance for all POWs would be as follows: For Officers, fifteen ounces of staple food, normally rice or barley, per day; Enlisted men, one pound four ounces; or if working at hard labor, as we in Kobe House certainly were, an extra seven and a half ounces were added, making a total of one pound, eleven and a half ounces. This meant that we were getting about one-half of what an American soldier received in peacetime, at the most, a thousand five-hundred calories. It was no wonder that all we thought of was food, and liberating it from the Japanese not only helped us to keep going, but also made us feel that we had done what we could to help defeat them.

As of the 1st of January, we were being paid once a month for our work. The rate for NCOs was two yen per day. One yen eighty-five sen to pay for our board and room was deducted from the two yen, leaving me with a net of fifteen sen. They actually made us sign the payroll, too. A canteen had been started for our benefit, which sold small notebooks, pencils, tooth powder, tooth brushes, etc. The tooth powder and brushes were welcome, as most of the Bataan boys had nothing such as that. I bought one of the small notebooks and began writing down the names and addresses of all the Yanks, as well as those of the British I had become friends with. Once in a while you could buy something to eat, such as a mandarin orange, curry powder or fish powder, either of which could be added to your rice or soup, that is if you could stand the taste. The curry powder wasn't too bad, but the fish powder turned your rice green and had a horrible taste, so once was enough. It was so bad you couldn't even give it away.

There were a number of small restaurants on the docks, frequented by the dock coolies, so one day on our lunch hour, Rigdon and I just went into one of them and ordered something to eat in our rudimentary Japanese. Wonder of wonders, we were given a big bowl of noodles mixed with bits of meat, all for fifty sen. Nobody seemed to see anything strange about us being there except a few coolies who mumbled a bit. The next day we had another good meal, but on our third try we were informed that we were not welcome. We did get two good lunches, anyway. Another of our noon expeditions around the godown paid off when we came across a large crate in a dark corner. I pried up a board with my *kagi* and found that the crate was full of what looked like dead leaves, but which turned out to be dried mushrooms, which we had never seen before. We enjoyed a thick mushroom soup that day. The Japanese pickled or dried lots of edibles which didn't look too appetizing, but the dried stuff, when soaked with water, was pretty good, and the pickled things went well with rice. The looks of anything didn't bother us. Our motto was, if you could eat it, it must contain some vitamins and therefore had to be good for us. Some days I was so hungry I waited for a coolie to finish his lunch and threw away the wrapping, usually a banana leaf, whereupon I pounced upon said banana leaf and picked off any grain of rice still stuck to it.

We soon became expert at moving railway cars around the docks. There were no yard engines, coolies and POW gangs being the motive power. Getting a fully loaded car moving was the hardest part of the job. Usually there was a coolie on hand with a long iron bar which had a chisel-shaped tip, which he placed under one of the back wheels and used it as a lever to get the car started, after which all the gang kept it going. The coolies had a chant they used to keep everyone in the proper rhythm. It went *yoi-tsa, yoi-tsa*, everybody pushing at the first *yoi*, resting at the second, and pushing again at the third. With all of us pushing at the same time, the car rolled along nicely. The coolies had a lot of these chants, all used to make the work easier by applying maximum force at the proper time. If the two men lifting hundred kilo bags didn't lift at the same time, injury to the back could easily result. The chanting kept the lifters in proper rhythm and made their hard work easier.

Another dock job was called Minatogawa. This was a smaller dock where produce from the numerous islands in the Inland Sea were off-loaded. Fruits and vegetables were the main cargoes. One day I worked on a shipment of dehydrated bananas and of course I managed to steal a couple. Bananas in dried form are pretty small, so you could put a whole one in your mouth while it softened up. This was the closest thing to candy we ever got. Dried pineapple was available at times, and was very tasty. All this stuff we stole to eat was packed loose in boxes or sacks, and not up to American standards of cleanliness, but that was no bother to a hungry POW. I'm sure the EPA would have fits about the poor packaging. Thank God they weren't active in Kobe harbor, or we wouldn't have had much to eat.

Returning to Kobe House after work was quite interesting at times. Some days the street outside the gate was empty, we just lined up and counted off for the duty Sgt, who checked us off in his book and let us go in. Other days it was quite different. Marching up the street, what you saw was mass confusion, with Japs all over the place, screaming and yelling. Usually it was because someone on one of the first jobs to get back had been caught with contraband on him, or had been reported for punishment by a guard. This always got the Sgt. and his crew worked up, which was pretty easy to do, and they proceeded to make it tough for all the rest of the jobs. As soon as your gang arrived, it was made to line up and remain at attention until it could be inspected. Hopefully, the inspector would turn out to be Darky or the Angel, but the odds were against that happening. Usually it turned out to be someone like Horseface or Gentleman Jim, in which case you were in trouble, because even though you had been on a job that had nothing to steal, you were still gone over with a fine tooth comb. If your cap wasn't on just right, or a button left unbuttoned, you were in for a bashing. This we got used to after a while, seeing what was coming out of the corner of your eyes and riding with the punch or slap. It was a good thing that most of the guards never learned to punch American style. If they had, none of us would have had a tooth left in his head.

One other thing that caused a lot of trouble was our issue blankets. Some of the British who were too sick to go out to work began cutting up one of their four blankets to make vests, which they sold to the working POWs so they could buy a little extra food. I had been given a vest by one of my Scottish friends which I wore to work under my overcoat to help keep me a bit warmer. About a week after I had acquired my vest, our work gang turned the corner and saw the whole street filled with POWs with their overcoats off, and the guards confiscating blanket vests. I could see what was happening, and while marching down the street, tried frantically to ditch mine to avoid being caught with it on. Unfortunately, the buttons were fastened Chinese style by string loops, and as my vest was pretty snug, I just couldn't get those darn buttons unbuttoned. Having an overcoat over the vest didn't make it easier, either. So I was stuck with it and just knew I was doomed, but wonder of wonders, the guards weren't on the usual rampage. The Sgt Major happened to be on duty and he kept everything pretty calm. All the guards did was to take the names of all those caught with blanket vests on, and of course confiscated the vest. After supper, all the ones on the list had to stand inspection and show their blankets. Most of those whose names were on the list didn't have the four we were issued with, and were immediately taken down to the alleyway between our two buildings, where there was a small empty shed. The guilty ones were packed in this shed, so many that they had to remain standing. They were in the shed for the next three nights in the freezing weather, as well as working their regular jobs during the day. I only escaped the shed because, although my name was on the list, I still had my four blankets as issued, and the guards thought they had made a mistake. Sometimes you got lucky, as I did this time, but usually you were just lumped in with the rest, guilty or not. Those who were punished were not allowed to take a blanket with them while in the shed, so the end result was that those who had been sick were sicker, and some of those who had been reasonably well got pneumonia. Always something going on in good old Kobe House!

Chapter 25

Monotonous Misery

Life at Kobe House became a daily grind consisting of backbreaking work on the outside, and a struggle to get enough to eat and to try to keep warm on the inside. Our food ration never improved. The rice was all right, as far as it went, but the soup ingredients were tops and leaves of sundry kinds of vegetables, and without taste. Once in a while a stray turnip or potato found its way into the soup, but most of the time it was the ubiquitous *daikon*, which was just an enormous white radish. Radish soup is exceptionally tasteless. One so-called vegetable we called whistle-weed, for its hollow stalk, and another one looked just like a pistol-chamber, having six holes in a circle. Both were hard to chew. Once a week, we got a fish soup, I can't remember whether or not we got it on Friday, but it was so bad that no one would ever eat it if he had a choice. It consisted of ground-up fish heads, bones, etc. Evidently it had been put through a grinder. If you were lucky, you might find a tiny bit of fish, or some fish eyes, which I looked for because they had a nutty taste. The soup we liked best was soy bean soup, which tasted good, and best of all, at the bottom of the bucket a few whole beans remained, which were rationed out by the spoonful. If you were lucky, you got a spoonful every other week. On such a skimpy diet it was no wonder than we were hungry all the time. The noon meals we got at most jobs were a lifesaver. I really pitied those who had to stay inside Kobe House every day, even though they didn't have the hard work outside.

It became a real chore to keep my coveralls together. They were my only working clothes and were coming to the end of their career. Every Sunday I had to sew up rips and tears, and patch the new holes. What with all the odd colors of my patches, I began to look like a circus clown. When I finally did get something else to wear, I counted forty patches on the bottom half of the coveralls. I had used the top half to patch the bottom half. Washing clothes was most difficult, unless you wanted to spend a day at Showa Denki. Any soap you could get was used to wash your face, so about all you could do was rinse your clothes in cold water. Cleanliness suffered in our soapless environment. In the morning, it was usually just a dash of ice water to open up your eyes. Brushing teeth in ice water wasn't too pleasant, either, so was usually passed up unless you were a fanatic. Even that wasn't as bad as having to shave for the Sunday inspection. It was a good thing that a few Red Cross supplies began trickling into camp. Most of the Red Cross stuff was stolen by Fishface and his buddies, and what we received for our section of thirty men might be a couple of tooth brushes, a can of tooth powder, one razor with a half-dozen blades, a comb or two, and, if we were lucky, a sewing kit. Anything issued to us was doled out by a lottery run by roster, those getting something one time were crossed off the list until we all had gotten something, then the process started over.

There were a few improvements made from time to time. The cookhouse began to issue hot water and a spoonful each of soya sauce an hour before lights out. A canteen cup of hot water mixed with the soya sauce made a drink that tasted just like beef bouillon. It was a very nice nightcap when you were shivering. Then one Sunday we were notified that we would be able to write letters home. Each section was allotted two letters of one hundred fifty words and five letters of fifty words once a month. As with everything else, this monthly issue became one every two months, but at least we were able to write home. It was odd, but nobody in our section wanted the long ones, so I got one each time we were allowed to write. Jimmy Barrett usually took the other one, which he sent to his mother in Manila. Each letter had to be printed in block letters and consisted of just four paragraphs, each of which had to conform to what the Japanese wanted you to say. The first paragraph had to say that you were in good health and being treated well. The second said that you were working and receiving pay. In the third, you wrote that you hoped the war would end soon so that you could join your loved ones, and in the last paragraph, you could write about old memories, such as family get-togethers, trips, etc., so that whoever you wrote to would know it was really you. Some POWs wrote in a sort of code, such as the writer was healthy and weighed as much as Bobby, who was his six-year-old brother, or twice as much as Jeff, who happened to be a pet dog. I used to print Jimmy's letters for him, his English being none too good. At any rate, it was good to able to write home, even though what you wrote was dictated by our captors.

Much discussion went on as to how the war was progressing. All we knew about that was what we heard at work, and that was all bad. Most of us had faith in our countries winning in the end, but we had no idea as to when that would be. Faith in our country kept most of us going, although all the bad news made it pretty hard at times. Some of the prophecies making the rounds were "Over the sea in '43," made by the most optimistic. Another one was "A Frisco whore in '44," which I thought nearer the mark, and the pessimistic "Back alive in '45." Nobody picked '46, probably because nothing rhymed with that. '46 seemed too far in the future to even think of the war lasting that long. We all knew that if we had to make it to '46, there wouldn't be too many of us left.

One thing that was easy was hair care. A couple of the older British who were unable to do heavy work were put to work as barbers. All they had were clippers and they became expert at their job, bald heads being the only style available. We all looked like denizens of Alcatraz, with the exception of our dear officers. Other older POWs became cobblers and tailors, who did as well as they could with the limited materials available to them, most of which had been stolen on the jobs and smuggled into Kobe House. There were a considerable number of British in their forties and fifties, as they were career soldiers, while most of the Yanks were in their early twenties or their teens.

My health had been improving slowly, but in March my legs began to swell up again for some reason, so one day I went on sick call. The nearest thing we had to a Doctor was a British medic who ran the so-called hospital. He took a look at my legs and then asked me if I had been working on a sugar job lately. I said that I had, as a lot of sugar was coming in from the southern areas by ship, and of course we had to move it from dock-side into godowns. This was hard work, because sugar leaked from the bags and gummed up the wheel bearings of our *nekkos*, which made them hard to push. Lumping sugar was miserable, too, because you got sticky when you got sugar down your neck, as well as some bags being hard as iron because they had gotten wet on the way up to Japan. Working on sugar was no fun, but eating it was nice. The sugar we worked on was a light brown and wonderfully tasty. Being starved for sweets, we gobbled pounds of the stuff. Anyway, the medic informed me that eating sugar was my trouble. It seems that the sugar I ate used up all my Vitamin B, and that if he gave me a shot of this vitamin and I ate one teaspoon of sugar, it would offset the shot, so I had better keep off sugar jobs, if possible. No POW had much vitamin B, anyway, because our ration sure didn't contain such. This British medic was the first person I had seen who knew anything at all about beri-beri and what caused it. I wished I had known about the sugar in the Philippines, because I would never have put any sugar in my *lugao*. From that time on, I ate very little sugar, and in a few weeks my beri-beri gradually got better, although it never completely left me. Other ailments soon took the place of the beri-beri, but at least I had learned my lesson about eating sugar.

Chapter 26

I've Been Working on the Railroad

One day in early March, all the Americans not having regular jobs were told that we were being assigned to a new job. There were only a dozen of us in this category, and we waited on the street until about an hour after all the other workers had left, when a truck pulled up and we got aboard with our guard. The truck headed east on back streets through the poorer section of Kobe for about two miles, then left, under what we thought was a bridge, but actually was a wide viaduct carrying the Japanese National Railways through the city of Kobe. Turning left, we arrived at Higashinada Station and were taken to a small hut next to the railroad office building, where we were to store our belongings when we were working and where we were to eat lunch. It was a comfortable hut with a stove to boil the rice which the railroad issued to us for our noon meal, as well as a pot for making our soup. One of us was detailed to do the cooking, usually someone not able to do the hard physical labor. Our railroad honcho was a man about thirty whose name was Sano. He spoke good English unless the guard was in the vicinity. Sano-San turned out to be one of the best of our honchos.

After we had settled in, Sano-San took us across the four main lines to a side track leading to a trestle, on which there were a half-dozen cars full of *sekitan,* or coal. Our job was to empty the coal cars into trucks waiting below the trestle, which was about fifteen feet high. Some of the cars were gondolas which had hinged bottoms. We liked to see gondolas, as the coal just ran out by itself and fell through the trestle into the trucks. Other cars were just flat cars with hinged sides from three to six feet high. When the sides were let down, half the coal fell out and the rest had to be shoveled out. This was our job. The shovels were pretty big, but the work wasn't hard, not much lifting but just shoving the coal out. Compared to work on the docks, we found this work pretty easy. Working with us were a couple of older coolies who showed us which car to work on and when. The work was sporadic, as trucks arrived and parked under the trestle. Half of the time there were no trucks, and we gathered around a coal fire in an empty drum. The coolies made sure that there was a good fire going as they liked to keep warm as much as we did. At every break they would get their little long stemmed pipes going. With bowls the size of a thimble, and tobacco so fine it looked like dust, a pipeful only lasted for three or four puffs, and then had to be refilled for the next smoke. Their pipes were tucked into the wide woolen sash that all the coolies wore around the stomach and abdomen. Wallets were stowed away in the sash as well. I never saw a coolie without his woolen sash, which was supposed to keep his insides healthy. They were worn all year, even in the hottest of weather. Probably they were worn in bed, too.

Noon arrived, and we went back across the tracks for our lunch. It was tricky crossing the main line, which had two tracks for passenger trains and two for freight trains. Higashinada was a freight station, so none of the passenger trains stopped, but zoomed right through doing about eighty miles per hour. A train came through about every three or four minutes, so you had to watch your step and move fast. Our lunch was pretty good, a bowl of rice and soup which was better than that we got at Kobe House. I think it was the same lunch the railroad people got. I forgot who the POW cook was, but it being his first try at cooking rice, it could have been better. After we had been at Higashinada a while, we decided to let one man become the permanent cook, after which the rice became fit to eat.

Lunch over, one of the coolies put his head in at the door and shouted *Hajime!*, which we ignored, seeing as we didn't know what that meant. After a few more *Hajimes*, he gave up and left. Pretty soon Sano-San arrived and told us that *Hajime* meant "Start work". One more Japanese word learned! We all hated that word. The word we liked best was *yasume*, as that meant a break. Back across the tracks we hopped, and found another string of coal cars on the trestle, just waiting for us. We had these done by the time Sano-San came to take us back to Kobe House. All in all, it hadn't been too bad a day. Nobody had shouted "Speedo" at us even once, and the food had passed muster, better than most jobs. Our backs did ache a bit and we had a few blisters on our hands from the unaccustomed shoveling, but it was far better than being half dead from lumping big bags all day.

Each day began with the truck ride through the back streets. We went the same route every day, and we got to looking for the same people. We waved to all of them and most began to look for us and wave back, all except one little boy about four years old with a snotty nose, who was in the same spot every morning with his little pile of stones, which he threw at us as we went by. He never hit anything but the truck, but he sure was persistent. We made fun of him all the time, and you never saw a madder kid. I have always wondered if he still remembers the truckload of POWs!

Some days when we arrived at the trestle, there were no trucks there, so we just unloaded the coal anyway. This was all right, except that after some time, the coal had built up to the top of the trestle. Then when we opened the bottom of the gondola cars the coal had no place to go, and we had to get down and shovel all that coal from under the car and to one side. This was hard on the back, as the whole car had to be emptied this way. Some of the cars were a bit bigger than the others, with sides six feet high. When the trestle was clogged up, it was a lot of work unloading these cars, too. After a while you began to wonder if you would ever be able to straighten up again. Fortunately for us, this didn't happen often.

Japanese trucks had all been converted to run on gas, which was generated in a little stove mounted just back of the cab. This stove used small pieces of wood for fuel, and every morning little columns of smoke could be seen all over the city while the trucks were warming up. The trucks seemed to have very little power and were always being worked on. I presume that was the reason they didn't show up every day. Then the coal pile began to pile up. At times the pile was so high that no more could be unloaded, and when this happened we were taken to the main station to unload miscellaneous freight. The first job we had there was to unload crates of mandarin oranges which we moved from the freight car to a waiting horse and wagon. Most of the time we formed a human chain and passed the crates along the line to the wagon. Two men worked inside the car passing boxes to the head of the line, and it was easy to open up a crate with your *kagi*. We all took turns inside the car, and when you finished inside, you took an orange out, stuffed somewhere in your uniform. When you took a trip to the *benjo*, your orange was eaten, rind and all. Nothing was ever left to be found by the Japanese. In this way we made sure that we would never have a hard time at Kobe House. The crate from which we stole the oranges was fixed up to look as normal as possible, and went along the line with everyone making it look as if it was as heavy as the rest. This was how we dealt with any shipment of vegetables or other edibles we had any use for.

At Higashinada we made our acquaintance with the popular vegetable named *Daikon*. *Daikons* were just a giant white radish which had a hot taste. They were about five or six inches across and up to two feet long, shipped tied together in bunches. They were a staple food in Japan, mostly eaten in a pickled form. When pickled they shrink to about a tenth of their original size and turn a bilious yellow, probably because of some spice added during the pickling procedure. A few small slices of pickled *daikon* were added to a coolie's rice to spice it up. We were issued some once in a while, but I don't know of many POWs who liked it. We got a lot of *daikon* soup in Kobe House which we didn't relish, as *daikon* when boiled have no taste, and I'm sure have no vitamins either.

Sometimes we were lucky enough to work on a car of apples. These came packed in straw bundles, which you could spread open enough to remove one or two from each sack; they didn't show at all. Of course you had to eat skin, core, seeds and worms (if any), which was all right with us, even the worms containing vitamins. We all thought that anything edible, no matter how repulsive it looked, had some food value, so down it went. Other good things to work on were shipments of assorted vegetables coming into the city people from their relatives in the country. These were also shipped in straw sacks, from which we neatly extracted potatoes, carrots, turnips, etc., all of which went into our soup for lunch. Other things were harder to work on, such as kindling wood, which came in bundles. The bundles were heavy, as well as hard on the hands, and with slivers aplenty. Not edible, either.

One day we were taken across the tracks to another siding at the west end of the yard. There was a small hut there with benches. Soon a couple of cars rolled up the siding for us to unload. They were filled with straw sacks of unslaked lime, which turned out to be the most miserable job we had at Higashinada. Unslaked lime comes in lumps, and is very dusty. Two men at a time had to get into the car, and with their *kagis* move the bags to the car door, where another pair of POWs loaded the bags into a wagon. Those inside had the rough part of the job, as the dust got in the eyes and mouth, as well as coating your body, burning anything it touched. It was almost impossible to breathe while you were inside the car. As we had twelve men, each team worked every third car, and it only took two cars to make you wish you had never heard of unslaked lime. The dust was especially bad on a hot day when you were sweating, as the dust got into the pores of your skin, where it burned for a couple of days. No amount of washing could get it off. The lime came in for two or three days at a time, and we hated to see it come, although we had lots of *yasume* time waiting for the horse-drawn wagons. There was a high board fence next to our hut, enclosing a few Japanese houses. There was a knothole in the fence which we peeked through to see what went on there, hoping to get a glimpse of a *musume*, or young lady, but all we saw were *mama-sans* taking care of *kodomos,* or children. I think they peeked at us, too, and saw how skinny we were, because every other day there was a basket of onions hanging on our side of the fence. They must have been for us, because no one ever complained about the empty basket.

We had noticed that all the wagon drivers had face masks which covered their nose and mouth, so we thought we should have masks as well. Old Luke had been coming to Higashinada with us as leader, so we asked him to get us masks. Luke didn't have to work, his job was to keep the work going and keep the Japanese happy, an impossible job and one that I hated when I had it. If the Japanese were happy, we weren't, and vice versa. It was easier to keep the Japs happy, and Luke hated to upset them by asking for masks, but after we threatened to make him look bad by slowing down, he knew he had to take some action. He approached Sano-san, who was as approachable as any Jap I ever saw, and the next time we headed for the lime cars, we each got a mask, which was a considerable improvement.

Everything considered, Higashinada was, to me at least, one of the best jobs I had been on. The work wasn't excessively hard and there were lots of times when there was nothing to do for an hour or so, when we could loaf in our hut, keeping warm and drinking tea. POWs can't ask for much more than that!

Chapter 27

Spring, 1943

Spring saw the POWs of Kobe House settling down to a changed routine, thirteen days of work and the second Sunday off. Working every other Sunday had become necessary to increase the war effort and we had to do our part. We were all for it, as Sunday in Kobe House was not a day we greatly enjoyed. It was better to be at work and get a good lunch. The weather had moderated and we didn't shiver as much as before. The guards were just as cruel as ever, but we had become familiar with each one's idiosyncracies to some extent, and were less likely to get into trouble. Our food ration remained the same, with the exception of a few more greens in the soup. With the extra food we were able to scrounge at Higashinada, most of us began to put on a little weight. In fact, I was up to a hundred and fifty pounds by April, and feeling a lot better than when we arrived in Kobe. My decision to volunteer for the trip to Japan was turning out well.

With warmer weather, the cases of pneumonia and the like started to tail off, but boils and ulcers became more numerous, caused by the deficiency in our diet of critical vitamins such as A, B and C. I had escaped these so far, but my turn would come. Old Luke developed boils on his rear end, and was told by the medic to keep it warm, if possible. At Higashinada, he thought of a good way to do this, by placing two benches in line about a foot apart, then building a small coal fire in the space between the benches. Then he laid on the benches with his rear end over the fire. Being leader and not having to work, Sano-San didn't object. After a bit, Luke dozed off. While the rest of us were working, we had to pass him from time to time. I don't remember who thought of it, but we began adding a piece of coal to his little fire every time we went by, and pretty soon Luke began to squirm in his sleep as the fire got hotter and hotter. Well, pretty soon old Luke let out a yelp and shot up off his benches. It was the funniest thing we had seen for a long time and we got a big kick out of it. Luke was pretty mad but he couldn't do much about it as all of us were guilty. It was just a sample of Kobe House humor.

One thing I had noticed about the railroad was that each car had a card in a slot next to the door with Japanese writing on it, which described the contents of the car. I figured that if I could read that card, I would be able to pick a car to work on that held apples or vegetables and avoid cars containing cement or wood, as at times the gang worked on more than one car at a time. I had been shooting the breeze with one of the older coolies on the coal trestle, and finally got him to scratch the *Katakana* characters on the ground with a stick. *Katakana* is used for all foreign words, because the Japanese don't have all the different sounds such as those in English or French. For example, there is no "L" sound in the Japanese language, so, for example, my name had to be written in *Katakana*. The *Katakana* alphabet consists of fifty characters, all ending with a vowel except "n". It is learned by rote, starting with ah, ee, oo, eh, oh, then ma, mi, mu, me, mo, ta, ti, tu, te, to, etc. By learning to read *Katakana* I would know what was in cars having cards with *Katakana* characters, and could avoid cars whose card read *cemento*, or cement. Normal Japanese, such as in newspapers or books, uses *Kanji* characters. *Kanji* consists of more than five thousand ideographs, had been adopted from Chinese and meant the same thing as the Chinese, but was pronounced differently. *Kanji* is pretty difficult, so all I managed to learn was a few common terms such as those for vegetables, sugar, coal, beans and fruit, as well as the symbol used by the Japanese Army which was stamped on everything belonging to it, like the U.S.A. on our equipment. Stealing anything that belonged to the Japanese Army was a capital offense, and you had better stay away from it. Everyone wanted to know how I was able to pick the good cars to work on, but I never told anyone that I could read the cards. If everyone could do it, I would surely lose my advantage.

Being permanent Higashinada workers, we soon became familiar with all the Japanese regulars. After they had gotten used to the POWs, we were treated just about the same as they were. There was a little newsstand under the arch in the viaduct which we came through just before we arrived at Higashinada, and we were allowed to visit it and buy small candies, that is if we had any money. They also sold a newspaper, called the *Osaka Mainichi*, or daily, which was printed in English. It was a famous paper which had been in existence for many years. English had been a required course in Japanese high schools and still is, so I imagine the paper was used in school. Other papers printed in *Kanji*, with any foreign word in *katakana*, were sold at the stand for ten sen. We never received any news regarding the war situation since we had surrendered a year ago, so these papers were very tempting. We couldn't buy one at noon because the stand was busy then and somebody would be sure to report it to our guard, but POWs are resourceful, and a plan was worked out to get us a paper. Some days we had no guard on our way to work, there being more jobs than there were guards, so one guard took care of two or three jobs, riding his bike from one job to the other. In fact, they wouldn't have needed guards at all, we sure weren't going anyplace. About all they did was to make sure we didn't get into too much hot water. So about once a week, when we had no guard on the truck with us, Sano-San was distracted by a faked argument or the like, giving Jimmy Barrett time to run back to the newsstand and buy a paper, then hide it up his sleeve or inside his coat. Being half Filipino, he could pass for an Oriental sufficiently well enough so he wouldn't be noticed as much as one of the rest of us. This worked pretty well, and about once a week we got a paper back into Kobe House where it was read in a hurry, then destroyed. What news it contained was relayed to all the section leaders and from them to the men. In this way we became up-to-date on what was going on in the war. Strangely enough, the war news in the paper gave a good account of the big sea battles and the island campaigns. When an island was taken by the allies it appeared in the papers, although claimed as a victory by the Japs, in which they had annihilated whole American divisions. The sea battles were also painted in glowing colors, with entire American fleets being sunk. Of course this was just propaganda for the Japanese people, and I don't doubt that they knew the truth as well as we did. For the rest of the war, we followed the course of events almost daily. From Guadalcanal on, we followed a trail of islands north. The news we gleaned from the newspapers gave us an incentive to keep going. The question was, how long could we keep going?

May arrived, and with it an issue of two summer working outfits. These were most welcome, as my set of khakis and my coveralls were barely hanging together. Wonder of wonders, both coat and trousers fit me as if they had been tailored. They were made of a greenish khaki material, the trousers without belt loops but having two long strips of cloth which were tied in front, and the coat buttoned to the neck, Mao style. The odd part of it all was that every POW in Kobe House got the same size as I did. Most of the British were six inches shorter than I was, and you can imagine how the new outfits looked on them. There was much cutting and sewing going on for the next week with people trying to cut their suits down to size. They sure finished with a lot of patch material! I didn't have any of that, but I couldn't complain. At least I was now decently dressed.

Along with the clothing issue, anyone whose shoes had worn out got a pair of Jap two-toed black rubber sneakers, odd-looking to us with the separate big toe. As with the clothing, every pair of shoes were size ten, and were much too big for most of the POWs. The British looked like a bunch of Charlie Chaplins flopping around in their new shoes, but soon found them to be of use in smuggling loot into camp. Some brought up to a half pound of sugar into Kobe House packed in a small bag which was tucked into the tip of their shoes. My own shoes were still in fair shape, so I didn't get any new ones. They would have been a fair fit if I had, as I wore size ten.

The weather was nicer in May, getting warmer and warmer, and even inside Kobe House it was almost comfortable. How nice it was to be warm again, as we had been half frozen ever since arriving in Japan.

Chapter 28

New Arrivals

One day around the middle of May when we came in from work, we found that our living arrangements had been changed. Above the top floor in "B" block there was a small storage area about thirty feet square, just a bare platform. Some native carpenters had been at work during the day, and had installed two sleeping platforms and a folding table in the aisle, as well as a railing around the edge. New matting and shelves completed the changes. The twenty Americans were moved up to this perch, just under the peak of the roof, after supper. Our new quarters were considerably roomier than our old ones, and a lot cleaner. It was warmer, too, any heat from the lower floors tended to rise to our level. Another advantage was that we could peek over the edge of our platform to see what was going on beneath us. This gave us plenty of warning when any of the guards came up the stairs, giving us time to hide any contraband and be at *kyotsuki* by the time he arrived in our area. There was also a ladder which one could climb up to a skylight in the roof and get a good view of Kobe, that is, when no guard was in the vicinity.

The Jap carpenters were still working on the railing when we moved in, and it was fascinating to watch them work. All the joints were mitred by eye, using their saws which were strange to us, cutting on the pull and not the push, as ours do. I can testify that their work was perfect. Everything in our new home was fresh and clean, and we settled in happily. The only thing about it I didn't like was that the *benjo* was four floors down, no fun when you had to go every couple of hours.

We were there for a week or so, enjoying the extra space, when we lost it just as quickly. The crew of a Greek freighter sunk by a German submarine, picked up and then dumped off the sub when it visited Kobe, were added to the population of Kobe House. I guess the Japs didn't know just what to do with this bunch of civilians, and Kobe House just happened to be handy. German subs came into Kobe frequently, to refuel and to replenish their food supply. When they had sunk a ship, the survivors were usually picked up and taken to the nearest friendly port, from Singapore north to Japan. We saw German sailors often on our way to work, and they always gave us a wave or a salute. The officers usually called at the German Embassy, which was next door to Kobe House.

The seamen who had unfortunately found their way to Kobe House were of many nationalities. Being from a Greek ship, one would think that the crew would be Greek, but only the Captain, the engineer and the mates were Greek. The rest of the crew consisted of one Maltese, two Egyptians, two Chinese, a half dozen Indians and one fellow from Argentina. The four Greeks and the Argentinean were moved in with us, while the rest were used to fill up those British sections short of men. The one from Malta was in dire straits as the only language he could speak was his native Maltese. How he got along on a Greek ship was more than I know, unless Maltese is near enough to Greek that he could make do. He was fortunate in that one of the English NCOs had been born and raised on Malta and could help him with all the rules we had to contend with in Kobe House. The Greek Captain and his engineer, who was a decent fellow, spoke passable English. However, we soon came to wish that they had been dropped off in Singapore instead of Kobe House, as they were noisy, uncooperative people who made our nights miserable with their never-ending arguments. They kept insisting that they were civilians, not POWs, and were always in trouble with the guards, who cared less about the whole deal. If they got punished, we did, too, as they were in our section. When the Japs forced them to go out to work, it was worse, probably because they were sent to Showa Denki and the graphite, which didn't tend to make them any happier. They only got worse, if that was possible.

Chapter 29

The Mad Doctor

About the same time the Greeks arrived, another Japanese officer was added to the staff of Kobe House. This was a 2nd Lieutenant Miataki, who was supposed to be a doctor, but never did any doctoring while he was in Kobe House. If fact, he put more people in the hospital than he ever got out of it. He made his presence felt the first time he was the Officer of the Day. When the work details lined up in the street to wait for the honchos, he was there, inspecting everything and everybody, passing out wallops right and left. It so happened that the Higashinada truck was late in arriving, so we became his sole preoccupation for all of twenty minutes. At strict attention, we numbered off all that time, while the good doctor cocked his ear at the nearby mountains, trying to hear the echoes when we counted off, shouting "Louder, louder", and emphasizing his demands with smacks with his saber. Thank the Lord he didn't take it out of its sheath. I was in the rear rank, trying to be inconspicuous, but he took care of both ranks that day. My number happened to be eight, or *hachi*, that day, which wasn't too bad to have to shout louder and louder, better than *ryokyu* or *shichi*, or six and seven. After all our attempts at getting an echo from the mountains, we could barely speak the rest of the day.

That same evening, Lt. Miataki made his presence known to the officers in "B" block. Any ash trays in Kobe House were made from tin cans, which had to be spotlessly clean and shining when inspected at evening roll call, or *Tenko*, by the Duty Sergeant. On this particular evening, one of the ash trays in the officers' quarters was found to have a cigarette ash in it. When the Sergeant asked who was responsible, no one would own up to it, and after a few minutes of fruitless questioning, all the officers were marched down to the alleyway in front of the guard platform, where they had to stand at attention while the guards tried to locate the culprit. My buddy Billy Johnson was at the end of the front line, as he was the officers' dog-robber and cleaned up their quarters. Pretty soon the guards became frustrated because nobody would confess, and they began going up and down the two lines, slapping them all in turn. A half dozen guards were engaged in this, which was to them a most delightful occupation, when who should arrive on the scene but our Lt. Miataki, who had already acquired the apt nickname of "The Mad Doctor". The sixty or so officers had been standing rigidly at attention for an hour by this time, and were showing the effects of it. It is humanly impossible to remain at *kyotsuki* for that long a time before trying to relax some of your muscles a bit, because if you don't, your body begins to quiver, and then you are in for it. The only way is to try and take it easy when the guards are occupied with another victim. The trouble with this is that your side vision is limited because you can't move your eyeballs, and have to rely on intuition. The Mad Doctor began with the group leader, an American Navy Commander, who was standing in front of a large tank of water which was there for fire protection, and when his questioning brought no results, hauled off and knocked the Commander right into the water tank. It was just like an old western movie when the bad guy is knocked into the horse trough. While the Commander was struggling to his feet, the Mad Doctor was repeating the procedure with the next one in line. One by one, they all went down like a bunch of tenpins. Those who had trouble getting up were helped along by hefty kicks in the slats or in other not so comfortable places. While all this was going on, the other ranks were all eager to see the show by going down to the wash racks where they could sneak a peek without attracting any attention. Of course the guards were too busy to bother with us, anyway. They were making the most of their opportunity to beat up on the officer class. It wasn't safe to take too much time at the wash racks, but we got a kick out of what we did see. None of the officers did any objecting when the other ranks were getting whacked, so we figured what they were going through was just a case of poetic justice.

After the Mad Doctor had gone through both lines a couple of times, even he was arm weary and took off for his quarters to rest up a bit. This left the duty sergeant and a couple of privates, who wandered around giving kicks in the shins to those looking a little slack. By midnight, all the officers were sagging and the older ones began to pass out, whereupon they were doused with a pail of water and kicked back into place. I'll wager those civilians who had taken a commission wished they had stayed a civilian, as they would have been interned in Santo Tomas University in Manila and not in Kobe House with the Mad Doctor. Of course all of them had to go to the *benjo* by this time, but the guards wouldn't hear of such a thing, and they just had to suffer. The result was that they all had to urinate in their clothes, after holding it as long as possible. The rest of the night passed on with the whole crew still standing at attention as best they could when we went to work in the morning. You never saw such a bedraggled looking bunch. As I passed Bill on my way out the gate, I told him he was looking great. I didn't get any answer to this remark. Bill never moved an eyeball.

After supper that night, I went over to "B" block to check on him. He told me that they had all been dismissed around eight that morning and allowed to go to bed. He was pretty tired and sore from all the beating and kicking he had suffered but thought he was going to live. He said that he had been pretty successful in anticipating the punches but had misjudged a couple of times and was belted pretty hard. He also told me that he had seen one of the officers smoking just before Tenko and flick ashes into the ashtray, not even realizing what he was doing. That put Bill between a rock and a hard place, because if he told the Japs who had done it, the officers would think he squealed on someone because he didn't want to be in the soup himself. So he had kept quiet and took the same punishment as the officers did. If he had confessed to having left the ashes in the ashtray himself, he would have probably got a slap or two and that would have been all, but you could never tell with the Japanese. Previous to this incident, the officers had been treated much better than the other ranks. The one thing that they had been made to do was to bail out the *benjo* when it began to overflow, about once a month. I think the Japanese made them do such a low-caste job was to humble them a bit. Otherwise, officer POWs had it fairly easy. They were paid hundreds of yen monthly, with which they could buy such edibles as were available for sale in Kobe House, most of which was smuggled in by those who worked on the plum jobs. The officer cigarette issue was triple that of the enlisted men, about three packs per week. Until the advent of Lt. Miataki, they had been living the life of Riley. From now on, they would tremble and shake every time they heard the sound of hobnailed boots on the stairs, thinking it might be the Mad Doctor again.

Two weeks after the cigarette ash episode, we came in from work and found that Bill Johnson had moved back in with us. All the officers, with the exception of Captain Houghton and Colonel Fliniau, had been shipped out to another camp which held officers only, on a small island in the Inland Sea. Zentsugi Officers Camp held hundreds of Allied officer POWs from the Philippines, Java and Singapore. This had ended Bill's cushy job. Instead of being a dog-robber, he would now be a working coolie. There had been one civilian lumped in with the officers, a mining engineer named Tex Howell, and he had been left behind as well. We all thought that Capt. Houghton must have pulled some strings with Jack Oakie to get the officers away from Kobe House and the Mad Doctor. He must have thought there was going to be more trouble and he didn't want to have to be mixed up in it. I don't blame him a bit, as the Mad Doctor would probably have lined him up with the rest if he had showed his face that night when they were all getting a going over.

Chapter 30

The Australians

The Sunday following the departure of the officers saw more changes in Kobe House. The British on the second and third floors of "B" Block were moved bag and baggage across the alley to "A" Block, leaving only the fourth floor and our attic perch occupied. We surmised that, since so many of the British had died during the past winter, the Japs wanted to fill up all the blank spaces in "A" Block. We were partly right, but that was not the real reason. Two days after this move, we returned from work to find both the empty floors filled with a new lot of POWs.

The newcomers turned out to be Australians who had been captured in Singapore in January, 1942. Out of a shipment of nine hundred POWs, they had been lucky enough to wind up in Kobe House with us. Their ship had arrived at the port of Moji, on Kyushu, after a journey of twenty-three days. The shipment, which was called "J" Force, had been split up on arrival, five hundred being sent to the northern island of Hokkaido. Another hundred and fifty, the sick and weak, were supposed to go to a convalescent camp, but instead wound up at Hakensho Coal mine No. 15, located across a gulf from Hiroshima. Nice place to go if you were sick!

The remainder went to other scattered POW camps in Japan. Moji was where all the ships carrying POWs docked when arriving in Japan, the POWs then were taken by train to whatever camp they had been assigned. I often wonder where I would have wound up had the Ryukyu Maru had dumped us off in Moji. It had been a lucky day for us when we wound up in Kobe.

The Aussies sent to Kobe were put on a train for an all-night trip, arriving early in the morning. They were then marched down the street to the cricket grounds next to Kobe House, where they had been greeted by Col. Murata, commander of all the POW camps in the Kobe-Osaka area, who gave them the usual welcoming speech that they were all cowards who had no right to live, should all be shot, and were only alive because of the wishes of the Emperor. I guess any POW of the Japanese must have heard this same speech a dozen times. After being forced to sign a statement saying that they would not try to escape and would work as required, the Aussies were counted, numbered, and placed into thirty-man *kumeis*, or work gangs. After this, they got a rundown on the Kobe House rules and what was expected of them in the way of work, given by Henry and then reinterpreted by our Cpl. Hoblitt to make sure they understood. They were then marched into Kobe House and into "B" Block, their new home.

These newcomers seemed to be in just about the same physical condition as we had been when we arrived in Kobe, that is to say they were walking skeletons, dressed in the remnants of what had been their tropical uniforms, consisting of khaki shirts and shorts, together with their distinctive hats turned up on one side, all of them brown as a nut from the Singapore sun. After supper, most of us went down to welcome them to Kobe House and give them a bit of advice on what they could expect in their new home.

I found that it was a lot easier to understand the Aussie dialect than that of the Scots or English. Other than pronouncing "ai" like "eye", they were easy to understand. They did use a lot of slang words, such as *bonza*, meaning wonderful, *sheila*, girl, and *good-oh*, which means just that. They were all as tall as us Yanks, much taller and bigger than the English, whom the Aussies called "Poms" for some reason, and with whom they didn't get along. They were all bitter about their quick defeat in Malaya, and placed the blame on the British. They could have been right, but like any POW, they had to blame someone for their predicament, just as I blamed Roosevelt and Eisenhower for mine. One thing that struck me was the number of older men among them. There were quite a few in their forties and fifties, most making out as well as the younger ones. All the Aussies were volunteers, no draftees or inductees, and hardly any came from the regular army. I became acquainted with one of the older men named Karl Sinclair, who came from Armidale, New South Wales. He had been in the lumber business, and I learned much about life in Australia from him.

Their first week in Kobe was essentially the same as our first week had been, learning basic Jap Army close order drill and saluting with the aid and encouragement of the usual whacks from wooden swords, slaps in the face and much screeching in Japanese. As with the British, the saluting came hard to the Aussies, as they also used the British salute. They got something that we hadn't, which was a class in basic Japanese, taught by some old civilians. A bit different than the way we had to learn it, which was the hard way, by experience.

One other thing that happened when the Aussies arrived affected the whole camp. Every POW in Kobe House received a new number, and for some reason, the Americans led off with number one. I couldn't believe it when I got my new tin badge with my name and number on it, in *Katakana*. When I saw the number thirteen, or *Ju-San,* in Japanese, I thought that now I really have had it. However, it was my number, like it or not, and after I got used to it, began to believe it was my lucky number, and it still is. At the time, though, I thought I was a goner. After the Americans came the British, and then the Aussies, starting with five hundred eighty-two. With twenty Yanks, four hundred twenty British, twenty Greek and other seamen, and the two hundred and fifty Aussies, Kobe House now held nearly seven hundred POWs. That made for a lot of rice and soup!

After their week of basics, the Aussies began work. They started out by getting the three factory jobs, Showa Denki, Yoshihara and Toyo Steel. It was easy to tell those who had been at Showa Denki by their black eyes. Of course it wasn't long before those in good shape found out how to get on the good jobs, and managed to be in the front ranks in the morning when those jobs were filled. Even then, they had to battle for the choice spots, because the work leaders were all British, who had their favorites for the plum jobs, and it was an uphill battle for them all the way. One example of favoritism was an incident on one of the ships that Sen Paku was unloading out in the bay. These ships were anchored quite far from the docks, and the POW gangs were taken to the ship by barge. Upon arrival, the POW leader assigned his special favorites to the hold having the choicest cargo, such as canned meats, fruit or fish. The rest of the gang was sent to a hold containing coal, iron ore, or some such cargo which was hard work with no loot. The Aussies really resented this, and one morning they happened to be the first aboard a ship, found out what was in each hold, and climbed down into the one that promised the best chance of loot. The POW leader that day happened to be our own CWO Walter Shaputnick, who had been left behind when the officers moved out, but was allowed to remain in the officers' quarters along with the new Australian arrivals. Of course Shaputnick didn't like this, and ordered the Aussies out of the good hold so he could put his own pet crew in. Whereupon the Aussies informed him that his crew had been getting the pick of the jobs too long; they were there first and were going to stay there. Shaputnick then tried to pull rank on them by giving them a direct order to get out of the hold, but they still refused, even when

Shaputnick threatened to turn them into Kobe House. When they got back to camp, they had to appear before Capt. Houghton, the Camp Commander. Shaputnick had told him that the Aussies had disobeyed orders given them by a superior and had used obscene language, which I don't doubt for a minute, knowing them as I did. Capt. Houghton then told them that this was a matter of military discipline and that he had to punish them, whereupon Major Campbell, the senior Australian officer, spoke up and said that they were Australian soldiers and no British or American officer was going to punish them. After some argument, it was decided that the guilty ones would be punished by sending them to Showa Denki for three months. That was some punishment, I would rather had taken a whacking from the Japs than gone to Showa Denki that long. The Aussies began to get their share of good jobs after this flare-up, so the punishment they got was probably worth it to them.

One thing the Aussies had in their favor; they arrived in Japan when the weather was warm, and had the chance to acclimatize themselves before winter arrived again. The Americans had come from the tropics straight into winter in Japan, and were frozen until May of the next year. The Aussies were also fortunate in having officers who didn't hesitate to stand up to the Japs when one of their men was being mistreated, something I never saw any of our American officers do. One of their officers was a doctor, the first one we had had in Kobe House. Capt. Boyce was a good doctor, who worked all hours of the day and night with

Capt. Clive R. Boyce, RAMC.
Photo taken in Malaya while preparing for evacuation.

those unfortunates who found themselves in sick bay. He did all that any doctor could do when placed in such an impossible situation, with almost no medicine or medical supplies of any kind. He was what you would call a good man and a good officer.

Chapter 31

Summer in Kobe

The coming of our first summer in Kobe was welcome to all the POWs. We had all come from service in tropical climes and the hot weather was more to our liking. Summer in Kobe was about the same as that in Baltimore, which is about the same latitude, and the sea breeze kept the docks fairly cool. Nights in Kobe House became uncomfortably hot due to the window shutters being closed. With no fresh air and so many bodies being crammed together, it was pretty stuffy. We inmates all slept in our *fundoshis*, and the heat would have been bearable except for the Japanese orders requiring every POW to have a blanket across his midsection to keep his insides healthy. The guards made periodic inspections to make sure we had our blanket on, and many were the slappings suffered by those who tossed off the covers because they were too hot.

Life in Kobe House became monotonous to the Nth degree. We got up at the same time every day, ate our meals at the same time every day, went to work and went to sleep at the same times every day in the week. The only break in this routine was on every other Sunday, when we stayed in. We hated Sundays, cooped up in our warehouse with no lunch, and subject to the whims of the interior guard. There were Sunday services of a sort, conducted by one of the officers, as we had no chaplain available. A couple of hours in the sports ground across the street would have been enjoyable, but the Japs were not amenable to this. In my almost three years in Kobe House, we were allowed in that park just once, and that was for propaganda purposes. Kobe House must have been the only camp in Japan that didn't have a bit of space for exercise or for a vegetable garden. So after the Sunday inspection was over, the majority spent the rest of the day sleeping, hoping to dream of home and apple pie. Those who couldn't, or didn't want to sleep, wandered around looking for someone to talk to. Card playing was allowed, but for one hour only, and no gambling, so that was useless as recreation. By Monday, we were ready and willing to go to work.

Our gang at Higashinada had become experts at shoveling coal, and other than the days we had to unload the lime, the work there wasn't too bad. Working on lime was worse in the hot weather, due to the fact that we sweated so much the lime dust got in the pores of the skin and was almost impossible to remove, burning like fire. We were all short tempered when on lime, and there was always an argument about whose turn it was to go into the box car. Rigdon and I got into a scrap one day, set off by some remark about the Civil War, which was always being fought amongst the Yanks and the Rebs in our group. The first thing I knew, Rig was swinging at me. I was straddling a bench and couldn't get out of the way, so I picked him up and held him off the ground. It was a good thing he was as small as he was or I could never have done it. Sano-San came running and the result was that we both had to stand holding a bucket of water overhead for an hour. This is hard on the arms and all the rest of your body, believe me. Even that was better than being turned into the guard at Kobe House. I was surprised that Rig got mad enough to want to fight, but should have known that mentioning General Sherman to someone from Louisiana was bad policy. Rig and I remained good buddies, though, for the rest of the war.

The biggest fly in the ointment in Kobe House at this time was our "Mad Doctor", Lieutenant Miataki. He was the best reason of all for us wanting to go out to work, as he made staying in Kobe House a hell. It was impossible to avoid him, as he was continually roving around the compound looking for some poor devil to bash, generally an Australian. He seemed to have a particular dislike for them, and hardly ever got past the second floor of our block, it being full of Aussies. He could usually pick one as a suitable candidate for punishment. The Mad Doctor made his own rules, such as whacking some POW for smiling when he should have been serious, and the next time for not smiling when he should have been. One evening after *tenko*, an Aussie named "Tibby" was caught by a guard with an unlit cigarette between his lips, and even though Tibby was not smoking, this was a definite breach of the rules. The guard took Tibby down to the guardhouse, where he punished him by striking him in the face and knocking him down time after time. After an hour of this, Lt. Fuller, who was in charge of Tibby's section, was told to report to the Mad Doctor at the guardhouse, where he found Capt. Houghton and Cpl. Hoblitt. The Mad Doctor proceeded to question Tibby, who told his side of the story through Hoblitt. While this was going on, one of the English, Lipscombe by name, came out of "A" block on his way to "B" block. He bowed to the Mad Doctor as per rule, but due to all the people crowding around, not quite in the right way. The Doctor made him repeat the bowing a couple more times, began hitting him in the face until he was knocked unconscious, then started on him with the buckle end of his sword belt. After poor Lipscombe was helped to his feet, he was knocked down again. This was repeated over and over, until he was unable to stand at all. Finally, the Mad Doctor allowed him to be carried away to the hospital, then proceeded to deal with Tibby. He declared Tibby's story to be a lie and preceded to beat him with his belt buckle the same way as he had beaten Lipscombe. Each time Tibby was knocked out, the Doctor took a breather, then, after bringing poor Tibby around by dousing him with a pail of ice water, continued with the beating. This brutality went on for another hour, when Tibby was finally completely out and couldn't be revived. Only then did the Mad Doctor allow his victim to be taken back to his quarters, his face covered with blood, cut up by the belt buckle, eyes swollen shut, lumps and bumps all over his head, and bruises everywhere. Lipscombe was in nearly as bad a condition. This was just one example of Lt. Miataki's cruelty. Cruelty seemed to be a common trait among Japanese Army doctors assigned to POW camps. Just another good reason to avoid going on sick call at all cost.

The Mad Doctor had many other ways of finding people to beat on. One of his worst habits was making a visit to Kobe House late at night and calling a *tenko*, say around midnight. This meant that all the POWs had to get out of their sacks, fold their blankets, get dressed and stand at attention in their bed space until every POW in camp had been accounted for, which might be for two hours. He would follow the duty Sgt around to each section hoping to find an unbuttoned button, a blanket out of line, or an imagined smirk on someone's face. The culprit was admonished to do better by a hefty whack over his head with the Mad Doctor's saber. The Aussies called this procedure "knighting", and by the end of the summer most of the inmates of Kobe House had become royalty. Section leaders were at high risk due to their having to give a long report in Japanese at each *tenko*. Old Luke had this unwelcome duty and was knighted just about every time he reported to the Mad Doctor.

I had one close call one hot summer day when I was taking a shower after coming in from work. The hot baths had been stopped with the advent of warm weather, and the bathroom was usually filled with POWs cleaning up just before supper. There were a dozen or so of us there when who should stroll in but the Good Doctor. I happened to be facing the door and saw him first, so I shouted *Kyotsuki* as loud as I possibly could, then *Keirei*. Everyone came to attention, then bowed. This bow had to be held until whoever being saluted returned the salute, so we were all frozen in the bowing position, not daring to move. Unfortunately for some, they had been caught facing away from the door, and in their bent over position, their naked rears were looking at the Mad Doctor. Of course he took this as an insult, and proceeded to knight the unlucky ones, not once but a dozen times, with the flat of his sword. Their butts showed red wound stripes for a week after their elevation to royalty. I could see what was going on from the corner of my eyes, but facing in the right direction saved me this time. I was just lucky that the Mad Doctor didn't go into his usual frenzied tantrum and lump me in with the rest.

One summer day I decided to take a break from shoveling coal and swapped with a fellow who worked at Minatogowa. My sweet tooth was satisfied that day, as most of what we worked on were dried bananas. I must have eaten a dozen, which probably upset my innards, but no POW ever worried about that as long as what went down helped to fill the ever-empty void in our stomachs. While we were taking our noon break, what did we see but someone swimming up to our dock. It turned out to be an Australian who belonged to another POW camp in Kobe. The POWs in his camp worked in the big ship yard just across the bay. This Aussie was trying to swim to Australia, but headed for our dock when he got tired. Of course he was slightly off his rocker, but working at the shipyard where there was nothing edible to steal would affect anybody to some extent. We fed him a good meal and took him back to Kobe House with us, where he had supper with some of his cobbers from home. Before long, a guard from his camp arrived, and he was taken away. I doubt he was even punished, as mental cases among POWs seemed to be allowed to do just about anything they wanted to do, short of escaping.

Another thing that made that summer interesting was the frequency of earthquakes. It seemed that we had one good tremor about every week. At times, when sleeping, you would be awakened by being rolled around on the platform, as if someone was shaking you. This was a bit unnerving the first few times this happened, with our location up above the fourth floor of the block on our little platform, but after the first few times we got used to it. One morning we were on the train halfway to the factories when the train stopped and we had to get off because of a quake. You could see the tracks going up and down like a snake. Another time I was in the freight elevator at Mitsui Soko when the elevator began shaking. I got off as soon as possible and went out to dockside, where an extra big wave had just broken over the dock. My worst experience was one evening when I had just come out of the cook-house with the supper soup when everything started shaking. Of course there was no place to run, being cooped up between two four-story warehouses, so I could do nothing but stand there and take whatever came. If you looked up, you could see the top of the brick walls swaying back and forth at least a couple of feet. I expected the whole place to tumble down, but I guess whoever had built the warehouses had done so with earthquakes in mind, because after the shaking had stopped, not a bit of damage could be seen. Quite scary, though, while it lasted. After Japan, earthquakes have never bothered me.

Chapter 32

Den of Thieves

Everyone knows about Ali Baba and his forty thieves, but they couldn't hold a candle to the POWs of Kobe House. With the exception of a dozen or so who had more scruples or religion than was good for them, every one of us became expert *dorobos*, or thieves. Of course the prime reason to steal was to get more to eat, and, as well, to get some satisfaction by outwitting the Japs. Most of what we stole went into the noontime soup pot, but much was smuggled into Kobe House to be sold to the officers or to trade for other things such as cigarettes or sugar. Those working at Sen Paku had access to canned goods such as salmon or corned beef, most of which was eaten on the job, but a few brave souls were always trying to get a can or two into Kobe House where corned beef commanded premium prices.

The different duty sergeants, who met and inspected each work detail coming in at night, all had their individual routines. Some made a strict search, some hardly bothered to search, and others were careless about it. The POWs soon found a way to signal to the jobs coming in by hanging towels of different colors in one of the windows, where they could be seen before the party reached Kobe House. A signal of a certain color meant that the Mad Doctor, the Sgt Major, or some other of the duty sergeants who had the habit of making a rigid search was on duty, thus warning the party to ditch any loot they might have before reaching Kobe House. Of course there were always those who took their chances anyway and sometimes got away with it. There were rare days when we knew it was safe because all the baddies were absent, and everyone loaded up, but those days were rare indeed. The "go" signal was not all that sure either, as some guard other than the duty sergeant and his assistant might take it into his head to help out with the searching.

Australians were famous thieves, the British almost as good. The Yanks had one of the best, young Dick Morris. He and Spider Griffin worked at Mitsui Soko, where sugar was plentiful. I saw Dick come in from work many times with his long johns filled with the stuff. He would stand on a piece of cloth, untie the strings around the bottom of his long johns and let the sugar pour out, ten pounds from each leg. He waddled along with legs looking like an elephant's, but never seemed to get caught. I wouldn't have taken the chances he did for anything. I surely would have been caught, as the Japs were always looking for a chance to beat any tall POW up. Dick was just sixteen years old and was so innocent looking. I suppose they thought he was incapable of doing anything so bad as stealing the Emperor's sugar.

Sugar was by far the most popular article to steal. It was used to sweeten our evening tea, to make the rice palatable, to trade for cigarettes and to sell to the officers and office staff for cash or favors. It was about the easiest stuff to smuggle in, as it could be packed so as to be almost undetectable in a search. Those who wanted to bring in large quantities wore long underwear with the bottoms tied and with trouser bottoms wrapped with strips of cloth over the shoe top. As the majority of the Japs wore a sort of wrap leggings, both civilian and military, POWs doing the same were not particularly noticeable. The leggings helped to keep the sugar from leaking out on the march back to camp. Some of the big time operators had stolen full bags of sugar, which were hidden someplace in the godowns, where they were easy to get at on a day when no search was expected. Nothing was ever sure, though, and if and when someone was caught with sugar, the result was usually six hours standing at attention, with beatings thrown in when some guard felt like having a bit of exercise.

The most common method of bringing in small amounts of sugar was to make a small sack which held a quarter of a pound or so, and hang it on your body under your uniform. The favorite places were in the crotch, under the arm, down your back, or even sitting on your head under your cap. Another way was to sew a tube of cloth a half inch or so in diameter, pour it full of sugar, hang it from your belt and just walk in. A tube this size would hold enough for a week's supply, and being so small was hard to detect in a perfunctory search. Each of the guards seemed to have a certain place which they nearly always searched; some searched crotches, some legs, some backs or armpits. If you knew who was going to be on duty, you could make a good guess as to where to stash your loot. It was all chancy, though, as at times when you were lined up at the gate, the Sgt. Major or Jack Oakie might just stroll out the gate and join in. Jack Oakie was dangerous at these times, as he had a nasty habit of hitting you in the face with whatever loot was found. Many a POW was knocked cold by being swatted with a two-pound sack of sugar. It was like being hit with a blackjack. When the poor guy woke up, he was usually allowed to go inside, that is, unless the Mad Doctor had appeared on the scene, then it was a disaster. Jack Oakie was equally handy with his saber, hitting other culprits over the head with it, fortunately leaving it in the scabbard.

This usually left the recipient with a large lump on his head and a big headache. He thought this was quite funny, and of course all the Japs around laughed along with him. I will always remember the day when old Luke was caught with a china teapot which he had found somewhere. Leaders were hardly ever searched, but on this day Jack Oakie wandered out and caught poor old Luke with the teapot under his jacket, which made quite a noticeable bulge. He really wound up with that teapot and when it hit Luke's head it broke into a thousand pieces. I doubt if it hurt Luke that much, as he had a hard head, and it gave the rest of us a good laugh. The expression on Luke's face was something to see.

Smuggling in cans of salmon or corn beef was much harder than smuggling sugar, due to the difficulty of hiding them, but many a POW succeeded in getting a can or two into Kobe House. Other strange articles were brought it, such as a large bottle of sake, or rice wine, that Rigdon smuggled in one day. We had been unloading a boxcar full of the stuff, and when we started on the car, someone took the cap off one bottle, and each time we went back into the car for another load, we took a little nip. When the bottle was finished, it was stuck back into its crate and carried out. Rig was just a kid, and a few drinks of the sake got him feeling good. He must have liked it a lot, because that evening after supper he proudly brought out a full bottle which he had smuggled in, stuck in his belt. No one knew he had it, and as Higashinada was rarely searched because we never worked on anything good, he got away with it. I shudder to think what would have happened had Jack Oakie or the Mad Doctor found the sake. Anyway, Rigdon never tried it again.

When the Aussies began work, they were assigned to factory jobs where little loot was to be had. All there was at Showa Denki was coke and carbon dust and no edibles. There was nothing but iron ore at Toyo Steel. Yoshihara Oil was a different story. Peanut and other oils processed there were for the exclusive use of the Japanese Air Force, and any civilian or POW who was caught stealing this oil was liable to execution. This was just a good challenge to the Aussies, who, after getting used to the factory and its routine, couldn't resist the urge to get some of that oil. Our POW food ration never included oil of any sort, and the lack of it was one cause of the vitamin deficiency diseases we all suffered from. The Aussies used the peanut oil first as a spread on their noonday roll, which I imagine tasted pretty good. They then began to devise ways of getting some of that oil into Kobe House. One of the ways was to modify a water bottle, or canteen, by cutting it in two, soldering a false bottom on the top part, and fitting both parts together so closely one could hardly see that it had been touched. The modification was done by four English POWs who had been assigned to the factory machine shop some time before. It was then easy to take the canteen apart, fill the bottom half with oil, join the two parts, fill the top half with water and put the canteen back into its cover. All that remained was to get by the guards and the Kobe House inspection. The guards rarely checked canteens, and if they did, only the water in the top half would ever be noticed. Only a few canteens were fabricated in this way, and they had to be kept secret from the rest of the POWs because of the danger involved. Some oil was smuggled in, in small bottles which could be hidden on the body. The Aussies also had a racket going which involved the Japanese security guards at the factory, who knew the POWs were stealing oil, but were afraid to steal it themselves for good reasons. All these guards had bicycles, so some of them were modified by making it possible to carry oil concealed in part of the frame. Upon quitting work, the guard would have POWs push the bikes out of the gate, so if anything did happen, the POWs would be blamed. In return, they saw that the POWs had access to the peanuts, which were a good source of protein. The same four English machine shop men did the bike modification and of course, got their cut of any oil carried into Kobe House. These men did much of the maintenance at Yoshihara, and sabotaged much heavy machinery, while having success repairing the smaller machinery.

The peanut people also had an advantage in that the gangs from Toyo Steel and Showa Denki met the Yoshihara detail at Nishinomiya Station for the train ride back to Kobe. While waiting for the train, a POW from one job was able to visit a friend on another job, thus, if a Yoshihara man had oil or peanuts to smuggle into Kobe House, he could swap haversacks with this friend, who of course got a cut of whatever he brought in. Showa Denki and Toyo Steel people were never searched at camp because there was nothing to steal at these jobs, and anyone from either job could carry a haversack loaded with peanuts back in without trouble. However, there were POWs other than the regulars, who had swapped jobs for a day in order to fill up on peanuts, and who sometimes got carried away and tried to smuggle in a full canteen of oil. One POW who tried this was knocked senseless by Horse-face, who used the full canteen to do the job. The regular workers at Yoshihara tried to keep the smuggling down to a safe level and avoid trouble, but couldn't prevent these unforeseen actions completely.

Two dock jobs that offered good opportunities for stealing were Mitsui Soko and Mitsubishi. Their godowns held quantities of canned goods, usually belonging to the Japanese Army. These canned goods were stored in locked storerooms, open only while goods were coming in or going out. The Aussies found a way of getting into these storerooms by making an impression of the keys on a piece of soap, which was given to a POW working at Toyo Steel, who would make a key blank out of a piece of scrap metal, which he brought in and returned to the dock worker, who did the necessary filing to make the key work. Of course the Toyo Steel man got a share of any goods stolen using that key. Much salmon was added to the noon rice thereafter, and some few cans of condensed milk were smuggled into Kobe House for the use of the hospital, thereby helping keep alive desperately ill POW patients who of course were on half rations.

Most of the stealing was on the sugar jobs. Sugar, being unobtainable on the Japanese market, made it easy to bribe the honchos and their helpers by loading their bicycles down with sugar and pushing them through the gate. They repaid the POWs by closing their eyes to what we were doing, besides seeing to it that we got on the better jobs.

Just about everything movable was stolen by the POWs. Pieces of cloth were brought in, to be made into underwear by the invalid tailors or used as patch material. Any bit of scrounged leather could be used by our cobblers, wire of any kind was used to make a device to boil up a cup of rice if you could steal the rice, string to keep your pants up, a glass tumbler to strop your old razor blade in, if you had a razor blade. Buttons were always in demand. There was always a shortage of toilet paper, our issue never was enough and we were always on the lookout for any scrap of paper to augment the supply. Everything came into Kobe House, even a bicycle chain one of the English sneaked in around his waist, for what purpose nobody ever found out. Probably it was just to say he had put one over the Nips. As for myself, although I stole a lot of edibles which were added to our midday soup, about all I ever brought into Kobe House were small amounts of sugar which I could carry in a pocket. Not being a smoker, I could trade my cigarettes for the few things I needed or wanted.

I would say that the Australians were the best thieves in Kobe House, for the good reason that they worked well with each other, something the Americans didn't do, or perhaps because they were just naturally thieves who took after their ancestors who were shipped out to Australia when it was first settled. The English and the Scots also worked together well, being members of a regimental family which still kept its discipline, even in a POW camp. We Americans had little feeling of belonging to a family, all of us being from different outfits. Any discipline seemed to be nonexistent, except for that imposed by our captors. With us it was dog eat dog and every man for himself, unless you had a good buddy. I am sure that this selfish attitude was the reason many of the American POWs died, because everyone looked after number one and ignored the helpless. I will always give credit to the Aussies, who always gave part of their loot to the patients in the hospital, something very few Americans ever did.

Chapter 33

A New Job

By the end of August, the Higashinada POWs were getting tired of the same old job, day after day. Shoveling coal was one of the easiest jobs, but enough was enough, and we began to hate the sight of it, especially as the trucks that came to take the coal away began to break down more often as the war wore on. They couldn't keep up with all the coal coming in, and most of the time the top of the pile was higher than the trestle, so that when the bottoms of the cars were opened, the coal would not run out, and we had to shovel it out from under the car and move it to the side. This was really backbreaking work. We were tired of the unslaked lime and its burning dust to boot, so one evening in Kobe House when volunteers were wanted for a new job, six of us, including Rigdon, Marshall, Lucero, Barrett, Janiec and yours truly signed up. Volunteering for a new job was taking a shot in the dark, as it could be a winner, rarely, or a bust, most of the time. We had hopes it would be a winner for once.

The next Monday saw the hopeful six fall out in the street along with a half dozen Aussies and the same number of British. A truck and two honchos from our new job were at hand, and we headed west through Kobe for about a half mile, following the railroad tracks and passing a giant pile of coal while we all held our breaths, and thanking the good Lord we hadn't stopped there. In another hundred yards we stopped at a large railway station which turned out to be the Kobe City station, where we disembarked, lined up, were issued a large shovel each, and marched back down the tracks to that monster coal pile we had just passed. Our rosy dreams of a cushy job with lots of loot came crashing to earth. On this job, shoveling coal was the one and only reason for our being there, no working on vegetables, sake or fruit, such as we did from time to time at Higashinada. Woe were us! The name of our new job was Hyogo Iki, the freight division at Kobe City Station. We were treated very decently there, having a nice coal heated hut to lounge in when not working. The midday meal was a good issue of rice and soup, cooked by one of our crew. We were all experts with a coal shovel by now, at least we Yanks from Higashinada were, and the work here was about the same, except that there was no trestle. Trucks arriving for a load of coal parked alongside one of the coal cars and a crew of six POWs shoveled the coal from the car into the truck. Usually there was only one truck at a time, so the two crews not working could stay in the hut. The result was that we worked in spurts of perhaps twenty to thirty minutes, then had a good rest break in the hut. All this was fine until there were no trucks. Then we had to just shovel the coal out onto the ground so that the string of cars, usually five or six, could be put back in service. If there were no trucks for a couple of days, there were piles of coal twelve feet high along the siding. Then, when trucks did come, we had to load them from the ground, which was much harder on the back than filling them right from the coal cars. This went on until enough trucks had come in to clean up the pile, and then we could go back to the easier work of unloading directly from car to truck again. We got so good with the shovels that we could fill a truck in quick time, pleasing our honchos but not the truck drivers, who would have liked a longer break to have a smoke and a cup of tea. We finally adjusted our speed so that they were all pleased, and settled down to a humdrum existence. There was one nice thing about Hyogo Iki, as in Higashinada. We were able to do a bit of clothes washing in a drum of hot water, with no lack of coal to fire the boiler up. If we had had more soap if would have been nice.

During our rest breaks, we got acquainted with the Aussies who were on the job with us. Two of them were brothers, Jack and Luke Carey, who lived near Sydney but seemed to have spent most of their time at the famous Bondi Beach. They had another brother who had been captured with them but had missed the detail for Japan, and they had no idea where he was. Then there was Alex Olley, called "Dada," who came from Victoria, a nice easygoing fellow. They had been POWs since January 1942, and had been on work details there, similar to those we had been on in the Philippines, but had been returned to Singapore because of sickness. The detail which was shipped to Japan had been made up of convalescents who were in no better physical shape than we were, so shoveling coal was a good job for them.

The teams went out to load trucks by turns, and there always seemed to be an argument about what team was next, especially on cold and rainy days. The honchos finally picked team leaders for each team, and of course I got the job as leader of the American team, to see that we were on the job on time, and that the truck was loaded fast enough. Most of the time this went well, but one of us, "Slim" Marshall, was forever grumbling and making things hard for me. He was a tall, skinny guy from Cajun country in Louisiana, had a mean disposition and was always making remarks about Yankees. If he was a typical Southerner, it was no wonder we fought the Civil War. Anyway, we got into an argument one day which ended with us tangling in a coal-car. We had just got in a couple of blows when the *Honcho* arrived and stopped us. We weren't reported for fighting this time, but the *Honcho* informed us that any more of this behavior would be reported to Kobe House, so things quieted down some from then on. Slim and I avoided each other from that day on.

We had a bit of fun now and then, too. As the loaded trucks left the coal yard they had to make a sharp right turn. The road there was such that when the trucks made the turn they listed to the outside. Just across the street from the gate were a few houses and the old *mama-sans* used to wait by the gate in the hopes of finding stray lumps of coal. All of them had babies tied on their backs, their clothes were in rags, and looked as though they were starved to death. Of course we POWs pitied them, and if there was a bit of rice left over from our lunch, we would make up a few rice balls and hand them over the gate to whoever was there. I think that they were worse off than us POWs, if that was possible. We would talk to them in our pidgin Japanese and show them pictures of our families, those that had any pictures, and the *mama-sans* showed us pictures of their sons who were in the army, or had been killed in battle. They depended on what little bits of coal they could scrounge for heat and cooking. They never got enough, as the railroad people wouldn't let them near the big piles of coal in the yard. We POWs found a way to get them some coal. We made sure that every truck we loaded was heaped higher on the left side, and as it went through the gate and rounded the corner, about a quarter of a ton fell off the truck right in front of all the waiting *mama-sans*. You should have seen the scramble. We did this for a couple of weeks until one day the *honcho* happened to be watching and from then on kept his eye on how we loaded the trucks. I guess by that time every *mama-san* had accumulated enough coal to last a year. They are probably still talking about the good old POWs.

Nothing much happened at Hyogo Iki except the eternal coal shoveling. I had shoveled a whole lot of coal at Higashinada, but at least we worked on other things there. Not so at Hyogo Iki, it was just coal, coal and more coal. I would bet that during my time on these two jobs, I shoveled enough coal to run the Queen Mary across the Atlantic twice.

One morning we were surprised to find a couple of officers lined up with us. They had volunteered to work just to get out of Kobe House. These officers were nothing but trouble, bitching about taking their turn shoveling, and got us all in trouble by buying a chicken from one of the *mama-sans* and trying to cook it over our fire. I guess they thought they were on a picnic outing. The honcho didn't like the chicken business at all, took the chicken and reported it at Kobe House. That was the last we saw of any officers, thank God. We also had the Greeks for a week or so, but they argued and fought all the time and the honchos got rid of them in short order.

As the weather got colder, many of the coal cars coming in were filled with snow. This made our work harder, as we had to shovel the snow off before getting to the coal. I believe most of these cars came from the far north of Japan, where the winter is much worse than in the Kobe area. Shoveling kept us plenty warm, though, and we had a good warm hut, so it wasn't too bad.

Returning to Kobe House one evening, we got some good news. The Mad Doctor had been shipped out! Heaven help those in the unlucky POW camp that got him!

Chapter 34

Tempus Fugit — Very Slowly

Very little out of the ordinary happened in Kobe House during the last half of A.D. 1943. The ordinary being, of course, thirteen days of hard labor, then one day *yasume*, which was welcome for just one thing, the hot bath which had been placed in action again with the coming of winter. Otherwise, we would much rather have been out working. *Yasume* day was bad for the stomach, as all we got for lunch was a cup of hot water and a spoonful of soya sauce. The Sunday morning inspection usually resulted in a few poor devils having to stand at rigid attention in front of the guardhouse for not saluting properly, or for some other reason at the whim of some guard who needed a bit of recreation, which he got by slapping some POW. As the cold weather advanced, our soup declined in quality, if that was possible, due to the seasonal lack of the usual vegetable tops and stems available in the summer. About the only thing available to us was the everlasting *daikon* in the soup and a couple slices of the same, pickled, to eat with our rice. Once a week or thereabouts, we got what was optimistically called bean soup, but was really hot water with some *miso*, or bean paste, stirred into it. You might find two or three real beans in your bowl. Perhaps once every two weeks, the famous ground fish bone soup was on the menu. I could hardly wait to see if there was a fish eye in my portion. If you could stand the thought of chewing one up, they tasted very good. As nobody else wanted them, I usually was able to scrounge a dozen or so. They had a nutty taste and must have had some vitamins in them.

Every POW in Japan had to exist on the same basic food ration, which was supposed to be sufficient for those doing hard labor. It must have been bad for those who had no chance to implement their ration as we did at Kobe House. Even though we usually were given a good meal at dinner and stealing what food we could, I doubt if our total calorie intake was more than fifteen hundred. I know we were hungry most of the time. It was a wonder than anyone going to the hospital ever got well on the half ration issued to the sick. Going to work, even if you were half dead, was better than going to the hospital.

The cold winter weather didn't seem to be as bad as it was during our first winter in Japan. I suppose we must have become acclimatized to some degree, and our location up under the roof was much warmer than on the floors below, especially the second floor, where the wind blew up through the open stairwells. We were warm enough so that we didn't have to cuddle up with some dirty body to keep warm, but were able to make up a bed of our own and sleep decently. I didn't even have to wake anybody up when I made a journey to the *benjo*, which was at least three times each night. We still had to dress properly on these trips, and when I remembered the beating I had received the past winter for sneaking down there in my shorts, I made darn sure that I was dressed according to regulations when I had to go. On the job we were warm enough while shoveling our coal, and our hut was plenty warm when we were not shoveling. The only time I felt really cold was during the morning P.T., which had been reinstated for some silly reason. Being bare to the waist in that cold wind off the ocean was something I don't care to remember. The back scrubbing with that little brush was forgettable too.

Occasionally there were small lots of odds and ends available in the canteen, nothing of real worth, but which was bought just because it was there. Sometimes what was on sale was divided up by section and sold to us by the section leader. There was never enough that we all got one of each article, so a lottery was used. For example, one month the American section got two packs of razor blades at fifty-four sen each, three cans of tooth powder at twenty-two sen, and four cans of curry powder at one yen, sixty sen. Those who won something in such a lottery paid for it by having the amount deducted from his accrued pay, which was held for us by the Japs. We were no longer getting paid in cash, although we had to sign the payroll. My daily wage as an NCO was two yen per day, paid by the companies where we worked as contract labor, but my net pay was fifteen sen per day, one yen eighty-five sen being deducted by the Japanese Army for my board and room. So if you were lucky enough to get to buy a can of curry powder, it would cost you almost eleven days of hard work, but as there was no other way to spend your money, you might as well buy all you could get.

On the 14th of November, a few Red Cross parcels were delivered to Kobe House, and after the Jap staff took their cut we got what was left, at the rate of one parcel for each nine and a half men, one for each two officers, and one for the camp staff. The Aussie officers suggested that their share be lumped in with the other ranks, but were rebuffed.

However, they added theirs to those of their own men anyway, and all the Aussies received one parcel per each nine men. It was a pity that all the officers weren't like them.

On the 1st of December every POW was issued an almost new Japanese army overcoat. Believe it or not, I was lucky enough to get one that was big enough. Wonderful! This made going back and forth to work bearable. Later in the month winter uniforms similar to those we had been given in the spring were issued, and believe it or not, every uniform was the same size as before, and fit me like a glove. Even though we could not wear them to work, they were made of warm material and made life in Kobe House much more liveable.

Thanksgiving Day had come and gone unnoticed. I guess none of us could imagine having turkey and the fixings. It was only an American holiday, anyway, and we were a small minority in a British camp. Christmas Day was another matter. The Japanese knew about Christmas and I think many of them celebrated it, because on the day before Christmas, the powers that be at Hyogo Iki gave us an extra issue of rice and an extra good soup. When we got back to Kobe House, we found that the inside staff had decorated the place and it looked really Christmassy. The insiders had made cutouts which were hung on all the light bulbs, paper wreaths, and signs printed in red which said "Merry Christmas, Digger," "Merry Christmas, Jock," etc. Their efforts made for what was a nice Christmas Eve. For Japanese POWs, anyway.

Christmas Day was declared a *yasume* day, and it turned out to be quite a day, the best day that I had as a POW. We were allowed to sleep in and there was no inspection. Church service was held at eleven by one of the officers acting as Chaplain, and the few Catholics also had a ceremony. The canteen was open for business, and we could buy all the cigarettes, curry powder or fish paste you wanted, as long as you had credit on the books—I passed up on the fish paste, it had such a horrible taste. Curry powder was good for spicing up your rice, though, and I liked the flavor. For once, on *yasume* day, we got a good meal, the soup being much thicker than usual, and a Christmas Day extra, a small piece of fried fish, which tasted as good as turkey. I had by this time forgotten what turkey tasted like and was as happy as a clam with my little piece of fish. Besides the fish, we received an issue of one apple, a couple of mandarin oranges, a few candied bananas, and a half inch slice of Christmas pudding, courtesy of the mess cooks. This repast wasn't the end of this wonderful day, because after dinner everyone got a set of woolen long johns, from the Red Cross.

And as if this wasn't enough, there was a concert in the afternoon, with a musical group, the "Variety Harmonists," and a number of music hall skits put on by some of the English. The different acts were really funny and the singing couldn't have been any better. All the performers were in costumes which they had made from spare bits of whatever could be scrounged, put together with much work by the two old tailors. Some of the acts had female impersonators; I didn't think that any of the POWs in Kobe House could be that good looking. The whole show was much appreciated by all, especially by the Americans, as the whole thing was put on just below us on the fourth floor. We had the best view of all, as we could lie on our platform, look over the edge, and see everything. You could say that we were in the first balcony, just above Jack Oakie, the Sgt Major, and all the Japanese staff not on duty. They were the honored guests and sat in the front row enjoying it all, and joining in the singing, even when the festivities were closed with 'God save the King,' the British National Anthem. We were asked to sing the 'Star Spangled Banner,' but had to pass on this, because not one of us could remember the words. Disgraceful, to say the least.

After the finale, the camp commander announced that concerts would be held every *yasume* day from now on. We were happy to hear this, as it would help to make our mostly miserable existence more bearable. I don't know how those who put the concerts on ever found the time or the energy to rehearse, make costumes and musical instruments, considering they worked every day just as I did. I have to give the British full marks for keeping the camp morale up as high as it was. They just seemed to bear up better under difficult circumstances than any of us.

1943 ended on a high note. On the 30th of December, a Red Cross parcel was issued to every POW in Kobe House. I had made friends with a couple of the Scots, Tootie Greig and Duncan Cameron, and we three lumped our parcels together, and every night for the next ten days we enjoyed a sandwich made from one of our lunch rolls and a third of a can of corned beef, Spam, or pate, together with one good cup of coffee from a Nescafé tin, with powdered Klim milk and a lump of sugar. A lot of the POWs ate their whole parcel at one sitting, but stretching the eating out made you feel full for quite a while. We were supposed to get one Red Cross parcel a week, as enough had been shipped to Japan, but had been stored in godowns and never got to us. I imagine most of the parcels were taken by the Japanese army, because it was known than our staff at Kobe House got their share before we got any. I guess we were lucky to get anything at all, considering our lowly POW status, and disgraced forever in the eyes of the Japanese because we surrendered and didn't commit suicide, as any Japanese soldier would have done in like circumstances.

One Red Cross parcel per week would have made an enormous difference in our diet. The majority of POW deaths in the Pacific area can be blamed on the vitamin deficient diet of rice and soup on which we subsisted for almost four years. In contrast to our death rate of 33%, POWs in Germany, who were in most cases issued Red Cross food parcels weekly, incurred a death rate of just 1%, less than the death rate of civilians in peacetime. The blame for the high death rate of the Japanese POWs rests squarely upon the Japanese Army, as the Red Cross certainly shipped enough food parcels to Japan. Even common humanity would seem to have called for at least a monthly issue. I presume the Japanese didn't think we were humans.

Chapter 35

Another New Year

It was hard to believe, but by New Years Day of 1944, we had been POWs for almost two years. The most optimistic among us were still hoping the war would be over in 1944, but what news we were able to get, however favorable it seemed, showed that progress by the allied armies was proceeding at a snail's pace. We knew of the battle of Midway Island, of Guadalcanal and other small islands, won by the Americans but trumpeted by the Japanese in the newspapers and on the radio as Jap strategic victories, claiming that our fleet had been sunk many times over and our air forces all shot down. Reading between the lines, we knew their claims were impossible, just propaganda for the civilian population to insure the popular support for the war. Working and talking with the common people as we did, we never found much popular or any other kind of support for the war. They just wanted an end to it as soon as possible. We heartily agreed.

Late in January the canteen offered cigarettes for sale at two yen fifty sen for a pack of ten, mandarin oranges at fifteen sen, apples at ten sen. The fruit wasn't of the best grade, but sold well. One pack of cigarettes being worth seventeen days of work, you had to be a heavy smoker to buy them. For one week in January, we were issued barley instead of rice. I had no idea of the caloric content of barley as compared to rice, but it was a change, and tasted rather good. Greens in our soup were very scarce, but the *daikons*, as always, were still in plentiful supply.

Also in plentiful supply were lice and bedbugs. We all had lice, which congregated in the seams of what underwear we had, and were a constant source of irritation. Those POWs able to boil their clothes, such as we at Hyogo Iki with coal fires, were reasonable free from infestation, but most of the others had to spend their *yasume* days searching for and killing the little devils. Lice seemed to know when someone was sick, and they swarmed on such people. One of the Aussies called "Blind Harry" was an artist at dodging work of any kind by claiming he was too sick and couldn't see, was a special target of the lice; he hardly ever moved from his bed and seeming to welcome their attention. When the lice became so thick that Harry's mates could stand it no longer, he would be put in sick bay for a bit, but shortly came back to his section to repeat the process. He must have been the only POW at Kobe House who never worked at all.

In March, the civilians began digging trenches and air raid shelters. A few shelters were built around Kobe House, for the use of guards only. Nothing in the way of shelters for us POWs seemed to be in the works. The only place we could have been accommodated would have been on the cricket ground across the street, and I doubt the Japs would wanted that place dug up. I doubt very much if they cared whether we had any protection at all. All these preparations were just another indication that the war was coming closer, which was OK with us. The sooner, the better.

April Fool's day brought another issue of Red Cross articles. Each section received an assortment of pipes, tobacco, cigarettes, combs, razors, razor blades, hair clippers, scissors, shaving cream, tooth brushes, tooth paste, shoe polish, shoe laces, toilet paper, sewing kits and needles. The usual lottery procedure was used to decide who got what. I would end up getting a razor and a comb. Combs were of no use, as we were all skinheads for the sake of cleanliness. The new clippers were given to the two old barbers, who were too infirm to work. New clippers made their work easier and more pleasant to the cuttees. Giving haircuts to over six hundred people wore out clippers pretty fast. Shoe polish was useless, more toilet paper would have been in order. I had left Bilibid with a new pair of shoes, which were now on the verge of extinction, and they sure didn't need polish. They needed soles. Along with the Red Cross issue the Japanese delivered a shipment of mail to the British and the Australians. Nothing for the Americans. This was the first mail to arrive at Kobe House and of course was well received. After more than two years as a POW, news from home was nice to get, even if some of it was bad, such as death notices or Dear John letters. Our lack of mail was pretty disappointing.

Later in the month the Aussies were given permission to again wear their famous hats. They had been giving the Japs a lot of trouble because their hats had been taken away and old Jap Army caps issued to them. The British had lost all their caps when their ship had been sunk, and we Yanks had only had an assortment of odds and ends, such as my old mechanic's cap, so we didn't mind our new ones that much, but to the Aussies, their famous hat with one side turned up was the only part of the uniform they had left to signify who they were. That was about the only issue that I can remember on which the Japanese gave in, so it was quite a victory.

Later in April the British received another shipment of mail and we were left out again. We began to wonder whether we would ever get any mail. Along with the mail came an issue of one and a half oranges. I often wondered how the orange issue always came to one and a half, never just one or two. No complaints, though. Anything extra was always welcome.

I was still shoveling dear old *sekitan,* coal in our language. If all the coal I shoveled in Japan had been piled up in one pile, it would probably have been higher than the four storied Kobe House. If anyone was qualified as an expert coal shoveler, it would be me. Coal jobs were deadly monotonous. Even though it was easy work compared to the dock jobs, we all yearned for a change of scenery and a chance to steal some article of food to augment our ration. Hyogo Iki was by all odds the worst job if you were a thief, as you couldn't eat coal or trade it for anything. All we could do with it was to keep the hut fires burning and to see that the *mama-sans* at the gate got their share. We couldn't even sabotage anything at Hyoko Iki.

One day in early May we arrived back at Kobe House to see two long lines of POWs which we joined. At the head of each line was a Japanese wearing white jackets, giving each POW an injection of something, like it or not. Reaching the head of the line, I took my coat off and was jabbed in the upper arm with the same needle that had been used on all those before me, and with that dull needle and my skinny, fatless arm, it was quite a job. I was glad not to be the last one of six hundred to be jabbed with only those two needles. We never knew what the shot was for, but it stung like a bee. It wasn't to get rid of us, as the Japs would never get rid of us good war workers. Mitsubishi would never have stood for that.

In the middle of May another ration change took place. The one and a half buns we had been issued for our noon meal were discontinued and raw rice issued in their stead, to be cooked on the job. The excuse for this was that too many of the POWs were not eating the buns at work, but were bringing them back into Kobe House for trading purposes. Each job was equipped with a wooden box to carry the raw rice. This just made another opportunity for the POWs to smuggle, as it was easy to make false bottoms for the boxes. The bad part of this deal was that the POWs had to cook the rice on the job, and for a week or so we ate a lot of almost raw rice, or overcooked, burnt to a crisp rice. The burnt rice was said to be beneficial if you had loose bowels as most of us had, but tasted like charcoal, so were glad when the designated cook learned his business. In a short time, the cooks learned to produce well-cooked rice in the Japanese manner.

On the 27th of May 1944, the Americans received their first batch of mail from home. It had been two and a half years since I had heard from my folks, and it was quite a day. I got nine letters, seven from my mother and two from friends. All my mother's letters had been limited to fifty words, by order of the U.S. government. This didn't allow for much news. I found out that the post card I had written in Bilibid had made it home on my birthday in 1943, about a year from the time I had filled it out. I also learned of the death of my father in May 1943, at the age of seventy-six. It was quite a surprise, although I suppose that he had lived his allotted lifetime. I could never figure out why the government limited the next-of-kin to fifty words per letter, as the letters I got from friends covered three or four pages. All the letters had been censored and passed by the Japanese, so this wasn't an issue they were worried about. It must have been some Washington bureaucrat's stupid idea. Short letters or not, those that got mail were happy. Some parcels of food, mostly cookies, also came in, but were in pretty bad condition after a year in transit. My mother had sent parcels to me, but it was a waste of time, as none of them ever reached me. I hope the Japs liked my mother's cookies.

Early June saw an issue of strawberries, the first since the war began. Even though we had to pay ten sen each for them, I received eight and enjoyed them tremendously. On the same day, another batch of mail arrived and this time my share was ten letters, seven from my mother. Not much news, except that the letters I had been writing had all arrived safely. Most had taken around six months in transit, as all mail to or from POWs were processed through a neutral nation, which happened to be Switzerland. Better late than never, so said we all!

Chapter 36

Two More Moves

On the first *yasume* Sunday in June, we watched a good concert from our perch under the roof. A band had been organized by this time, and with music, the skits were fabulous. Most of the instruments had been made by hand, although some had been bought by the Japanese staff. As was usual, 'God Save the King' was played to start the program, and was sung by all of us, even the Japanese staff. The band even played 'The Star Spangled Banner,' although nobody knew all the words! The concerts usually lasted a good hour or so, and were one of the bright spots in our dull existence. This one terminated abruptly, however, as the act being put on portrayed a POW working party on the docks which included a guard punishing one of the POWs. We all though it very funny, but not so the Japanese staff, who as usual occupied the front row seats. The aftermath found those in the skit at attention in front of the guard house for two hours. Other than that, the entertainment was just fantastic. After the concert, the band played over the camp speaker system for an hour, and we were given an issue of fruit. Quite a day!

Everyone was relaxing after the program, when Cpl. Hoblitt arrived on the scene with what was to us bad news. We were to vacate our warm attic perch and move over to "B" Block, leaving our Aussie friends behind. We moved over to the fourth floor of the block, which meant that we would still be warm the next winter, if we made it that far. Everyone was hoping to be out of Kobe House before that. In one way, I benefitted by the move, as we were allotted our spaces alphabetically, and as I was in the middle of the list, wound up at the end of the left-hand row next to the outside wall, and had a window to look out of. I could look out onto the cricket grounds, all nice and green, and wish they would let us out there sometimes, which they could have, but never did. The bad part of "B" block was that the guard house was directly opposite the door to the alley, and every time you went to the wash racks or to the shower, it was necessary to halt, come to attention, and salute or bow to the sentry, both on the way out and on the way in. This wasn't too bad except when you were on the mess detail. Then it was necessary to set your buckets down, salute, and pick up the buckets again before you could go inside, which was inconvenient to say the least. Another advantage to this move was that we were only three floors from the latrine, instead of four and a half. This meant fewer stairs to climb during our nightly visits to the *benjo*.

Our section had picked up another member on the move, a seaman named Hector Godoy, from the Greek ship. He was from Argentina and could only speak Spanish and about as much English as I could speak Spanish. The Greeks had been given our attic perch when we vacated it, as they were nothing but trouble and their new quarters more or less isolated. Hector was a quiet, inoffensive sort, and was probably put in with us because of the language problem. With us he could talk in his native language to Jimmy Lucero, at least. I got along with him well, and began teaching him English, with him teaching me Spanish in return. He seemed to have some mental problems which I think were caused by what he thought was an injustice by being treated as a POW by the Japs, Argentina being a neutral country. Hector didn't think this was legal, even though he was serving on a Greek ship. The Japs wouldn't let him near the Argentine consulate in Kobe, so he was just stuck with the rest of us in Kobe House.

The next day we went to work at the coal yard as usual, but on arrival, the honcho told us that this was our last day, as the job was shutting down. I don't think any of us were sorry at the news, as we had seen more than enough coal. We made sure that the old *mama-sans* got enough coal that day to last them the rest of the year. I'll bet they hated to see us go. When we got back to Kobe House after work we were greeted by the same two so-called Jap medics who had given us the shots before, and who repeated the process using, I presume, the same two needles, as they were duller than before. Hoblitt told us that we had just completed a course of dysentery shots. They must have been effective, because dysentery was almost nonexistent at Kobe House. We were also vaccinated for smallpox. I think the Japs wanted to keep us from dying of disease; they wanted to work us to death instead.

Another surprise waited for us inside. Cpl. Hoblitt was being shipped out to Tokyo, together with Bill Johnson, my buddy. Rumors had it that they were going to be doing propaganda work on the radio there, Bill being a radio operator and Hoblitt able to speak Japanese. When I came in from work the next day, they were gone. I found a note that Bill had left for me, saying that he would be seeing me *"Asta, Asta."* He must have meant *ashita*, which means "tomorrow" in English. In this case, tomorrow meant over a year. I missed Bill a lot. We were the only New

Englanders among the Yanks, and we spent many hours shooting the breeze. The staff interpreter, Henry, had also been replaced. We couldn't understand the replacement any better than we could Henry, and we missed Hoblitt, who had usually interpreted what Henry had said.

The displaced Hyogo Iki workers, having lost their regular job, had to go to work at any old job that needed extra men. Most days we wound up on the docks, some days going out in barges to unload ships anchored in the bay. I was unlucky my first day out. Every POW not on a steady job was barged out to a dingy old freighter which had to be unloaded in one day, and you can guess what the cargo was, the worst possible stuff to work on, especially on a hot day in June. You guessed it; *cemento*, and of course I wound up down in the hold, loading the bags of cement into cargo nets. Usually there are four nets to a hold, with a crew of POWs on each net. The loaded nets were hoisted up and out of the hold by winches, which means that three nets were being loaded at one time, the fourth crew taking a break. Not so with cement. Every sack had to be loaded onto the net by hand, as *kagis* would have torn the sacks. Unfortunately, most of the bags had been ripped open, and most of the cement had to be shoveled. This made for much dust and the honchos had to issue us face masks so we could breathe. Soon, everyone was streaming with sweat mixed with cement dust which got into every pore of your poor skinny body and into your eyes and ears. All we had on were our *fundoshis*, as nobody wanted to have their clothes covered with cement. What a scene it was in that hold! If Hell was anything like it, I knew I didn't want to go there. It was some relief to get out in the air and sluice off some of the dust before getting into our uniforms. I think that day was the absolute worst day I spent in Kobe and I doubt if I could have done another like it. Thankfully, there wasn't another. It took a week to get all the cement off.

Dock work at this time seemed to be slacking off, as most of the work was moving hemp, rubber and sugar out of the godowns into railway cars. The number of ships coming into Kobe had dwindled considerably since the first of the year, which we took to be an indication of the number of ships being sunk. At Dai Ni Shinko, most of our work was unloading barges and small coastal ships which never strayed into the open sea. We spent a lot of time in our hut drinking tea and talking about all the good food we were going to be eating in the future. There were barges full of cement to be unloaded at times, but not being down in a hold and in the open air it wasn't too bad. Most of the bags were intact and we could take our time. Dai Ni Shinko seemed to be at the end of the rail system on the docks, and we spent much time pushing cars around. This was easy work after a coolie had started the car moving.

Mitsui Soko had a lot of rubber which the Japanese had looted from Singapore, and now it was going out to factories. This rubber came in blocks about two feet square and weighed a hundred kilos. One block was placed on a *nekko* by two POWs, then was trundled to the elevator and down to the freight car, where other POWs moved it into the car and stacked it. Some of it had been shipped in the hot tropical summer, and at the bottom of the hold lost its square shape. The rubber still weighed the same but looked like lumps of play dough after a kid had played with it. These blocks were harder to move, and hard to stack up in the cars. One day while we were working on rubber, someone had the bright idea of bypassing the elevators and just dumping the rubber out the open door at the end of the godown. You can imagine what the result was when a block of rubber hit the deck from the third floor. Of course the rubber bounced in every direction imaginable, some wound up in the bay and some across the street. All the coolies and piggy women dove for cover and the horses took off down the dock with wagons bouncing and their owners in full chase. A few windows were broken as well. For a few minutes there was quite a commotion, which we enjoyed from our third floor perch. Needless to say, we didn't enjoy the three hours in front of the guard house that evening. We were lucky that no one had been hurt, or we would have been made to regret it.

One Japanese habit we found very strange. In the hot summer heat, everyone working on the docks got thirsty in short order. The companies put large pails of ice water out where we could get a drink on our break, and that wonderful icy cold mountain water sure tasted good. That is, until you took a big slug, only to find that some Jap had stirred in a couple of pounds of sugar, making the water sickeningly sweet. I suppose they did this because their sugar had been rationed so long they were starved for it. We learned to get our ice water before they got to it with the sugar.

Food was becoming scarcer as the war went on. We still got our bowl of rice, but the soup was mostly *daikon* or cabbage, with ground fish or bean soup perhaps once in a couple of weeks, and sometimes only a half issue. It was a lifesaver to us to get the company lunch. Everything we could scrounge in the way of edibles was thrown in the soup pot. I suspect the honchos looked the other way when we stole food, as otherwise we would never have been able to do the heavy work we did. Of course they always got their cut of what we stole. The Japanese civilians fared worse than the POWs, as they didn't dare to steal as we did, or had no chance to do so. They were all as sick of the war as we were.

At the end of June the camp commandant, Lt. Morimoto, was transferred. Everything considered, he had been a lot better than any of the camp commanders I had been under. He punished you when you did something wrong and were caught, but he wasn't as vicious or as cruel as most camp commanders were. His worst fault was not curbing the Mad Doctor. We would come to miss him. The new camp commander, a Lt. Takanaka, was fluent in the English language, having been in business in Australia. We would have to wait and see what his idiosyncrasies were, and pray that he wasn't another Mad Doctor.

Chapter 37

Aches and Pains

It became evident that, by the middle of 1944, our almost two and a half years of life as Japanese POWs was drastically affecting our health. We had been living and performing hard labor on a diet which would be inadequate for someone sitting behind a desk all day. Our rice and soup ration amounted to some one thousand calories, and what we stole in the way of food might have added another couple of hundred. The Japs weighed us each month, and nearly all of us were losing a pound or two at each weighing. Boils, carbuncles and ulcers became common, due to what the medics said was the lack of essential vitamins, especially vitamin B. This was the prime cause of the horrible disease, beriberi, which among other things, destroys the nerve sheathes in the extremities, particularly the feet and lower part of the legs. A dozen or so Kobe House POWs were afflicted with the dry form of beriberi, or tender feet. With dry beriberi, the slightest pressure on the foot causes exquisite pain. The feet become red-hot, and the only way to get any relief is to keep them cold. In Kobe House, the only way to do that was to hold the feet under a cold water tap. The pain was so intense that the sufferers slept on a bench at the wash stands with their feet under icy cold running water, even in the winter. Another effect of dry beriberi, besides the pain, is that the toes turn black and begin to drop off. After the toes are all gone, the rest of the foot starts to go. Several of the English finished up the war with nothing but their heels left. The medics tried one way to treat these men, a sort of kill or cure method. Cold water doing nothing but dulling the pain, they thought that applying heat might do something, so they wrapped up a couple of patient's feet in blankets, put their feet in an orange crate and nailed up the crate. It didn't take long to find out that this method wouldn't work—nobody could stand the screams. Wet beriberi, which is the type I and most of Kobe House suffered from in varying degree, had no associated pain. In fact, there was a loss of sensation in the lower legs and feet, together with muscle weakness. I found that as long as I laid off the sugar, I could do most of the dock work, as long as it wasn't climbing up ramps with a hundred-kilo bag on my back.

For most of the summer, I, along with most of the Kobe House POWs, was afflicted with batches of ulcers, located mostly below the waist and on the abdomen, privates and upper legs, a dozen at a time. These ulcers were another evidence of vitamin deficiency, which reduces resistance to infection, and were common to all Japanese POWs. Some POWs working on the Death Railway in Burma suffered from ulcers so large they could not be cured, due to lack of any medicine, and amputations of the legs became necessary. My ulcers were fairly small, about the size of a pencil, but all very painful. The only treatment ulcer patients received at sick call was the painful removal of the scab and a dousing with purple gentian, which was all the hospital had in quantity. They had no salve or antibiotics to waste on ulcers, as any such available had to be saved for patients in danger of dying. The treatment I got was so painful that I hated to go on sick call every evening, but it must have helped, as after a month my ulcers were healed, leaving dents in the skin and scars which I still have. Later in the year, I developed little pimples on the back of both of my hands, like small boils except that they came to a small whitish head. Thank God they cleared up in a week or so, because they were so painful. It was a good thing that they were only on the backs of my hands, otherwise I wouldn't have been able to work at all. As it was, any time I had to bend my hands it was hell. The medics said it was septicemia, or blood poisoning. With no medicine, all I could do was to sweat it out. Capt. Boyce, the Australian doctor, had a really tough job, caring for over six hundred POWs, all undernourished and overworked. The Japs insisted that anyone able to walk was able to work, and the Doc had to fight them daily in order to keep the worst cases in camp. He finally got permission that allowed him to keep some of the older and weaker men in camp on permanent duty, to keep the barracks clean and to do light repairs. A job was found for convalescents in making envelopes. This was done in groups of three men, the first man drew the outlines of an envelope, the second man cut around the markings, and the third applied paste and folded the envelope. There was no particular hurry as long as they kept working. Weaker men on dock jobs were given light duty such as sewing up rips in bags and sweeping the godowns. They were not pushed and half of them usually went to sleep while the other half worked and kept an eye out for the honchos. Compared to the majority of the POW camps where everybody had to work, half dead or not, Kobe House was heaven.

Hot weather brought on another unhealthy situation, that of an enormous number of maggots in the *benjos*, which could have resulted in an outbreak of fly-borne intestinal diseases. Flies became a bother because their population grew daily. Complaints to the Japanese were fruitless, their solution was to require each POW to turn in so many dead flies each day. No one paid any attention to this order, and for once nobody was punished. Flies flourished until the *benjo* was emptied. As most of our officers had been transferred to Zentsuji, the job was done by regular coolies who did this work as their regular occupation. They had to be forced to work on the Kobe House *benjos*, I guess they thought that waste from POWs wouldn't be good for their gardens. The Japanese Army changed their minds.

In addition to the physical troubles, many of the POWs had mental ones. It was a terrific mental strain just being a POW. We were in a situation not unlike that of Damocles and his sword, which hung over his head ready to fall on him at any time. We never knew what the next day would bring, or even if you would be around to see it when it came. A jail sentence would have been much easier, at least you would know when you were getting out. We had no idea as to when that happy day would arrive, if ever. Sometimes we thought we would end up as coolies for the rest of our lives. All one could do was to try and take every day as it came and not to worry about it.

Three of the POWs had gone off the deep end already, one Englishman, one Australian and one Scot. They had been moved to the hospital, where they sat all day long in their corner doing nothing. They were treated well by the Japs, who never punished them, even when they called the Japs all the names in the book, so their existence could have been worse. Some of us thought they were faking it. Maybe so, but I wouldn't have tried to fake being crazy, if it meant having to sit in a corner all day, every day, just to be able to swear at any Japanese.

Some of the Americans were beginning to act oddly. Walt Bohannon never had been much of a talker, but now he never spoke at all. Owen Barnett was another of us who rarely said anything. He had a really heavy beard and it was torture for him to shave every day. I guess he got fed up with it and just stopped shaving. Of course his beard became readily noticeable and it wasn't long before he caught some guard's attention. When he was told to go and shave, he refused, and of course was slapped around. He still refused to shave and down to the guard house he went, where he spent the night at rigid attention. In the morning, the Sgt. of the guard showed up and treated him to a more forceful drubbing. He still refused to shave, and after all the punishment he had gotten, I think the Japs got tired of him, as he was finally allowed to grow a beard, the only one in Kobe House. He certainly earned the privilege!

Del Busta was another one about to go off the handle. He was in better health than most of us, but always worried about food and how many vitamins he was getting. No matter what he acquired in the way of edibles, the first thing he did was to ask the nearest POW, usually me, "How many vitamins do you think is in this?" I would usually tell him, "Jesus Christ, Busta, just eat it. Everything has some vitamins in it." He always did just that, anyway, so there was no use his asking such a silly question. One time he and old Luke got into an argument about something. It was fast developing into a real fight when Busta jumped on Luke, who was sitting down, got one arm around Luke's neck and one of the supports holding up the shelf, and refused to let Luke up until Luke promised not to hurt him. Busta had powerful shoulders and arms, and had Luke in such a situation that Luke couldn't move, so finally, after an impasse of half an hour with the rest of us cheering Busta on, old Luke had to give in and promise not to hurt Busta. This was one of the fun times we had in Kobe House. Busta caused us a lot of trouble at another time. One night after *tenko*, when lights were out and we were in the sack, Busta just sat there on the end of his bed, and pretty soon pulled the switch chain to put our one light bulb back on. Pretty soon a guard showed up and put the light back out, growled a bit and went away. In a couple of minutes, Busta had the light on again. When the guard came back, Busta told him he was afraid of the dark. The guard must have realized Busta was a bit off, as he sat and talked to him like a father would, asking about Busta's family and showing him pictures of his kids, etc. This was nice for Busta, but the rest of us needed our sleep, so we finally told him to get that damn light out and go to bed. This went on for two or three nights, until we threatened him with much bodily harm if he didn't cut it out.

Our new bunkie, Hector Godoy, from Mendoza, Argentina, was another of the unstable ones. Being from a neutral nation, he was always complaining about being a POW, but the Japs paid no attention. On our way to work, we passed the Argentine embassy, and every time we neared it, Hector would make a dash for the front door of the embassy and ring the bell. The guards got a kick out of letting him get to the door before grabbing him and heaving him back in line with us. This only made him more frustrated and angry, until we all wished he was back with the Greeks. He wasn't a bad fellow at heart, though, and he taught me a good bit of Spanish and much about his country. I remember once when we had a lottery of mixed goods and he had picked a can of jam. When he opened the can, he was really disappointed, thinking that he had a nice tin of ham, as *jamón*, in Spanish, means ham.

Some of the Yanks were hard to get along with, too. Barnett and Bill Janiec were both surly types who were useless to talk to, Slim Marshall didn't get along with anybody, Gabby Sutherland wore you out with his endless gabbling, and our Navy Warrant Officer, Mr. Shaputnick, never associated with an enlisted men if he could help it. With my buddy Bill Johnson gone away to Tokyo, my closest friends were Al Rigdon, Jimmy Lucero and Earl Loughner, my Scots muckers, Tootie Grieg, Dunc Cameron and Claude Barker, and of course Karl Sinclair, the Aussie.

It was certainly hard keeping your sanity under the conditions we were living in, but I found that keeping my mind busy and active, learning what I could from any source available was the best thing for me, and I think I came out of it all with my brain still functioning on all cylinders, as they say. I'm sure that what I did was better than just sitting doing nothing but thinking of food.

Chapter 38

Summer Drags On

One Saturday evening in late July, we were each given six monster size pills, three to be taken with our supper, and three the next morning. They turned out to be worm pills, and the guards saw to it that they went down. It was a good thing that Sunday was a *yasume* day, as there was much coming and going from the *benjo*. These worm pills were probably a good idea, as I had heard stories about worms a foot long coming out at night to get some air. I don't know if I had any worms, but if I had had any, those pills would have done them in for good.

That same *yasume* day also saw a visit by a Catholic priest, the first of the scheduled monthly visits which the Japanese had agreed to. The Catholic POWs had Mass and received Holy Communion, but trouble started when the priest said some of the service in Latin. This caused the guards supervising the service to object, as they didn't understand what he was saying. After a bit, he was allowed to go on with the service, but after it was over, he spoke in English to wish the men a safe and early return to their families. At this, the guards marched the priest to the guardhouse, where he was grilled for some time before he was let go. That was the one and only Catholic service in Kobe House.

During the summer, a new POW hospital was established in a former school in the foreign area of Kobe, to serve the POW camps in the Osaka-Kobe area. Evidently there were quite a few camps in this area unknown to us, except the one at the Kawasaki shipyard across the harbor from the Kobe docks. This new hospital was described by Capt. Boyce, our doctor, as "a cold place of cruelty, starvation and death, under the slope of a grandstand," to which he never sent any patient unless by a direct order from the Japanese.

On the third of August, I celebrated my twenty-ninth birthday, no cake, candles or presents. Just being alive and kicking was enough of a present for me. The odds were pretty long on whether or not I would ever see the next one.

The physical condition of the entire POW population was gradually worsening, as the following remarks taken from Capt. Boyce's notes for August attest: "Coughs and colds more frequent, but sick parades heavy with minor surgical... *viz* boils, carbuncles, abscesses and pustular degenerations of axillary lymph glands; patellar bursae frequently fill with pus and respond to opening; all cuts and skin abrasions show an indolence due to malnutrition and take months to heal with an exuberance of heaped up cicatricial tissue at abscess margins."

Bandages were at a premium in the sick bay and every bit of cloth had to be washed and used over and over again. Any little piece of cloth we ran into on the docks was smuggled in and handed over to the medics for use as bandages. Most minor ulcers such as I had were never bandaged; probably that was one reason they took so long to heal.

Air raid practice had started in early summer, and became more frequent as time went on. To us POWs, this was just an indication that the war was coming closer and closer. We had been following the course of the war in the newspapers we had been able to smuggle into Kobe House and knew that the Japs were losing. We just hoped that they would have sense enough to quit before the real bombing raids began. If that happened, it wouldn't be very pleasant for the POWs cooped up in Kobe House. The port facilities of Kobe would be a prime target, and to date no shelters had been prepared for us POWs. It wouldn't be much fun sitting three stories up with bombs dropping on us. I had been through enough bombings in the Philippines to know what would happen in that case.

We had one red letter day late in August. On a Sunday *yasume* day the Yanks were told that we were to get up a baseball team to play the Australians after lunch. This was a problem, there being only twenty of us, half of whom could barely make it through a day's work. I knew I couldn't run, but having done a bit of pitching prewar, volunteered to pitch. My arms could still function even if my legs couldn't. We finally came up with the necessary nine men and practiced a bit on the road outside the camp. Early that afternoon, every POW and Japanese in Kobe House turned out for the game, which was to be played on the cricket grounds across the street, the first and only time we were ever let out on Sunday. The ball game went off well, the Yanks beating the Aussies by a pretty good margin, but it was a struggle to last the nine innings. It was good propaganda for the Japs, and the whole game was filmed. I would like to have seen myself doing all that pitching, but they never played that film for us. Anyway, it was a day to remember, with six hundred POWs sitting on the nice grass, guards and staff in the front row cheering us on. You would think it was the World Series the way they were jumping around. They really were baseball fanatics. So all went well, except that my arm was sore for the rest of the year.

By September, we had all been POWs for two and a half years, and it wasn't just our bodies that were wearing out, you should have seen what we had to wear. The Bataan boys had never had much of anything and always looked like tramps, and what clothing the more fortunate ones had started with were also about gone. Of course we had our Japanese issue, but only for wear on *yasume* days. Nobody had any underwear left, and had to wear our Jap issue *fundoshis*, comfortable enough, but a little embarrassing when working in just those. We all stripped down to our *fundoshis* when working in the hot weather. We must have been a pretty sight, gangs of skinny, scabby, bony POWs with nothing on but a strip of cloth between the legs. We all tried to find enough cloth to make a pair of shorts, such as cloth taken from a bale of cotton, or from bags that bran or flour came in. If you knew a piggy woman well enough, you might be able to trade a few cigarettes for enough cloth to smuggle into Kobe House, to get it made into a pair of shorts by one of the old men who worked inside doing tailoring. They would make a pretty good pair in return for a pack of cigarettes or a bowl of sugar. I finally decked myself out with a pair of flour sack shorts covered with Japanese writing, tied on with string. Shoes were another thing in short supply. The British had arrived in Kobe shoeless, and all wore the Japanese two-toed rubber ones. The Yanks and the Aussies had been wearing their issue boots, which, after two years or so of hard usage, were just about beyond repair. I was pretty lucky in getting a pair of Australian army boots from supply which were just my size. British Army boots were in great demand, as they were made from water buffalo hide which wore like iron, and, in addition, were fitted with hobnails and seemed to last forever. Getting those boots was just another stroke of good luck on my part.

More canteen goods were being made available, such as tea, cigarettes, fish sauce and curry powder. This last was a favorite of the English, who had been stationed in India before being sent to Hong Kong, but most of the Yanks hated the stuff. It took a while to get used to curry, but it did give our so-called vegetable soup a bit of a flavor. At the end of August, we began to receive a loose tobacco issue in place of cigarettes. Of course, with this loose tobacco, it was necessary to have paper to roll it in. The best paper was toilet paper, but with that it short supply, any kind of paper was used, from newspaper to a page from a book, if you had a book. One of the English who had a Bible started reading it from end to end. When he finished a page, he would tear it out and use it for rolling cigarettes. That was the story, most likely true. One day when I was scouting around a godown, I spied a crate sitting in a dark corner which hadn't been opened, so with my *kagi* I pried up one corner. Lo and behold, it was full of small packs of cigarette papers! This was worth a fortune and I made the most of it, carrying in a couple of hundred packs over a week's time, tucked under my wrap leggings. Each pack was worth a bowl of sugar or its equivalent in other goods, so I was all set for trading material for a good long time. Cigarette papers took up so little room and were so small they were just about undetectable in a search. No more trying to smuggle sugar or peanuts in, I had everything necessary with those cigarette papers.

Chapter 39

Autumn and Another New Job

September 1944 rolled around and with it cooler weather, making our work on the docks more bearable. Very few oceangoing ships were coming in, and most of our work was shipping out what was already in the godowns, which had been stacked up to the ceilings with loot. There was still a lot left, though, and the lumping of bags never ceased. What was different, we were now taking bags from the great stacks instead of adding to them, and going down ramps instead of up. Not too much easier, but a little.

Our new camp commander, Lt. Takanaka, inspected all the jobs and the working conditions at each one. He seemed to take more interest in his job that Jack Oakie ever did, even ordering the men working at Sumitomo to steal all the soya beans they could, being careful not to get caught, and to bring them into Kobe House. The beans were to be used to make hot soya milk for the patients in our hospital. A strange order for a Japanese officer to give! He also allowed Capt. Houghton, who had been an entertainment officer in World War I, to use the camp intercom system to put on an entertainment three times a week. These were a mixture of songs, music and skits, and were a hit with all the POWs. Anything that livened up our boring evenings were appreciated. The new Sgt. Major, Morita, although a terror when administering punishment, was a music lover and bought musical instruments for our POW orchestra, which was allowed to visit the area hospital and give concerts to the patients there.

Canteen issues were becoming few and far between. The two in September were one pear and one candied banana per man. Our food ration seemed to be declining, the beans in the bean soup were almost nonexistent, the weekly ground fish soup tasted worse than ever, and the usual so-called vegetable soup consisted of mostly leaves and little pieces of *daikon*. Japan will never run out of *daikon*! Once, for a period of two weeks, the rice was discontinued, with white potatoes of the same weight taking its place on the menu, but there were so many complaints that the potato experiment had to be abandoned and the rice brought back. This may sound funny to Americans, but if they had to live on a diet of very thin soup and a small bowl of plain boiled potatoes for a week, they would get sick of potatoes in short order. We POWs loved our rice and never could get enough of it. We all became rice connoisseurs in Kobe House! However, it was still a very monotonous diet. I tried to vary it some by putting my rice in the soup one day and the next day putting the soup in my rice. This didn't do much to help anything but was a bit of a change, at least.

On the tenth of October, the whole camp was given a holiday to celebrate the second anniversary of the establishment of Kobe House. We even got a special dinner; two potato-flour rolls, a spread of bean cheese, and for once a thick soup. After dinner we all paraded in the street outside, where presents of food were given to POWs who were designated "good workers" by the honchos. One of the Aussies received an award for saving a piggy woman from drowning, and one of the British an award for stopping a runaway horse and wagon. Another banner day in Kobe House!

Later in October there was another call for volunteers to go on a new job. By this time, nearly everyone in Kobe House had found a job he liked and wanted to stay on, so there were just a few, including me and Rigdon, who wanted to take a chance on this new job. The next morning when we met our new honcho we weren't too happy, because he was a tall, dark and ugly fellow with a hole in one hand, who was promptly christened "Old Black Joe." We soon found that appearances can be deceitful, because Old Joe turned out to be the best honcho we had ever worked for. Our new job was called "Kobe Go," and was about a ten minute walk from Kobe House. It was located in the large railroad yard at the eastern end of the dock area. Both of my railroad jobs so far had been shoveling a lot of coal, but on Kobe Go I never saw any of that stuff. Our gang was given a small hut beside the freight station where we made ourselves at home.

Kobe Go seemed to handle all the odd jobs around the docks, so every day saw us going to a different place, mostly unloading single railway cars here and there. One day we were unloading ingots of pig iron from a flat car by sliding each ingot down a wooden chute into a barge below. Each ingot weighed about forty pounds, and it was easy to get the barge's owner into a towering rage by missing the chute and hitting the bottom of his barge with the ingot. No wonder he got mad, as one iron ingot could have sunk the barge if it hit in the right place. The whole family lived on the barge, and the lady of the house and the kids screamed at us as well.

With the warehouses full of rice, barley, peanuts and beans, there were rats galore. The Japs kept the rat population down by keeping a couple of ferrets in each godown, which we spotted now and then. When a barge was loaded with anything edible, rats went right along. Every bargie owned a dog, who was Johnny-on-the-spot when the last bag was unloaded and the rats had no place to hide. A good rat dog would usually get them all.

Kobe Go turned out to be a good job for eating. All along the railroad tracks were small gardens belonging to the railway employees, most of them about six feet square. They sure hated to see us go by, because anything edible in those gardens ended up in our soup. Old Joe cared less about our stealing as long as he got his cut, and his bicycle was usually well loaded down when he took us back to Kobe House after work. Best of all, Joe made sure that we had plenty of soya beans for our daily soup. We had a bean box in the hut, and when the beans were about to run out, we would find a carload of soya beans shunted to a stop right outside our hut. Needless to say, a bag of beans mysteriously disappeared, a third of the bag went into our box, a third was packed on Joe's bike, and the other third to the railroad men who had shunted the car to our hut. These soya beans were a godsend to us. They were chock full of protein and gave us the energy to do the hard work of a coolie. I believe that if I hadn't gone on the Kobe Go job, with Old Black Joe for a honcho making sure we got our beans, I doubt that I would have survived to the end of the war. The Kobe House rations were by now almost devoid of anything that could be called nourishing. We could see that the civilian workers were getting less food as the war went on, and they never got extra food as we did. I'm sure old Joe was dealing in the black market with the loot he carried home every night on his bicycle. We hoped he didn't get caught, as that would be the end of our good fortune.

Our usually monotonous existence was upset one fall day when Del Busta, who had been acting queerly for some time, jumped off a dock and was pulled out by a coolie. Evidently he had gone off his rocker and tried to commit suicide. This was the story we heard, anyway. He was put into the hospital, and the next morning dove head-first out of a window, probably twenty feet from the ground, somehow landing on his feet in the middle of a sand pile next to a bomb shelter. He hadn't hurt himself a bit. All that resulted from his dive was that the Americans had to furnish a man to watch him day and night. This was a pain, as none of us wanted to spend two hours a night standing guard. This went on a couple of weeks, until we all wished that coolie had let Busta sink. We complained so much that the Japanese finally built a small cage out of two-by-fours, into which they moved Busta and one of the English, where they sat all day. Eventually, a Scot and an Aussie became occupants as well, which made it an international affair with one each of the four nationalities in Kobe House. This ended the guard duty, thankfully.

Capt. Boyce, the Australian Medical Officer, was undoubtedly the finest officer of all those with whom I had any contact during my years as a POW. He had the guts to stand up for any mistreated, overworked or underfed POW, and did his best to see that those least able to work were either given an easy job or allowed rest while recuperating from an illness. Capt. Boyce never hesitated to lodge a complaint to Jack Oakie or Lt. Takanaka if he thought it was necessary. I think the Japanese respected him for his devotion to duty, and were inclined to give him much of what he wanted. If all the officers had been like Capt. Boyce, things would have been much better for all the POWs. Unfortunately, this wasn't the case, as the majority of the officers tried to avoid any controversy which might upset their relatively easy life. This was easy to do as long as they obeyed every Japanese order without complaint, no matter how stupid or unjust the order might be. Capt. Boyce deserved a medal if anyone ever did. His notes for the month of October contain the following: "Rations ever lower and mainly rice and vegetable tops, so bad in fact that troops are asking not to be kept in when too ill for work, because they can get decent food on their jobs. Nip psychological attitude towards food and work is peculiar. By ruling as soon as a man is unfit for work from any cause whatsoever, he is supposed to go on half rations. They would let a broken leg or a pneumonia case die of starvation, with no chance of getting better on half an already meager ration, rather than as we would, feed up such cases, to have them better in quicker time to be fit as workers again. At most camps, I understand their rule holds; at Kobe House we obviated the rule and gave our sick extra food at the expense of the commonwealth."

And from his notes of November: "General health of camp good; but troops fed up, 'browned off,' tempers frayed and quarrels easy and fights getting common. Rations very scanty, rice and *daikon* mainly, but some beans added, and slowness of healing and chronic sepsis are evidence of prolonged inadequate diet."

In November, the Catholic Archbishop of Japan, with the representatives of the British and American governments as well as a Swiss representative, paid a visit to the Kobe House hospital. They inspected the patients, the food conditions, and also had an hour's talk with the officers, no Japanese present. They also gave a gift of a thousand yen for purchase of medical supplies and medical books, and promised they would try to secure better rations, including meat, for the patients. Sorry to say, but try as much as they did, the rations stayed the same.

Work on the docks was very slack in November, most of it seeming to be just maintenance work such as sweeping and cleaning up. The dock workers didn't complain about the lack of work, they enjoyed sitting around and drinking tea. This showdown didn't affect us that much, as the railroad was always busy moving things from one place to another, and the lack of large cargo ships wasn't too much of a factor. The railroads had not been bothered by the war, as submarines couldn't sink trains, and there had been no bombing in the homeland to date, with the exception of the Doolittle raid.

Toward the end of October, rumors began to the effect that there were seven thousand letters at Osaka for the whole Osaka area, which included Kobe House. We did get a shipment of mail but very few, if any, from the U. S. I know that I never got any mail after the June 1944 shipment. Another rumor had it that a party of sixty Aussies would be required to go to Showa Denki and live there on a permanent basis. This would do away with the daily work party and the travel time involved, thus increasing the work hours at the plant. It turned out that there had been quite a hassle between the Aussies and the British over the composition of this detail. Capt. Houghton, being English, declared that none of the English would be sent to live in such a filthy place. There had been dissension ever since the Australians came to Kobe House about the English having all the good jobs. Of course this came about because we and the English had been working in Kobe for a full year before any Australian began working, and of course all the good jobs had been taken. There was never any love lost between the Aussies and the Poms, as the Aussies called the British. We Yanks, being so few in number compared to the others and having but one useless Lt. Colonel to speak for us, had to find our own niche in the scheme of things.

A further indication of the Japanese policy toward the sick came when an order came down from Osaka that men in hospital, on light duty in camp, and camp staff were not to have any entertainment in future. They were not to have books to read, could not play cards, and were forbidden to smoke. In other words, if you were not a full-time worker, your life was to be made more miserable than ever.

Late in October, Gen. MacArthur's landing in the Philippines made the headlines in the local papers, along with the usual Jap propaganda saying that all the Americans had been annihilated, but somehow had landed in spite of this. Cheering news to us POWs, even if it didn't alter our situation that much. We just wish it had happened a couple of years earlier. The news was just another indication that freedom was approaching slowly, if we could last long enough to welcome it.

On Armistice Day in November, a Red Cross ship arrived at Kobe. Eighty POWs from Kobe House were detailed as a work party to unload the ship. They reported that there were seventy thousand individual parcels, enough for every POW in Japan to get at least five, as well as cases of clothing, boots and medical supplies. All this was stored in the Mitsui and Mitsubishi godowns for distribution. Kobe House received hundreds of parcels and cases which were stored in the supply room. We had never seen a Red Cross parcel since last year's New Year's Eve and our tongues were hanging out in anticipation of the goodies we thought we would be getting soon. Our tongues hung out a long time!

Our next *yasume* day was a national holiday, on which the Emperor offered sacrifices to the gods in thanks for a good harvest. We didn't thank them, as our share of the harvest didn't amount to much more than the usual *daikons*. What we did get was a visit from a Protestant Japanese clergyman, and we had a good service with no trouble from the guards.

We had a nice surprise at the end of November; all twenty-one Americans and all the Australian officers and NCOs were taken to the Kobe POW hospital, where we made radio broadcasts of Christmas greetings to be sent to our families. Major Campbell ordered the Aussies not to make the broadcasts, as it was against their Army Regulations, but after the Japanese threatened to cancel all incoming and outgoing mail privileges, he agreed under protest. Everyone was given a mimeographed form which had to be filled out and checked by the interpreter before we could broadcast our message. As was the case when we wrote letters, we had to show our benevolent captors in a favorable light, and included the following: Name, age, rank, unit, home address and name of addressee, fifteen words; was POW being treated well by the Nipponese Army, twenty-five words; health, all right and well, ten words; ask for mention of family's health, twenty words; reunion with dear ones and hope to see them soon, twenty words; memories of family and good times before the war, forty words; season's greetings, ten words; remarks in ending, ten words. We were allowed two and a half minutes to make our broadcast, a total of a hundred and fifty words.

These messages were not actually broadcast at the time, but were recorded, and were to go on the air later. Nobody ever thought they would actually be broadcast, but after I finally got home, my mother showed me four small records of my broadcast, which had been picked up by U.S. Navy ships and forwarded to her. I played one, but it was unintelligible because of the great amount of static. My mother and my sister-in-law had played the same record continuously all one night, getting a word here and there, until they had the whole message written down. At least the Japs had kept their word and followed through with the broadcast.

In December, Red Cross parcels were finally issued, one parcel per two POWs, so Rigdon and I shared one. It seemed as though that with all those parcels in the supply room, they could have done a bit better, but as the saying goes, half an apple is better than none, and we were happy to get our half parcel. After all, it had been a year since the last one. Australian and British overcoats were also passed out, one to every NCO and to a few lucky other ranks. The rest had to settle for Japanese Army overcoats, which were essentially the same. No matter what the nationality of the overcoat, we were all happy to get one.

My third Christmas as a POW was spent at work. Nothing special about the day except that a concert was given in the evening. We expected to get a Red Cross parcel at least, but none was forthcoming. I presume the guards got one to celebrate, as those POWs who had access to the supply room had noticed a perceptible shrinking of the stacks of parcels.

Just before Christmas, the city of Osaka, thirty miles to the east of Kobe, had been bombed. We could hear the explosions as well as antiaircraft fire, and the honchos had rushed us back to Kobe House, where we had to close the iron shutters over the windows. No guards were around, as they were all down in their air raid shelters, so we left the shutters open to see what was going on, but the action was too far away to see any of it. The next day at work, we saw all the Japanese looking up and pointing at something. Of course we all looked up too, to see what was so interesting. What we saw was a shining silver speck, so high up we could hardly see it, but we knew it must be American. We were pretty happy to see an American airplane, and it was a wonder we didn't get a good bashing from the guard for jumping up and down and cheering. If we had but known what the future held in the way of American bombers, we wouldn't have been that happy!

So ended the year 1944. It had not been too bad a year, all things considered. All the Americans were still alive and kicking, even though some weren't in too good a shape. Thanks to the Red Cross, we had warmer clothing for the cold weather, which didn't seem to bother us as much as it had the past winters. This being our third winter in Japan, we had more or less become acclimatized. The morale in Kobe House was high, Lt. Takanaka pretty decent, the guards more lenient than they had been, and the work was getting easier all the time. The one negative aspect of our Kobe House life was the declining quality and quantity of our food ration. If we got any less food, we would certainly be pretty hungry by spring.

Chapter 40

And Another New Year

January 1945, turned out to be a cold month, with sleet and snow about every day. The two small charcoal fires on each floor had been discontinued early in the winter because of the charcoal shortage. One small fire was allowed in the hospital, but it being in a wooden building, the patients and orderlies suffered more than the rest of us. At least there were no drafts in the brick warehouses the rest of us lived in. There was an influenza epidemic, and everyone seemed to have either a cough or a cold; nothing in the way of cough syrup or aspirin was available. If you went on sick call, all you got was sympathy and a dose of quinine. The quinine was a mite late, when we had malaria we could have used it, but now, in a place where there was no malaria, there seemed to be a plentiful supply. Strangely, the dose of quinine seemed to help our colds. Most of the influenza cases were among the Aussies, who seemed to feel the cold more than either the British or the Americans, probably because they were used to a warmer climate than we were. Because of the influenza, many POWs were being excused from work. This soon exasperated Lt. Takanaka, who refused to believe the cold weather had anything to do with it, and said that none of the other POW camps in the Kobe area were affected. Capt. Boyce was blamed for the epidemic, and was ordered that there be no more influenza cases. All the sick had to go to work, no matter how high their temperature was, and were allowed to sit by a fire all day. Capt. Boyce obeyed the order and there was no more influenza, but bronchitis showed up instead.

Tex Howell, our lone civilian, developed an ulcerated tooth which caused him much pain. We had no dentist in Kobe House, and the doctor had no pain relievers, so Tex just had to suffer. He stood the pain for a week and then begged to have somebody pull it with a pair of pliers. This turned out to be quite an operation. Two men held Tex down and one of our medics got a hold on the aching tooth with his pliers and began to pull. Nothing gave, so Al Rigdon grabbed onto the medic's arm and added his strength to the pulling. The only result was that Tex's face got red and his veins swelled up almost to bursting, but the tooth just wouldn't budge. Finally, Tex mercifully passed out, and the tooth stayed where it was. Tex had to suffer until late spring, when a dentist finally visited Kobe House. It didn't pay to have teeth trouble in our camp!

We had a lot of fun with old Luke, our esteemed leader, who wasn't too well liked by rest of us. As usual in cold weather, our bladder troubles increased, making *benjo* trips necessary every other hour. Old Luke had found a ceramic battery jar someplace which held about a gallon, which he used as a chamber pot during the night to spare him the frequent trips down the three flights of stairs to the *benjo*. Luke had a habit of going over to "A" Block after supper to gossip with some of his British friends, getting back just before *tenko*. About ten minutes before he was due back, all of us would empty our bladders into Luke's jar, and if there wasn't enough to fill the jar, we would recruit enough British to complete the filling, then ease the jar under the edge of the platform. Of course, after making up his bed and taking his clothes off, Luke would reach under the platform for his chamber pot, while we all waited with bated breath for the explosion which came when he stuck his fingers into the full jar. Then, of course, he had to carry the full jar down the three flights of stairs to the *benjo*, the jar slopping over at every step. This went on until he finally got rid of the thing. Luke was a great talker and could discourse for an hour on any subject. One of the Englishmen sleeping directly in back of Luke had the habit of asking Luke a question just after lights out, such as "Luke, how is the fishing where you live?", which would start Luke off, and the monotonous dissertation which followed would put the Englishman to sleep in a couple of minutes. Unfortunately, most of the Yanks couldn't get to sleep with that going on, and we had to tell his friend to refrain from getting Luke started.

The cold weather seemed to bring out the worst in our ever present lice. I suppose they liked to go where it was warm just as we did. It was just too bad that the warm spot they found was us POWs. We also had an invasion of bedbugs, not at all pleasant. They appeared at night on the walls, almost like a trail of ants. They seemed to know just where they were going, and evidently certain POWs must have tasted better than others, two or three of us being the target. The unfortunates chosen by the bedbug tribe had to spend half the night shaking out their blankets trying to get rid of these pests. I was lucky to be one that the bedbugs avoided. In fact, I was only bitten once in all the time I spent in Kobe House. That one bite was enough; I was certainly glad I wasn't on the bedbug menu.

Air raid sirens began to sound in February. For the first couple of weeks after this, the POWs double-timed back to Kobe House, where we stayed until the "all clear" signal was sounded. This disrupted the work details, and finally someone with a bit of common sense decided that we should dig our own shelters so we could stay on the job. This was fine with us, as no one wanted to be stuck in Kobe House if there was any bombing. At Kobe Go we dug the deepest and best bomb shelter around. When an alert was sounded, we all disappeared down the ladder about twenty feet to our shelter, where we were joined by Old Joe and the regular coolie gang, where we sat and drank tea for the duration of the alert. We enjoyed such breaks from work, and I guess the Japanese did, too.

More Red Cross parcels arrived in camp, but were not issued to the POWs directly. Milk, cheese, butter and jam went to the patients in the hospital; meat, raisins, coffee and sugar to the cook-house to supplement our regular ration, and the cigarettes to Capt. Houghton for issue to all of us. Some mail came in also, but none for us Yanks.

On the 14th of February, twenty Aussies, including Lt. Goddard, left Kobe House for Showa Denki, where they would live and work. It must have been a wrench, leaving Kobe House and their buddies for that filthy job. It's a wonder they didn't ship the twenty Americans there if that was all they wanted, and were we glad they didn't think of us! We heard later that they joined some eighty other POWs already there, some British and a group of Americans from the Philippines, who had spent six weeks at sea on what they called a "Hell-ship." I bet that when they arrived at Showa Denki they thought they were still in Hell. I know from the dozen or so times I had been there the heat made you think you were.

About this time Kobe House acquired another Doctor. He was an Aussie named Longbottom, whose specialty was "rough medicine and surgery." He loved to cut boils, abscesses and such open in cold blood, without anaesthetics. After a few POWs got a taste of his medicine, a POW wanting to go on sick call would ask which doctor was on duty, and if it was Longbottom, they went to work rather than have him operate. It was bad enough to be taken care of at all, but at least Capt. Boyce tried to be as gentle as possible. The two doctors didn't get along at all and soon had a good feud going. Needless to say, we were all for Capt. Boyce.

The air raid sirens sounded nearly every day in late February, but so far we had seen nothing much except for single planes flying at high altitudes. This state of affairs changed in short order. Late one night we heard explosions, and from my window, which was on the east side of the block we could see Japanese searchlights sweeping the skies about ten miles away, which would be half way to Osaka, in the area of Showa Denki and Toyo Steel. After a few sweeps, one of the searchlights picked up a single bomber coming in from the sea, and followed it inland until it had dropped its load of bombs. Then all the searchlights went back to the spot where they had picked up the first bomber. This went on for a long time, as I counted each bomber, and there must have been at least a hundred, all bombing the same target, which must have been blasted into oblivion by so many bombs. We knew there were aircraft factories in that area, so one of them must have been the target. If so, no more planes were ever manufactured there. The Americans didn't get off lightly, either, as the Japanese had plenty of antiaircraft along the coast, and at least ten bombers were shot down that night. I had what you could call a ringside seat, three floors up, and saw it all, even the flaming bombers heading for the ground. This bombing became almost a nightly occurrence, until it seemed to me that there couldn't be a factory left in the twenty miles from Kobe to Osaka. We began to wonder when they would start on Kobe, and after what we had seen, didn't even want to think about it.

The Japanese staff was becoming very touchy, probably due to the air raids. Sgt. Major Morita and the interpreter had searched the officers' quarters and found a small bottle of oil in Lt. Fuller's bag, as well as other forbidden articles in other officers' bags. Oil being a prime article in the war effort, Sgt. Morita was determined to find out who had brought it into Kobe House, and Lt. Fuller was promptly taken down to the guardhouse, where he was made to stand at attention while being questioned by Morita. Questioning getting no results, Lt. Fuller was sentenced to stand at attention in front of the guardhouse for ten hours. This meant that the culprit would be at the mercy of every Jap who happened to be in the vicinity and had an urge to bash a POW. The bashing usually took the form of kicks, spitting, hits with rifle butts or wooden swordsticks. During his punishment, Lt. Fuller was kicked in the groin, as well as having one of his teeth broken. He was given no food or water for the whole time. A little before the ten hours was up, the pay sergeant happened to show up and asked Lt. Fuller why he was being punished, and when told the reason, asked who had brought the oil in. Getting no answer, the pay sergeant proceeded to bash the Lt. all over his body with his sword stick. Lt. Fuller tried to tell the pay sergeant that his honor as an officer would not permit him to tell who had brought the oil in, whereupon the sergeant went up to talk to Capt. Houghton about "honor," as he didn't understand the word. Evidently Capt. Houghton gave him a good explanation, as the pay sergeant went back down and let Lt. Fuller go, to report to him in the morning. When he reported in the morning as ordered, the pay sergeant asked how he was, and then was dismissed. He heard nothing more about the oil. This was an example of extreme punishment which we had not seen too much of since the Mad Doctor had been shipped out. Some unlucky POW was usually seen standing at attention in front of the guard, but only for a short time, and if he was lucky, he might not have been slapped or kicked at all. Lt. Fuller was a big man, over six feet tall, which may have accounted for what he got. The Japs liked to beat up on the larger POWs, as I knew from my own experience. Any way you looked at it, being punished was no fun.

Chapter 41

War Comes to Kobe

By March the air raid sirens were sounding nightly, but all the action seemed to be in the Osaka area. The daily papers carried accounts of the raids, listing the numbers of enemy planes shot down, usually so many that if true, none of the bombers ever returned to Guam or wherever they had come from. One paper even carried a picture of a Japanese fighter pilot, complete with sword, who had landed his plane on a bomber, captured the crew, and forced it to land! If the Japanese civilians believed this baloney, they were stupider than I thought. The papers also informed us of General MacArthur's return to Manila in February, too late to rescue me by three years. We even found out what the bombers were; when one appeared during the day, all the Japanese would be point at it and say *Bi-ni-ju-kyu,* so we knew it was a B-29 bomber. We had never heard of a B-29, but we knew it must be a lot bigger than a B-17.

St. Patrick's Day came on the 17th of March, and with it came a whole lot of excitement. The air raid sirens had roused Kobe House just before midnight of the 16th, and everyone had to get up, dress, and pack whatever he owned. It didn't take me long to pack what I had in my old *nipa* woven shopping bag. Nothing further happened for half an hour, when we heard the drone of airplane engines and the antiaircraft batteries around Kobe opened up. Our window shutters were supposed to be closed, but as during the previous raid, there were no guards around, and we left the shutters open for a good view of what was going on. I presume all the guards were safe in their air raid shelters, leaving the POWs locked in as usual. The first wave of bombers dropped flares on that part of Kobe east of Kobe House to light up the target for those following, who dropped ton after ton of incendiary bombs which we could see falling like snowflakes. The resulting fire was a holocaust. The city was a tinderbox of small wooden houses, which caught fire almost immediately, flames shooting high in the sky. No fire department in the world could have stopped a fire like that. It looked as if the whole eastern half of Kobe was on fire and heading our way. We watched the fire come closer and closer until the large office buildings on the other side of the cricket grounds caught fire. At this time, around four in the morning,

Kobe under attack by B-29s. *(USAAF photo.)*

the last of the bombers finished their runs and headed for home. With the fire just across the street, the Japanese opened our doors and we were herded into the cricket grounds where we stayed for four hours. The heat from the fires kept us toasty warm except for our feet, as there was snow on the ground. Finally, about eight o'clock, all the bombers had gone and we were allowed back into Kobe House, where we had a late breakfast.

We were kept in for the next week, and as we were not working, only got two meals a day, nothing at noon but tea. There was no heat and no electric power, as all the poles carrying the power had burnt down. Kobe House was like a tomb, and our numerous trips to the *benjo* in the pitch dark were quite adventurous. An owl would have had trouble navigating in Kobe House. With nothing to do except visit friends to shoot the breeze, most of the POWs just crawled into their blankets and tried to sleep. During this period of enforced idleness, I found that the private areas of my body had become the home of a family of those unwelcome creatures called "crabs," which called for a complete shave of all hair. With ice cold water, a dull razor and only a scrap of lye soap, I finally got the job done, but not without quite a few scrapes and cuts. I have no idea where my crabs came from, certainly not from any female contact, so they must have come from some sleeping platform I had sat on. As far as women were concerned, they never entered a POWs thoughts, except as a dim figure dishing up a huge apple pie. The Japanese women we had contact with certainly didn't warrant any sexual yearnings, all being dressed in the same drab, baggy outfit called *mompei*. Even when we were talking among ourselves, women were rarely mentioned. I suppose the fact that we were all so undernourished had something to do with that.

When we were finally allowed to go back to work, we could see first hand the extent of the damage caused by that one raid. From the street that ran from the docks past Kobe House to Sannomiya Station and up to the mountains, everything to the east for miles was a still smoking ruin, except to the north of the railroad viaduct. This was the area where foreigners lived, and the houses were built of stone or cement with large open areas. In the burnt area, nothing remained except the gutted shells of large cement buildings. All the small wooden houses the poorer people lived in had been destroyed, and with the houses, hundreds of small factories which had been turning out war materiel. Thousands of people must have perished, regrettable but also inevitable in a large-scale incendiary raid such as this one. On the docks, half of the go downs and their contents had been burned. The big Kawasaki shipyard had been badly damaged, and a large aircraft carrier, which had been partially completed and was sitting in the harbor minus its engines, had been nearly sunk. It had been quite a raid; one more of the same and Kobe could be crossed off the list of targets.

One more thing that should be mentioned regarding this raid was the performance of the POW population. In contrast with the performance of our guards, who seemed to be scared witless, rushing here and there like ants, the POWs kept good discipline and remained calm throughout the whole raid. In fact, POWs volunteered to fight fires, and some of the British went up to the top of the Naval building across the cricket grounds and brought down wounded Japanese who had been hit while manning a gun there, even though they were enemies. I doubt very much if the Japs would have done the same for us.

A couple of days after the bombing, the Australians were formed up in the street while the guards searched the second floor of their barracks, pulling up floor boards in search of hidden loot. Evidently an informer had been at work, because a considerable amount of loot was found. It was later reported that six hundred and thirty-eight items had been found, consisting of shirts, dresses, socks, sugar, medicines, cigarettes, home made knives and other odds and ends which made quite a pile. As some of the stuff was Army property, the theft of which was punishable by death, the Aussies who were waiting outside had good cause to worry as to what their punishment would be. However, the guards soon realized that if this was reported to higher headquarters, they would be in the soup themselves for allowing such an amount of stealing to take place, and the upshot of the whole affair was that the guards divided the goods up amongst themselves and the Aussies got off with a little slapping.

What was more serious, a number of diaries had been found along with the loot. They were the property of one of the Aussie warrant officers, one Ian Doherty, who had been keeping a record of all the events since the day they had arrived in Kobe House. The diaries had been read by the interpreter, who decided to notify the *Kempeitai*, or secret police. This was bad news, as a Captain in the *Kempeitai* outranked a Colonel of the Army, and had the power of life and death over any POW. Ian was taken to a cell under the guard room where he was questioned by the *Kempeitai* Captain. In one of the diaries, Ian had written, "The Japs are obviously losing the war, more raids could be expected, and the future was terrible to contemplate." The Captain deduced than Ian must have had a radio, otherwise he couldn't have forecast what had happened. Ian was asked where his radio was; how powerful it was; where it was plugged in; and could it pick up the B.B.C. Of course the existence of a radio was denied over and over. Finally Ian was told that he would be executed the next morning! The next morning the Captain came into the cell, slapped Ian, handed back two of the diaries, said that he had decided that there was no radio in Kobe House, but that Ian had violated the rule that POWs were not to keep diaries. Then Ian was handed a sheet of paper and told to write exactly one hundred words as to what his opinion of what would happen to the towns and cities of Japan as a result of another incendiary raid. He was then told by the Captain that he had decided not to "severely execute" Ian, but that he had violated their rule of "no diaries," and was to be severely punished. The punishment consisted of kneeling with a two-inch pole resting on the back of the knees, then having to squat. This causes intense pain, and Ian fainted a number of times, being brought back to consciousness by a bucket of water poured on his head. Finally, he was allowed back to his quarters, and the next day had to go out to work. He never wrote another word while he remained a POW.

On the 27th of March, more letters were distributed, none of which were from the States, and what was more important, each POW received one Red Cross parcel! It was about time, I for one was so hungry that I had been eating tea grounds to help fill the void. I had never cared for tea in the first place, but on *yasume* days that was all we had for the noon meal, so I drank it for the sake of having something warm in the stomach. I have detested tea ever since Kobe House!

If I remember rightly, we were issued the Red Cross parcel because it was the Emperor's birthday and we were to celebrate it by eating well. One parcel was supposed to be issued to each POW every week, and if that had been the case, we could have told the Japanese to stick their rice and soup. My parcel contained the following: two packs cigarettes, half pound cheese, one package sugar cubes, one package prunes, one can Spam, one bar chocolate, one can corned beef, one can pate, one can slim milk, two cans "C" rations, one can instant coffee and one can opener. Each parcel varied a bit as to the contents, but what I received was about the norm. A slip of paper which gave the name and address of the packer was usually found in each parcel. They were mostly girls' names, and I think that some of the POWs wrote thank you letters to the packers.

By the end of March, all the officers except the two medical officers were transferred away from Kobe House to a special officers' camp. Ian Doherty, who had had the trouble with the *Kempeitai* Captain about his diaries, was told by Sgt Major Morita that he was now the senior Australian, a promotion he would have gladly done without. Most of the POWs were glad to see the last of the officers, with the exception of Major Campbell and Lt. Fuller. They were good officers and would be missed. We Yanks lost our Colonel Fliniau, who had never been much use to us anyway. This left old Luke as the senior American, and he wasn't too happy about that. So ended a very eventful and exciting month.

Chapter 42

Sweating It Out

The St. Patrick's Day bombing of Kobe made it abundantly clear to us POWs that we would be in the thick of things from now on, working as we did in areas sure to be attacked such as railway yards, docks, and factories. Kobe House was in the center of all these, as it was only a quarter of a mile from the docks in one direction and an important railway about the same distance in the opposite direction, and had no markings on the roof which would indicate that it was a POW camp. Located where it was, markings would not have made much difference anyway. What the POWs wanted, in case of an air raid, was to be at work where we had some protection in our air raid shelter, and not be cooped up in Kobe House where a single bomb could kill hundreds of us.

It was a relief to get back to work at Kobe Go. None of the workers there seemed to have any resentment against us because of the air raid, even on the docks, where so much damage had been suffered. The railroad was still undamaged, and although there was little movement by water, we were kept busy enough unloading barges and small coastal craft. Once in a while a freighter made port, having by good luck avoided the submarines. On our journeys around the dock area, we found out what havoc one high explosive bomb could do. The Mitsui Soko godown had been hit by one bomb, which had exploded on the second floor after having gone through the roof and the upper floors. This floor was made of reinforced concrete three feet thick, but the bomb had blown a hole in it twenty feet across. This made quite an impression on the Japanese, not to mention us POWs. One bomb that size hitting Kobe House would have taken out the whole building. The few high explosive bombs that had been dropped during the big raid must have been just for the nuisance value, to show the Japanese what they could be in for.

As usual, the Kobe Go gang scrounged around in the burnt godowns to see what we could salvage. In one godown I found a box of razor-blades, brittle from the heat of the fires, but still usable if you were careful. In another place I found a real prize, a book. It turned out to be a handbook of Japan, printed in Spanish. It was a source of much pleasure to me, as it was the first book I had had in my possession since the start of the war. It had a lot of information about Japan in it, history, geography, commerce, business, railroads, you name it and it was in the book. It took me the next two months to finish reading it, but with the help of Hector Godoy and Jimmy Lucero I read every word. To an avid reader such as I had always been, that book was the most wonderful thing to have, and it kept my mind so busy I didn't have time to worry about the future.

Old Joe was still able to keep us supplied with soya beans, which was a godsend, considering the state of our Kobe House ration. Old Joe had a pet chicken which wandered around near our hut, and we tried for months to catch it in the act of laying an egg. We really wanted that egg, not having even a taste of one for more than three years. All our plans came to naught, Old Joe had his chicken timed, perfectly, and every time that fool chicken laid its egg he was Johnny-on-the-spot to collect it. We did get lucky one day, though. We were in the hut eating our noon bowl of soup when we heard a horrendous noise outside. When we looked out, we saw a cattle car on the siding, filled with cows all mooing like mad. From the looks of things, those cows hadn't been milked for quite a while, as they were literally dripping milk. It didn't take long for the gang to grab whatever they could find that would hold milk, and rush outside to milk those nice cows through the bars. I had an empty Klim tin which probably held a quart, and it didn't take much time to fill it with milk, which was promptly guzzled and refilled as fast as possible. Even the city boys who didn't know one end of a cow from the other managed to get their share. Nothing I had ever drank had tasted better than that milk, and nobody worried about whether the cow had been tested for tuberculosis, either. That was a red letter day on Kobe Go!

Air raid warnings were sounding daily, but there were no more actual bomber raids. We were just left on the job, and spent a lot of time down in our air raid shelter, which we were glad to be in. The one thing we didn't want was to be cooped up in Kobe House if there was another raid. I had made another good friend at Kobe Go, one of the Middlesex named "Buck" Jones. He was from High Wycombe, in Berkshire, and although he had the Cockney accent, it wasn't as bad as that spoken by the majority of the Middlesex. I learned quite a bit more of the life around London from him. We spent a lot of time swapping stories about our past experiences in the service. He was just about my age and had served in Palestine, India and Hong Kong, so had a lot of interesting stories. In turn, I told him about my own past service in the U.S., China and the Philippines. We worked on the same team from then on, including my buddy Rigdon, and shared what look we could steal.

On our next *yasume* day, the sirens went off as usual, and we got a pleasant surprise when the guards told us to form up outside, after which we were marched up the street past Sannomiya Station, under the railroad viaduct and on into the foothills of the mountains to a nice park area. It was a beautiful spot where we enjoyed a couple of hours, just lying on the grass and taking it easy. There were quite a few civilians there, who must have wondered what such a horde of barbarians were doing. We would have liked to stay there all day, but no soap, we were marched back down to Kobe House and inside we went. It was a pleasant outing, though!

From about the middle of April, Kobe became subject to sporadic raids by smaller American planes, evidently carrier-based. These planes were a real nuisance, as they cruised around Kobe looking for targets to strafe with their machine guns, and from what I saw, they must have had about four on each wing. They had a nasty habit of coming down almost to street level when they spotted any body of men, and POWs in Japanese uniforms were fair game. These fighters, as we presumed they were, flew so fast that they would be on you before you knew it, and a sharp lookout had to be kept all the time we were going from job to job. We had to dive for cover many a time while the street was being chewed up by machine gun fire. It would have been just our luck, to be killed by our own planes. Besides their machine guns, they carried a couple of pretty big bombs which they were liable to drop at any time. With all this going on, it was no wonder we became a bit jumpy.

Another tactic used by the Americans became very annoying. This was the dropping of mines by single bombers who sneaked around at night. Some smart guy in operations must have been worried about the subs missing a few Japanese ships and figured out a way to get any that got through to Japan. So every other night a bomber would drop a load of mines into the Japanese harbors. Kobe, being the second largest port in Japan, received its share. Any ship making it into Kobe harbor had to watch its step, even while it was docking. One night we heard a gigantic explosion which broke every pane of glass in Kobe House. We figured it must have been a mine that missed the harbor and landed on shore. Good thing it didn't land on Kobe House!

In late April there was more good news in the papers. The battle for Iwo Jima had been fought and won by the Americans. None of us had ever heard of the place, and couldn't imagine why it was important. We soon found out when the B-29s started coming over by the hundreds.

The landings on Okinawa made the headlines as well. We knew where Okinawa was, and we knew that Japan itself would be the next target. An invasion of the homeland would most likely be the end of us POWs, as we couldn't have possibly survived anything like that. Every day we saw groups of women and children being trained with wooden swords, which meant that an invasion would be resisted to the last Japanese. The odds that we would ever get home alive were getting longer and longer.

The month of May arrived and with it an increase in the air raids. Just about every day the work was stopped by the sirens. Some of the time we were sent back to Kobe House, other times we found what shelter we could. Night alarms became common, and when the alarm sounded, we had to get up, get dressed, and remain in our sleeping area. All this did was to cut our sleep in half, and everyone was so tired our work output suffered.

The exodus of Australians continued with the transfer of fifty more, on the 8th, to another camp in the hills three or four miles from Kobe House. This camp was called Kawasaki Camp, because the POWs there, all Australians, had been working in the Kawasaki Shipyards since December 1942. Four days later, Kawasaki Camp was closed, and two hundred POWs were sent on an eighteen-hour train trip to a coal mine on Kyushu, where they became coal miners for the duration. Twenty-three Aussies from the Kawasaki Camp came to Kobe House in bad physical shape, but soon recovered enough to go out to work, due to the much better treatment they got in Kobe House, as well as extra food given to them by Aussies who worked on the good jobs.

Another plus was a gift of five hundred books for our library, as well as tea and cigarettes, given to Kobe House by the Swedish Consul. There was more good news when Lt. Takanaka informed us that there would be no more work at the three factories. A good thing, too, as it was reported that they were bombed the next day. On the 13th every POW was allowed to send a cablegram. I sent mine to my mother, as always.

The 18th of May saw a second batch of Australians, thirty-one in number, shipped out to another camp in the eastern part of Kobe. This camp was called the Wakinohama School Camp, because it was located in a burned-out school. The next day they left for their future home which was in Maibara, six hours by train from Kobe. On the 20th, another party of forty-six Aussies left Kobe House for a place called Notagawa, where they faced a life of hard labor. The Japanese interpreter at this camp was none other than our old friend, "Henry," who had been the interpreter at Kobe House when we first arrived there. After all this moving around of Australians, there were only fifty left of the original number, plus nineteen from the Kawasaki Camp. There must have been an increase in the sleeping areas with a quarter of the men of "B" block gone. Of course no Aussie volunteered to leave his snug home in Kobe House, and there were instances of men hiding out until all the draft had been selected. I would say they were lucky guys.

One day on the job the Japs seemed in a good mood, telling us with great glee, *Rooseveloto shinda,* over and over. In this manner we learned of the death of President Roosevelt. I can't say that I was very sorry, as I had always considered that he was to blame for all the misery I had suffered. When we asked about who was President now, we were told his name was *Taroomanu,* which meant nothing to us, nobody ever having heard of him.

Chapter 43

We Lose Our Home

As we passed the cricket grounds on our way home from work on the 1st of June, we noticed quite a change. An antiaircraft battery of four guns was being emplaced where we had played our baseball game against the Aussies. This may have made our guards feel better, but to us it was a big negative. What we saw was another good target for those pesky carrier planes, and if those guns were attacked, even a close miss would hit Kobe House, just across the street. All this didn't help our state of mind.

Our premonitions of impending disaster were fulfilled on the 8th of June when, just as we finished our scanty breakfast, the air raid warning sounded. I just sat by the window as always, thinking I would be safer there if Kobe House was hit. Any time the sirens went off, Kobe House was like an ants' nest, all those POWs like me, who thought we would be hit by high explosive bombs hurried up to the top floor, because we knew this type of bomb would penetrate all the floors and explode at the bottom. The others ran down the stairs because they thought we would be hit by incendiaries, which wouldn't get past the top floor. All this rushing up and down made for quite a commotion during the first minutes of an alarm. I preferred to stay where I was because the brick wall made me feel safer, and I could look out my window to keep up on what was going on.

A few minutes after the sirens began, we heard the drone of engines, so loud that we knew it was going to be a big raid. In no time at all, I saw a lot of dark objects falling through the air. I had no idea what they were, but soon found out. From my window I could see a section of the roof of "B" block thirty feet away, and as I looked at it, it just seemed to disappear. There were a few of us still in our area, so I shouted to them to get ready, as we were going to get it. A couple of the guys crawled under the platform, while one just sat there with his four folded blankets over his head. A couple of seconds later our roof disintegrated. What came through it was a stick of incendiary bombs, each of which was about four feet long and four or five inches in diameter. There must have been two dozen or so in our area, sticking up in the floor and spewing fire in every direction. All I could think of was the whole place looked like a gigantic birthday cake, only these candles couldn't be blown out. Fortunately, none of us had been hit, and we all grabbed what we could reach and wove our way between the bombs and down the stairs. My old shopping bag went with me as usual. I should have taken at least one of my blankets, but didn't think of that in my haste to get out of the building before I caught fire.

When we got down to the alley, we found a mass of POWs milling around, both of the gates still being locked. Fortunately, one of our guards had enough sense to unlock the gate leading to the cricket grounds, to which the guard pointed. We were glad enough to get out in the open, even if there were no shelters. To our amazement, we found the antiaircraft guns deserted. The gun crews must have thought that discretion was the better part of valor and had taken off looking for a safer place. They had the right idea, because the entire field was covered with burned out incendiaries, so many that the place looked like the back of a porcupine. The Japanese had dug trenches for air raid protection, which were promptly occupied by thankful POWs. I found a small hole holding range-finding equipment, into which I jumped, and made myself as comfortable as was possible. It was almost black as night, due to the black smoke clouds caused by all the fires, but through gaps in the smoke we could see wave after wave of bombers flying at a low altitude, probably around five thousand feet. They were dropping incendiary bombs in such numbers that they looked like a snowstorm, glinting in the sun. Between successive waves, POW volunteers went back to Kobe House, where the top floors were blazing furiously, and helped to save some of the food stores and cooking gear. The hospital had been evacuated and most medical supplies had been saved by the medics, who had been well prepared for an emergency. Nine patients were in hospital at the time, three of whom were stretcher cases, Jack Schlosser being one of these. Jack had been injured at work and had come down with severe tetanus and was unable to move. A field station was set up in the middle of the cricket field by Captain Boyce and his medics, where the many burn cases were taken care of, including some of our Japanese guards, three of whom died. Their dugout had received a direct hit by an oil bomb. The British living on the top floor of "A" block had the majority of the burn cases, while the British and Americans on the top floor of "B" block escaped with no burn cases at all, as far as I know. With all the bombs that hit Kobe House and the fires that followed, it was indeed a miracle that none of the more than five hundred POWs were killed.

I have no idea of the number of B-29s involved in the raid, but I know there must have been hundreds. They certainly did a good job of destroying the western half of the city of Kobe that had survived the St. Patrick's Day raid. We remained on the cricket grounds all day, dodging sparks and blazing bits of debris from the raging fires. By late afternoon, when the fires were dying down, we got a meal of rice that our cooks had managed to prepare on improvised stoves. Finally, after it had gotten dark, we were formed up and started marching westward past poor old Kobe House, now just a mass of tumbled bricks, still smoking. In addition to what possessions each of us had been able to save, we had to carry Jack Schlosser, as none of the sick or wounded had been taken to the area hospital. This was a problem, due to the fact that we had no stretcher to carry him on. The best we could do was to find a wooden door which by some chance had survived the fire, and load him on it. It took four of us to carry Jack on his door. Some of the Yanks were too weak, and some of the more able refused to do any carrying at all. This left just eight to do all the carrying, and we took turns with that heavy load for the whole of that miserable march, which lasted most of the night. We passed through the still smoking ruins of what had been the prosperous city of Kobe, and began to climb the foothills of a mountain range. The door we were carrying, with Schlosser and assorted baggage on it, weighed at least two hundred pounds, which meant that each of us had a fifty-pound weight on one shoulder, not a bag, but a hard edge of wood, which cut into the flesh and was very painful. This hike, up hill all the way, seemed to me never-ending. Finally, about two in the morning, we staggered through the gate of what turned out to be the Kawasaki POW camp, which was empty, due to the fact that its previous occupants, the Australians who had labored at the shipyard since late 1942, had been transferred elsewhere. I doubt very much whether we could have carried that door another yard. I almost wished it had been me on that door instead of Jack. We were all pretty glad to see the end of that hike. It had been a pretty traumatic day, I think more traumatic than the first day at Clark Field. The bombing of Clark had been short and sweet, but the bombing of Kobe lasted much longer and, of course, under much different conditions.

The living conditions at Kawasaki Camp were quite different from those at Kobe House. We found ourselves in single story buildings which held about eighty POWs each, with platforms on each side of a central aisle. We all hit the sack without delay, but as beat as we were after the hike up the mountain, most got very little sleep that night. As soon as we got down, something odd happened. Everybody began to feel something strange on his body, zipping from place to place, taking a nip here and there on the way. Not having lights to see what was causing such a commotion, we had to wait until morning to investigate. Lo and behold, we found that the platforms, as well as the POWs, were alive with big black fleas, a nuisance we had not had in Kobe House, although we had had most every kind there. The fleas turned out to be the hardest insect to get rid of, being almost impossible to catch. They bite pretty hard, too. I imagine the Aussies who had been here were glad to leave, if they had had to suffer those fleas all the time.

The next morning was spent in getting settled, with much counting of POWs, as all those who had been in Kobe House had to be accounted for. The Japs finally being satisfied that no one had strayed or been stolen, we were able to look around and see where we were. Kawasaki Camp was different from Kobe House in that we had some open space to walk around in, which was a big change for us, having been cooped up in two warehouses for so long. The camp even had a duck pond, although there were no ducks. They had probably been eaten by some POW.

We did nothing for two days, while the staff sorted everything out and reorganize things. The POWs needed this break, after what they had gone through. The trouble with this *yasume* time was that we only got two meals per day, and darned skimpy ones at that. Between the poor rations and the fleas, we became pretty disgusted with the place, and the sooner we got back to work the better. Another two days and we got our wish, as all the jobs started up again except one coal job. Transportation down the mountain to Kobe was another matter. Some jobs sent trucks up to Kawasaki Camp to pick up their workers, while those on other jobs had to hike to work, then hike back up the hills after work. The Kobe Go gang was lucky, as Old Joe made sure we got a truck ride back and forth. After a short time, the Japanese realized that this was an unsatisfactory state of affairs, and we were all moved back down to the city to Wakinohama Camp, about a mile and a half east of where our old home, Kobe House, was situated. As we passed the ruins of our home of almost three years, I would bet that every one of us wished we were back there instead of being shipped from pillar to post, not knowing where we would be the next night. We also thought of the hundreds of Red Cross parcels lost in the fire. We sure could have used them.

Chapter 44

Wakinohama

Wakinohama Camp was located in a former schoolhouse, a three-story building damaged in previous incendiary raids. The upper story had been gutted, but the lower two were habitable. There should have been plenty of living space for all of us, but for the Japanese penchant for packing POWs in like sardines. We were all jammed into just two floors in one wing, and had no more space than we had in Kobe House. All the windows had been boarded over, and we lived in a sort of perpetual twilight, without any ventilation. When all the POWs were inside, it was so stuffy and hot that the air was almost unbreathable. You could always trust the Japs to make things uncomfortable to the Nth degree. We did have toilets, which flushed for a short time, but which soon became blocked due to lack of water. This made it necessary to dig slit trench *benjos*, which were worse than those in Kobe House. The location of the camp, with the main railway to the docks running past the camp on one side, and a city gas storage tank on the other side, was a nice target for any carrier plane roaming around. Not a good prospect for our future existence.

Another worry was the state of our food ration, especially the rice, which had been salvaged from burned out godowns and was very dirty. The cooks did their best to clean it up, but despite their efforts, it was still in such a state that just about all the POWs developed diarrhea. The soup ration was a bit better, due to summer vegetables becoming more plentiful. For a couple of days we would have a good cabbage soup, then another couple days of onion, egg plant, pumpkin, tomato or potato soup. This may sound as if the soup was wonderfully filled with vitamins, but just how many vitamins are there in cabbage or pumpkin soup? Our calorie input was less than one thousand per day, and everyone was fast losing weight. The constant air raid alarms made it almost impossible to get a night's rest, causing a further loss of weight, as well as making everyone jumpy and nervous.

The Kobe Go gang was happy to get back to work, where we felt much safer, due to our deep air raid shelter. Old Joe did his best to keep us supplied with soya beans, but the supply became erratic due to the fact that most soya beans came from China, and very few ships were making it across to Japan. Another good thing about Joe, he never made work for us, as most of the *honchos* did. When there was no work, he let us loaf around in our hut and sleep, if we could, keeping one POW on the alert in case a guard came roaming around.

One day our gang was assigned to unload a small coastal ship which held rock salt. It was a hot July day and we were all sweating, but when we went down into the ship's hold, we began to feel cold and damp. It took most of the day to unload that little ship, and we were glad to get back into the summer heat. It was strange how the salt affected the temperature.

Another day we went to Dai Go, which was the last dock on the eastern end of Kobe harbor. Just across the slip from us there was an antiaircraft battery on full alert, all guns manned. Our job was one of my unfavorite ones, unloading a barge of my favorite stuff, *cemento*, although this time it was neatly stacked, with very few broken bags, and as we had all day to do the job, it wasn't that bad. We took our own good time, one bag each, up the planks and into a box car. One bag of cement was a lot lighter than the usual load, but in our poor physical condition, it was enough. Any other honcho than old Joe would have had us lumping three bags instead of one. At two o'clock we all went into a small room at the shore end of the godown which the coolies used for a tea break. A freighter which had miraculously escaped the submarines was off the end of the dock, ready for a tug to help it in. We had just gotten our cups of tea when there was a tremendous explosion and all the plaster fell from the ceiling onto us and into our tea. Of course we rushed outside, to see that freighter sinking, just the length of the dock away. Evidently it had struck one of the mines which the Americans had so generously strewn around Kobe harbor. The Japs manning the guns over the way must have been shell-shocked, as the ship had been pretty close to them. I would have liked to see their faces when that mine went off. It would have been worth all the plaster down our necks. Just another exciting experience. I began to wonder how many more of these exciting experiences I could take.

At the end of July the Japanese announced that our rations, such as they were, were being reduced due to food shortages throughout Japan. In place of rice, we began to get a mixture of barley and sorghum seed. The barley would have been all right by itself as a rice substitute, but the sorghum seed was almost indigestible, and was most irritating to one's stomach. Just about all the POWs in Wakinohama camp developed intestinal troubles because of the new ration, but it was either eat it or starve. We had all been suffering from avitaminosis, or lack of essential vitamins, for more than three years, and resistance to any illness had become practically zero. In searching for anything to eat, Al Rigdon and I started going through the garbage to find bits of discarded vegetable tops to add to our soup. Of course we were caught by a guard and got the usual punishment of standing at attention for an hour, along with the usual half dozen slaps to the chops. Anything that would help to fill the void in our stomachs received our attention. There were a number of horse drawn carts around Kobe Go, whose owners would put the nosebag on their horses and then go into their lunch room to eat their own dinner. It would seem unbelievable to a well-fed American that anyone could be so hungry as to steal a horse's food right out of his nosebag, but I saw starving POWs do just that, and what is more, I gave serious thoughts to doing the same. What stopped me was the thought of all the slobber I would have to get through. The first two weeks of August seemed to be a continuous air raid. Single B-29s and smaller carrier planes were overhead just about all of the time, not doing much of anything but looking around. Of course the city of Kobe, or at least everything burnable in it, was already destroyed. All you could see from Wakinohama was a waste of nothing but ashes with a few skeletons of burned-out cement buildings sticking up here and there. Any *yasume* time we had was spent in collecting charred bits and pieces of wood for the kitchen and cleaning debris from the area around the camp. After an area had been cleared and raked, small plots were dug up and sweet potato plants and other vegetables planted. Produce from these plots were destined for our consumption when ripe. I remember well one Sunday when I had to go on a raking detail. My legs were so weak I could hardly navigate, and the soles of my boots were falling off, to say nothing of a good sized ulcer on my left leg which refused to heal. To save what was left of the boots, I decided to try to work barefooted. That turned out to be a bad mistake, the day was hot and so were the ashes and other debris, which kept me hopping all afternoon.

On the 7th of August, we read in the newspapers that an unusual type of bomb had been dropped on Hiroshima, and pictures in the newspapers showed some of the damage. We had no idea of what type of bomb it was, but from then on, when the air raid sirens sounded, all the Japanese seemed to be scared out of their wits. To the POWs, all it meant was that it was just another thing that would possibly shorten the war. A couple of days later, the raid on Nagasaki was in the headlines. The general consensus was that the B-29s were dropping one monster bomb instead of the their normal load of five hundred pounders, or whatever size usual bombs happened to be. I know that we weren't unduly worried about the matter, as anyone could see that nothing left in Kobe would warrant the use of such a big bomb. Looking back at all that had happened since the day back in December of 1944 when we saw our first B-29, and all the alerts and air raids since then, what struck me as strange was that we had never seen a Japanese plane in the air during all that time. I know I never saw one, although a few bombers must have been shot down somewhere. I am sure of one thing, I saw a lot more American bombers and fighters than I needed to or expected to, and a lot closer than I would have desired.

Chapter 45

All Over But the Shouting

The 11th of August saw a low-flying B-29 cruising over Kobe, dropping leaflets. We managed to grab some of them before the guards began to get ugly. The leaflets were about nine inches by four, showing the Emperor on the edge of a cliff with a rope around his neck. Another rope held Hitler, already finished. They were printed in Japanese, which we couldn't read, but one was interpreted in camp to say that Kobe would be next for the new bomb, unless Japan surrendered unconditionally. The next newspaper we saw gave instructions to the citizens to get into the nearest underground shelter when the air raid sounded, and to cover the body with any white material that was available. We POWs had no shelters at all at Wakinohama, and nothing white; Capt. Boyce didn't even have any bandages. I guess we would have been out of luck if the big one had dropped on Kobe.

Every morning after the dropping of the leaflets, a B-29 came over the city. I presume it must have been taking pictures, as no bombs were dropped. What it did was cause a lot of commotion, because as soon as the sirens went off, thousands of civilians ran as fast as possible up into the mountains, as there were few underground shelters available. We POWs just went to work, or just kept on working wherever we happened to be. We hadn't been the subject of an air raid for some time and didn't expect another. If we happened to be in our hut at Kobe Go, we just climbed down into our own air raid shelter as we always had done.

On the 8th of August, we went to work as usual. While eating our sparse lunch, we noticed that all the employees of Kobe Go were gathered around one of the platforms, where a loud speaker had been set up. In a few minutes we heard someone speaking in a loud voice, which went on for some time. During this talk, or speech, all the women began to wail and cry. Of course we didn't understand just what was going on, but we knew from the faces and the actions of the Japanese that it must be important. What we didn't know was that the voice we were hearing was that of Emperor Hirohito, informing the Japanese people that he had decided to halt the hostilities, and thus save more people from getting killed or maimed, and cities, towns, and villages from being destroyed.

This was the first time the Japanese had ever heard the voice of their Emperor, which probably explained their reaction. I doubt that any of them were crying because the war had been stopped.

Right after the Emperor's radio broadcast, we were promptly marched back to Wakinohama by Old Black Joe, who told us on the way, *Senso awari*. We all understood that, I can tell you! We still couldn't quite believe it, but back at the camp, we found that the British had taken over, and very few of our guards were still around. Later than afternoon, Lt. Takanaka gave a speech in which he said that the Emperor had graciously given us back our lives, that we could all sleep securely because there would be no more bombs and no more sirens, and that tomorrow and in the future there would be no more work for prisoners. I had heard a lot of speeches by Japanese officers, but this was the only one that had any good news. We POWs certainly gave our sincere thanks to the Emperor for returning us to the land of the living. Too bad he hadn't thought of it sooner.

Lt. John Fuller, 2/18 Btn, AIF, taking sword from Lt. Morimoto ("Jack Oakie"), Camp Commandant, Kobe House.
(Australian War Memorial photo 3299)

Capt. Houghton spoke as well, telling us to remember that we were soldiers, and not to try to retaliate on the guards or civilians who had mistreated us in the past, as we were still in enemy territory, and nobody knew how the Japanese would react to the Emperor's speech. He also told us that the guards would remain on duty, not in charge of us, but to protect us from any harm from the Japanese. To the credit of the POWs, peace and order was maintained in camp, and very little revenge was taken by us, although the thought of it ran through our minds. I think we were all so happy with the war being over and being free again, thoughts of revenge took second place in the scheme of things.

On this day, there were sixty-nine Australians, around five hundred British, and nineteen Americans in Wakinohama Camp, all of whom were in a state of near starvation, with severe intestinal troubles and nearly all having skin ulcers. All had been losing weight rapidly since the big raid on the 8th of June. In the two months since, I had lost over twenty pounds and was down to a hundred and twenty. If the Emperor hadn't come through, we would all have been skeletons in another couple of months.

In the next few days, parties of the more able men were sent out daily to bring in food, and we began to get bigger and better meals. There was still a lot of foodstuff scattered around the docks, and as the POWs were now free to steal with impunity, it was wonderful to see all those edibles arrive in camp. The guards that remained on duty, without arms, were astounded to see what the *dorobos* could do when they had free rein. In fact, the guards began to ask for a bit of food for their families, and would you believe it, they were given a share of the loot. For their wives and children, of course. Even those honchos still around got gifts of food, as well as those coolies who had treated us like human beings. It was just like a big Christmas party for everybody concerned.

The days passed, and nothing much happened until the 20th of August, when a rumor began that an unconditional surrender had been signed, but the next day's paper had a short report about Gen. MacArthur's announcement that the ceremony would not be held in Manila, but in a different place, so we were still in limbo. The waiting began to wear on us, and as our bellies were now full, hanging around camp became boring. Small groups of POWs began to go for walks around the city, and one day Rigdon and I thought we might as well try it too. We filled up newly acquired haversacks with sugar, just in case we found something to trade it for, and headed for the mountains and the only unburned section of Kobe. It was wonderful to be free and to walk around without a guard after so long a time. It just didn't feel natural to be able to go where we wanted to. The people who had lived in this area had been mostly foreigners, and we hoped to meet someone who spoke anything but Japanese. We never did meet any such person, but were able to trade some sugar for a couple of bottles of beer, the first since December of 1941, a long, long time ago. It did taste good! The only white faces we saw on our walk were those of freed POWs, just strolling around and enjoying themselves. Before we headed back to camp, we got rid of a little more of our sugar in exchange for a bowl of noodle soup, which was somewhat better than our ration soup had been. Back in camp, we found a couple of strangers had arrived. They were Americans who had been captured on Guam and were in worse physical shape than we had been in. After a few good meals, they perked up a bit, and said they thought they must be in Heaven. Their entire experiences as POWs had been ones of brutal and ferocious punishment, which made us realize how fortunate we had been in ending up in Kobe House.

Our camp had been marked with a big, white "P.O.W." on the roof of the school, and soon a small Navy fighter appeared and flew over us, dropping a weighted message with the pilot's name on it, which said, "It won't be long, now." He waved to us, and then flew right into the only factory chimney still standing in the area. The pilot was Ensign E. J. Shea of Everett, Massachusetts, and I suppose was killed in the crash, although we never did find out if he was or not. He must have radioed our location to someone, though, as it wasn't too long before some low flying B-29s appeared and made a supply drop, which consisted of fifty-five-gallon drums, welded together in pairs, attached to parachutes. Their first drop was made at too low an altitude, many of the drums hitting the ground before the chutes were fully opened. This was a disaster, as the drums burst open when they hit the ground. There seemed to be a lot of canned fruit being dropped, and peaches and pineapple were strewn everywhere. A good share of the drop landed quite a distance from our camp, and the Japanese women got enough fruit to last them a long time. It was dangerous to be in the open while these drops were being made, because if one of those drums landed on you, you were a goner. One load went right through the kitchen roof and nearly killed a cook, so we quickly learned to stay under cover when the B-29s came over. Besides the canned fruit, we got loads of canned meat, field rations, candy bars and clothing. It was almost too good to be true, and everyone gorged himself on whatever he fancied. I had always liked sweets, and put away quite a few Hershey bars and a lot of fruit salad, which did my poor shrunken, overworked stomach no good at all. I have always wondered why Capt. Houghton and Capt. Boyce didn't confiscate all that food and see that it was issued in small amounts at first. I guess they thought that they would have a real riot on their hands if they had. Six hundred starving POWs who had been on a rice and soup diet for such a long time would have likely taken things in their own hands. We also had an issue of fresh-baked bread. Some of the British had found a bakery, whose owner had gladly baked a load of bread in return for some of the food drop, thereby making both he and the POWs happy. A lot of Red Cross parcels had been found in a godown and dealt out as another addition to our plentiful diet. The cooks, being British, even issued "chips" at one meal. They had also found a brewery, and barrels of beer began coming through the gate. We could hardly get used to such plenty. Talk about being in Heaven!

The parachutes from the supply drops were of all colors, and were in great demand by the locals. One thing we did with the chutes was to have some of the Japanese *mama-sans* make chute material up into our national flags, which we raised with proper ceremony. We had "Reveille" each morning, and a "Retreat" parade each night, complete with regulation British bugle calls, someone having acquired a bugle in exchange for sugar. None of us Yanks ever having blown a bugle, we had to do with the British, and it was all so wonderful no matter whose calls were blown. Now having flags, it was decided to have a "parade spectacular," which was to be a contest between the British and the Aussies. As only fifty Aussies could be considered able to march, the British picked the same number. The Yanks were left out of the contest, as we didn't have enough fit men to made up a squad. The parade was quite a show and we all enjoyed it. The participants, who had been marching and drilling in Japanese Army fashion for over three years, had quite a struggle to get back into the swing of British drill. In the end, it was decided that the Australian irregulars had won the honors from the British regulars. Another wonderful day!

On the 22nd, some of the officers came back to the camp. It was said that they had been sent for in order to maintain discipline, some of the men being quite uncontrollable. Capt. Boyce commented that this was just an excess of high spirits—and higher—by a few, otherwise there was little to complain about. On the 27th, various formations of fighter planes and bombers flew low over the camp, no doubt staged to awe the locals and the thousands of Japanese soldiers being sent home for discharge. On our walks around the city we had run into many of them, all armed and in God knows what state of mind.

Fighter planes flew over the camp on the morning of the 30th, dropping small bundles of clothing. At noon, a B-29 showed up and dropped its load of drums, the majority of which made like bombs and strewed clothing all over the vicinity. Half landed in our area and half quite distant from the camp. Civilians began showing up with cart-loads of uniforms, shoes, etc. There were enough uniforms on hand to furnish every POW with all the pants, shirts, shoes, socks, and caps he could possibly carry. It was nice to get out of our old rags and look like a soldier again. The powers that be had failed to include chevrons in the drop, so we were all privates together. There was so much clothing we couldn't possibly use it all, so a lot was given to those guards who had been good to us, along with a letter stating that the bearer had treated the POWs well, and should be considered for a position with the occupation army. Darkie and the Angel got the best recommendations, as they had been the best of all the guards. The Kobe Go gang even located Old Black Joe and fixed him up with a load of clothes and a letter. He certainly deserved it! Rig and I even took a trip out to Higashinada and found Sano-San, to fix him up with a letter of recommendation as well.

The last of August saw many Australians coming into Wakinohama in very bad physical shape, most having severe diarrhea or dysentery. These Aussies were from the Notogawa and Maibara camps, and were former Kobe House POWs. They had not known that the war was over until the 26th of August, and had been kept working all that time. They were cleaned up, fed and bedded down in the sick bay. It goes without saying that they were pretty glad to be back with their old Kobe House mates.

Chapter 46

Farewell to Kobe City

September rolled around, and everyone was getting tired of waiting around for something to happen. It seemed that by this time somebody would have shown up to take care of us. It was all well and good to have plenty of food and freedom to do what we wanted to, but until we were out of Japan we really wouldn't feel safe. With all the Japanese soldiers still around and under arms, some bad things could happen if we stayed in Kobe much longer. Spider Griffin, Dick Morris, Windy Sutherland and Ernie Burnette had decided that they were sick of waiting, packed up their bags, and left by train for Tokyo. I would have liked to have gone along, but all those Hershey bars and fruit salad had done their job, and I was spending most of my time sitting on the *benjo*, too miserable to do anything else.

Major Campbell returned to Kobe on the 3rd, and with Lt. Fuller set up an office and prepared it for use of whatever unit came for us. That evening a recovery unit arrived at last; a half-dozen American soldiers wearing a type of helmet I had never seen, a couple of Army nurses and two Australians. Next morning they inspected the camp, then began the processing of the five hundred forty five POWs still at Wakinohama Camp. We filed past nurses at tables, where our name, rank, age and nationality were taken, then were examined by a physician and a surgeon who determined our state of health and gave each of us a colored ticket which indicated our mode of travel from Japan, which would be by hospital ship, by other naval vessels or by air. We were then allowed to fill in a message form to be cabled to our families, to the effect that we were alive and on the way home. We then proceeded to Kobe station, the sick being transported by vehicle, the rest of us by foot. A special train was waiting for us, which we boarded for the overnight trip to Yokohama. This trip was a lot more comfortable than our other trips as a POW had been, crammed into a box car with doors shut. It was quite a long ride, and passing through the devastated towns and cities, we could understand why the Emperor made the decision to surrender. All you could see was burned out buildings and acres of ashes. The Air Force had certainly done its job.

Our train arrived in Yokohama early on the morning of September 7, to be met by a crew who directed us to whatever destination our colored ticket indicated. I wound up being taken to the hospital ship *Marigold*, at the Yokohama docks. The rest of the Americans from Kobe were taken to an airfield for transport to Okinawa and thence to the Philippines for rest and recuperation, together with the Australians and British, so I became an orphan of sorts.

Back on American territory, even though it happened to be a hospital ship, I could finally say that my war was over, and after one thousand, two hundred and forty-seven days as a Japanese prisoner-of-war, I could begin living again. No more slave labor, beatings, *daikon* soup, ground up fish or forced marches for me. Everything would be peaches and cream from now on! Of course all recovered POWs were put on a special diet so they wouldn't stuff themselves with pie and cake, but we did have all the ice cream we could eat. One of the hardest things to get used to was sleeping in a real bed. After hours of tossing and turning I began to wish for a platform of boards so I could get a good night's rest. Of course, our state of mind was such that sleeping was the last thing we wanted to do. We just wanted to stay awake and enjoy the wonderful feeling which went with freedom.

I remained on the *Marigold* for two more days and nights, doing nothing but eating and sleeping. On the morning of my third day of freedom, I and a couple dozen other POWs were taken to Tachikawa Air Base, where we boarded a C-54 transport plane, fitted up as a hospital plane complete with beds, nurses and a doctor. On the morning of the 10th of September 1945, I finally said goodbye to the Empire of the Rising Sun and headed east on the way home to New Hampshire. By the time I got there, I had been overseas for six years.

Chapter 47

Homeward Bound

My trip across the Pacific Ocean by plane was a lot faster and much easier than the other three times I had crossed it. It had taken a month on the old transport *U. S. Grant* at about twelve knots an hour, but this time I was in a nice soft bunk, looking out the window at the white clouds below and doing nearly two hundred miles per hour. Our first stop was at Guam to refuel and get a bite to eat. I had gone ashore there in 1937 on my first trip across the Pacific headed for China, and the total number of Americans stationed there had been just one hundred Marines. Now, there were thousands of people of all branches of the Service, and a gigantic air base. We had a good lunch in an Air Force mess hall, and I will always remember their iced cocoa. It looked so nice and tasted so good while it was going down, but after you stopped swallowing, you found that it had been about 20 percent quinine. For the next hour, that was all you could taste. If all the water on Guam tasted like that cocoa did, I didn't envy anyone who was stationed there and had to drink it all the time. Quinine must be one of the worst-tasting things there is.

Back in the air again, we headed for Kwajalein Island, where we made a brief stop to top up our fuel tanks for the long leg of our flight to Hawaii, crossing the International Date Line on the way and losing a day in the process. Hawaii was our final stop for fuel, and we all had a good meal there. Then it was up and away on the last leg of the flight home. By early morning on the 12th of September we saw the coast of the U.S.A., and flew over the Golden Gate Bridge en route to Travis Air Force Base, where at long last we could say that "Back alive in '45" had been the correct prediction.

All the POWs were loaded on busses and taken to the Presidio of San Francisco, where Letterman General Hospital was located. Our reception there was nothing exceptional: no physical examination that I can remember, or any special treatment. We expected a bit more than that after what we had been through, but I suppose it was because nobody knew much about Japanese POWs as yet, as only a few had been flown back to the U.S. The great majority had been taken to the Philippines for a month's rest and recuperation, then returned to the U.S. by boat. I had been one of the lucky few, and by this time was feeling pretty good and gaining weight fast. I had put on at least ten pounds in the past week and was now up to a hundred and forty pounds.

There were some fifty other POWs who had arrived before me, and to my surprise, one of them was my old buddy Billy Johnson, who had been shipped up to Tokyo from Kobe House to make propaganda broadcasts. When he arrived in Tokyo, he had played dumb to such effect that they gave up on him and sent him to Omori Camp, where he got a job as a cook. I don't know how he got to fly back, as he wasn't that sick. It must have been his gift of gab which had got him on a plane. It was good to see Bill and to have his company, as neither he nor I knew any of the other ex-POWs there.

The day after our arrival at Letterman, we began processing for our entry into active service. First on the docket was an issue of a new uniform unlike the one we remembered. Instead of the old belted blouse, we got an Eisenhower jacket without a belt, and an overseas cap instead of a garrison cap. It felt good to be in uniform again, no matter how different it was. Then it was a trip to the tailor shop to get our stripes sewn on. I got a nice surprise when I found that as of some time previous, 1st Sergeants had been given a rank equal to a Master Sergeant, so now I was in the highest enlisted grade in the Army. All returning POWs, with the exception of First and Master Sergeants, were given a one-grade promotion upon their release, so Bill Johnson, who had been a Technical Sergeant, was now a Master Sergeant. I missed out on a promotion because I was at the top already. Quite unfair, I thought; after all that time I should have been promoted to Warrant Officer at the very least. Privates had more reason to gripe: all they got was one stripe. Being a POW for most of the war sure didn't help a career.

After the clothing issue, the paper work began. No POW of the Japanese had any records, and we had to start all over again with a new one. We all had nearly four years pay due us, but for the present got partial payments only. Bill and I got $200 each, with which we enjoyed the next few days while waiting for transportation home. We didn't have to spend much money in town, because when people found out that we were ex-POWs, everything was on the house. With our new uniforms, complete with two rows of campaign ribbons and seven overseas bars, we hit about every night spot in San Francisco.

Bill and I had decided to go home by train, so we asked the Warrant Officer in charge of transportation to ship us both on the same train. We were told that, as we hadn't arrived on the same day, we couldn't leave the same day, either. When we persisted, what he said was, "Who do you think you are, anyway? Civilians can't even get a seat, to say nothing of a berth. You'll go when I say so and not before." I couldn't believe my ears, and to this day have regretted not having cold-cocked him. The reason I didn't was because if I had hit him I most likely would have been court-martialed. That wouldn't have worried me too much, because I would never had been convicted, but it would have delayed our trip home and we didn't want that to happen. So the upshot of it all was that Bill left one day before did. I boarded a train in San Francisco on the 21st for the four-day trip across the United States. The train was jammed full, but I knew another POW, a Sergeant named Sirois who was also headed to Boston, so we had a pretty good trip hashing over old times at Nichols Field. We finally got into Boston late in the evening of the 19th, where I had to wait until the next morning for a train to Manchester, New Hampshire, ten miles from my home town of Hooksett. Another half hour by bus and I had finally made it. Nobody knew I was coming, and when I walked the quarter of a mile to our house and knocked on the door, my mother almost had a heart attack. I should have known better. At long last, I was home again, after six years, about ten years older and thirty pounds lighter. A bit wiser, too, I think.

28 February 1946. (L to R) The author, Bill Johnson, Mrs. Johnson, the author's wife.

Chapter 48

Random Thoughts

Approximately twenty thousand Americans were captured by the Japanese in World War II. Thirty three percent, or one in every three of these American POWs died during their captivity, from malaria, beri-beri, dysentery, from beatings or being worked to death, and thousands more by drowning when the hell-ships carrying them to Japan were sunk by American submarines. Half of those who survived the three years and five months in the hands of the Japanese returned home in such physical or mental condition that their lives were never the same again.

Many people have asked me how I survived such an ordeal. I doubt that I have ever been able to answer that question in a way that people really understood. In the first place, no one who had never been a Japanese POW could ever understand how it really was, no matter how much you or any other POW told them. For one thing, every POW has his own particular story, none of which are identical. Some are so different you would think that they were in different wars, but the experiences of all the Japanese POWs were so horrible that most people refuse to believe that they are true, and think the POWs are stretching the truth a bit. They should have been there themselves!

There are many things that must be considered in the matter of survival. The first, and most important, is the will to live, no matter how hopeless life seems to be. Constant hunger, sickness, hard labor, cruelty and despair take such a toll on some, that they just want it all to end. Adaptability is almost as important. The change from normal American life to that of a POW is in itself traumatic to the fullest, but to be a prisoner of an Asiatic country was something that not everyone could cope with. The diet became a major problem. Rice is something that most Americans never eat except in rice pudding, but rice became the major portion of our diet as a POW of the Japanese. Many POWs died because they could not, or would not, eat rice. Moral scruples have to be considered as a factor in your survival, because stealing food, or anything that could be traded for food, could help to keep you alive. If a man's scruples kept him from stealing, his chances were reduced. Faith didn't seem to have much to do with it all, as those who read their bibles or prayed every night died just as fast as those who had no bible and never prayed. I would imagine, though, that prayer helped some to retain that will to live which was essential to survive.

How, then, did I survive? I had one advantage that the majority of those captured did not have. I had the knowledge and experience acquired in my five years in the Infantry, which helped me to avoid dysentery, the deadliest disease, which killed so many men, those having no idea of proper sanitation and who drank water from ditches containing dead bodies and never washed their mess gear. Another thing was that I was twenty-seven years of age, and required less food than one who was still growing, and had the strength to survive when most of the older men didn't.

Then there was the matter of making the right choices when a choice was available, which was seldom. I chose to fight on, instead of just dying, when I discharged myself from St. Peter's ward in the hospital at Camp O'Donnell and volunteered for the work detail which landed me in the hospital at Little Baguio. My next opportunity to shape my own destiny came a few months later in Bilibid Prison when the Japanese wanted fifteen volunteers to make up a shipment of fifty POWs to go to Japan. This called for a bit of thinking, for if I were to go to Japan, it would be for the duration. I knew that if I stayed in the Philippines I would be shipped out on some work detail in the jungle, without medical care, and would surely come down with malaria. That was something I didn't look forward to. Another thing that came to my mind was that, as time went on, ships heading to Japan from the Philippines would be in danger of being sunk by American submarines, and the sooner I left, the better. The third reason I volunteered was that I had always wanted to see Japan. I certainly saw it, but not as I expected it to see it. In the final event, my choice to go to Japan was the best choice I ever made. The great majority of POWs wanted to stay in the Philippines, where they thought they would be liberated in a short time. This short time turned out to be quite a long time, and in the end they had to make the trip to Japan anyway, under the worst possible conditions. In the latter part of 1944 and early 1945, thousands of POWs died when their unmarked prison ships were sunk on the way north. Japanese POWs were rarely offered any options or choices, and when they did, the right one was all important.

Luck had a lot to do with it, too. I could have wound up in a coal mine or a steel mill, but instead landed in Kobe House, the best POW camp in the whole of Japan. Lady Luck was with me all the way!

Chapter 49

Fifty Years Later

The fifty-three years which have elapsed since the end of World War II have seen many changes in the lives of the twenty Americans who were residents of Kobe House. Fourteen have passed away, most of them naturally, some not so natural. My mucker, Al Rigdon, died tragically just a week after we were liberated. He made it to Okinawa, where his group remained overnight, then was killed the next morning when the plane which was to take him to the Philippines crashed on takeoff. Talk about hard luck. My English friend, "Buck" Jones, was in the same boarding line as Rigdon, but as the plane was full, was the first man to have to take another plane and saw Rigdon's plane crash right in front of him. Poor Rigdon had been the last man to board. Good-looking Mike Burnette died a derelict in 1988. In the same year, Slim Marshall committed suicide by shooting himself in the head. In 1991, Del Busta took his last dive, from a third-floor hospital window. It was not known whether he jumped or fell, but as someone familiar with Del's past, I would say he finally made it his way. Mr. Shaputnick made the whole fifty years before he died in May of 1995. Bill Johnson's cigarettes finally did him in. He died of emphysema in 1995.

On Memorial Day in 1987, six of the former Kobe House POWs held a reunion in Colorado Springs, Colorado. Those attending were the author, Jimmy Lucero, Spider Griffin, Dick Morris, Carl Hayden and Jimmy Barrett. It was the first time any of us had gotten together since the war ended, when we were so sick of the sight of each other that we never wanted to see or hear from any of the others as long as we lived. We met at Dick Morris' Mexican restaurant in Colorado Springs and had a wonderful time, helped out by the plentiful food and drink furnished by Dick. We parted the best of friends, all the old irritants caused by living together like sardines forgotten.

As for the author, he remained in the Service, retiring from the Air Force in 1961 with the rank of Captain after twenty-seven years service. Since retirement, he has acquired two college degrees, worked as a field engineer for RCA and Westinghouse, served four terms in the New Hampshire Legislature and is still employed as a reference librarian in his local library. He and his wife Lorraine, a pre-war acquaintance who attended the coming-home party given him by hometown friends in 1945, recently celebrated their fifty-first wedding anniversary. He and Lorraine are the parents of two daughters, Linda Lea and Sandra Luana, who live in Florida and Georgia respectively. He is a member of the American Defenders of Bataan and Corregidor, the American Legion, and the American ex-POWs, New Hampshire Chapter, of which he is a Past Commander, and is a volunteer at the Manchester V.A. Hospital.

A.J. Locke
1998.

www.ingramcontent.com/pod-product-compliance
Lightning Source LLC
Chambersburg PA
CBHW030817190426
43197CB00036B/551